SOUND ADVICE

Praise for *Sound Advice*

"Guidance around health and wellbeing can often be overwhelming but *Sound Advice* does an excellent job of cutting through the noise on this vitally important subject as well as demystifying the fundamentals of our industry. Simply put, this is a must-read for anyone starting out in music today."
David Joseph, Chairman and CEO of Universal Music UK

"*Sound Advice* is a very accessible, comprehensive book which brings together key messages about how to sustain a healthy and successful career in music, illustrated by stories from musicians who have experienced and worked through some of the challenges. Delighted to see these important health messages embedded in a guide to success. This is essential reading for anyone developing a career in music."
Claire Cordeaux, BAPAM Director

"*Sound Advice* is a great resource for artists, songwriters, producers and musicians. The pressure of creativity and success in music is a heavy burden and can be overwhelming."
Nile Rodgers, Grammy Award-winning musician and producer

"I wish I'd had this book when I was just starting out as an artist and songwriter. The music industry is complicated and no one teaches you how to navigate through all of the different parts of it. *Sound Advice* really covers everything in a way that's digestible and accessible, and even after being in this industry for 10 years, I still learned new things!"
Lauren Aquilina, singer and songwriter

"This book is informative, accessible, and, at times, highly entertaining. We have a responsibility to create a healthy and sustainable working environment - music is no different to any other business. *Sound Advice* will be a valuable asset to all those artists and executives alike, trying to navigate a safe, successful and sustainable way through our world. Highly recommended!"
John Reid, President of Live Nation Europe

"*Sound Advice* combines up to date, practical career information with straight-talking discussion about many unwelcome companions to a career in music — the mental and emotional pitfalls, how to avoid them, or how to get help if you do fall in to the pit. Read this book - it might save your life one day."
Matt Thomas, co-founder of Music Support

"The whole industry needs a book like *Sound Advice*. From the artists at the very beginning to the artists who've been in the game for the longest time. This industry chops and changes but *Sound Advice* outlines the fundamentals that will never change."
Lucy Spraggan, singer and songwriter

"An important and sobering look behind the curtain of the archaic, mythical 'rock and roll lifestyle' and the effect it has on the mind, body and soul."
Jonathan Higgs, Everything Everything

"In this book, Lucy Heyman and Rhian Jones depict through the first-hand insight from artists as well as their own knowledge and experience, a highly realistic picture of stresses, strains and rewards of being a professional musician. It's an indispensable read for anyone embarking on a career in music."
Sarah Osborn, Incorporated Society of Musicians

"This book manages to combine academic and scientific insight with specific self-help techniques all within the context of the lived experience of many of the contributors. I will be sure to recommend it to all of the artists and acts I come across in my work within the music industry and my private practice."
Adam Ficek, psychotherapist, musician and Babyshambles member

"*Sound Advice* is a hugely needed resource for helping to deal with the incredible pressure to do great work and succeed in our business."
Merck Mercuriadis, founder and CEO of Hipgnosis Songs

RHIAN JONES & LUCY HEYMAN

SOUND ADVICE

THE ULTIMATE GUIDE TO A HEALTHY AND SUCCESSFUL CAREER IN MUSIC

This book would not have been made possible without the generous support of **Live Nation**, **Universal Music UK**, **Sony Music UK**, **Warner Music UK**, **IFPI**, **Spotify**, **Hipgnosis Songs**, **Vevo**, **PRS for Music**, **Polydor Records**, and **PPL**.

Shoreditch Press

SOUND ADVICE

The ultimate guide to a healthy and successful career in music

Rhian Jones and Lucy Heyman

Shoreditch Press
Unit 22511
PO Box 6945
London
W1A 6US

First published in Great Britain 2021
1

Paperback ISBN 978-1-8381949-0-1

Hardback ISBN 978-1-8381949-1-8

eBook ISBN 978-1-8381949-2-5

Printed and bound by CPI Group (UK) Ltd, Croydon, CR0 4YY

Edited by Peter Robinson and Gareth Dylan Smith
Interior design by Steve Russell aka-designaholic.com
Illustrations by rhileedesign.com
Front cover by music.agency

soundadvicebook.com

CONTENTS

START HERE

OVER THE LAST FEW YEARS, the mental health and wellbeing of musicians have been the subjects of much discussion. Research commissioned by the charity Help Musicians has said the UK music industry is experiencing a mental health crisis,[1] with musicians, in particular, facing significant mental and physical health issues.[2] There's also been an endless number of articles, documentaries, and panel discussions focusing on the problems and suggesting various solutions.

This book intends to help move the conversation into preventative action by empowering those who work in the music industry with some tools and information that will help them manage and prioritise their own health, as well as the health of those around them. It has been created with unprecedented music industry support — you'll find the names of those who helped to fund us on the previous page — which makes it the only industry-backed resource of its kind.

It may not be the kind of book you'll read cover to cover and we've written it in such a way that you don't need to — so feel free to dip in and out of sections or chapters. There will be future editions, and for that reason, we warmly welcome all feedback on this first version. Also, while there is lots of globally relevant information, this particular edition is UK-focused. We plan to produce an international version in future.

We were editing and writing during the coronavirus pandemic in 2020, which will no doubt have a considerable impact on the music industry for years to come. In the world of music, some artists responded by putting projects back, while others brought releases forward and even conceived brand new projects. Rather than waiting for an unknown date in the future when life returns to normality, we decided to bite the bullet and take the Dua Lipa and Taylor Swift route by getting the book out there while people might have a bit of time on their hands to reflect and think about their health and career. In times of crisis, fostering good health is more important than ever. We remain hopeful that the touring chapter, in particular, will still be helpful both now from a planning perspective and in future when venues and festivals are operating again under normal conditions.

This book is written with musicians in mind. When we refer to musicians throughout the text, we mean all those who work on the music-making side of music — performers, vocalists, composers, instrumentalists, DJs, producers, and songwriters. If you work on the business side, there will be lots of relevant information for you too. When reading the advice from any medical experts we've quoted, it's important to know that there are many different approaches to treatment and theories about the reasons for ill-health so don't be surprised if some things chime with you while others don't. Everyone has individual needs and life experiences, which is why it's vital to do some research and probably engage in a bit of trial and error before finding ways of managing your own mental and physical health. That said, we've also covered some universal truths that a host of research has proven to form the basic tenets of living a healthy and happy life. We've done our best to feature lots of stories from a diverse pool of musicians, too. And regardless of your individual experience, we've signposted the best services and information available in a resources section at the end, and also on our website. So if you ever need anything, you'll be able to find it instantly (maybe bookmark the page online).

The book is divided into three sections: the first covers the more business and career-related side of music and the second is all about health. The third offers lots of research-informed practical tips for setting and reaching goals; improving your ability to practise and perform; and managing and harnessing creativity. Especially in the pop world, so many musicians don't feel equipped with the skills they need to do their job, which contributes significantly to stress levels. We hope this last section will help alleviate some of that. Another thing to note: when you see quotes from musicians, as well as industry executives and health professionals, those without a reference are original interviews we've done for the book, and those with references are interviews we've sourced elsewhere.

Finally, the nature of this book puts a lot of onus on musicians to look after themselves. But it'd be remiss of us not to mention the significant responsibility that lies with those working on the business side too. The music industry is built on the creative output of human beings, and quite often that creative output is the result of dealing with the hardest things we have to go through in life. On top of that, the live music industry requires those humans to endure what can often be quite tough touring schedules in order to make a profit and bring their music to a global audience (which is especially true in the era of streaming when most income is made playing live rather than from record sales). As we'll discuss further, this creates an often conflicting cocktail of sensitive and passionate creatives who can struggle to meet the demands of a pressurised business that prioritises cash over care.

If we look to sport, athletes have a support crew consisting of physiotherapists, performance psychologists and nutritionists. In music, artists have people around them to further their career but little support when it comes to mental or physical health and wellbeing. If the industry wants to nurture and maintain career artists, support for mental as well as physical health should be truly baked into the business. That might mean sacrificing some instant gratification to reap the long-term benefits of happy and healthy musicians. Writer, producer, and musician, Catherine Anne Davies, who we interviewed for this book, says it best:

> *"This isn't just about a musician having to go and buy a book about how to look after themselves and their own health. It's not just about individual personal responsibility — health is something that needs to be looked at in terms of the infrastructure of the industry more broadly."*

For anyone who works with artists and doesn't consider their health to be a personal responsibility, Davies adds: "People need to stop passing the buck and saying, 'It's not my problem' or 'That's management's issue'. Everyone is economically benefiting from this ecosystem. Because the music industry is made up of these little pockets and there isn't one big umbrella, it's such a great get-out clause. Everyone can just absolve themselves of responsibility. But how long have we been passing the buck? As long as we continue to do that, nothing changes." Hear, hear.

Everyone must help to foster a culture of open discussion around health and a deep sense of understanding for any issues that might arise, no matter whether they affect artists, managers, staff on the business side, or touring crew. Music has such a powerful and positive influence on society by shaping culture; bringing joy and comfort to listeners and musicians; challenging the status quo;

fostering solidarity; and helping to shape the people we become. It's vital that we adequately support those who produce it.

There's no doubt that there's a lot more to be done, but there is evidence of the industry starting to take steps towards fostering a healthier working environment. This book is a case in point — as we said earlier, it's only been made possible thanks to financial donations from major record labels and industry organisations. They've been kind enough to leave us to it and have had no editorial say in what we included, suggesting that there is a desire to learn and improve. Time will tell what those changes continue to look like, but after writing this book, we have a few ideas. We'd love to hear your thoughts too. Head online to the *Sound Advice* pages on social media @soundadvicebook to get in touch with us.

It's been quite a journey to get this into your hands. The book started out as a shared idea between us (the authors), who had no idea that a simple catch-up coffee one Monday evening would turn into a two-year planning, writing, editing and publishing adventure that featured lots of highs — as well as a few tough moments and days thrown in to equal the balance of life. It's been a bit like making an album, really. There've been the surges of creativity, the frustrating periods of writer's block, the soliciting of many opinions and choosing which noises to drown out, then the joy and heartbreak of cuts made and chapters changed during editing.

We hope this book starts useful conversations and enables anyone reading it to manage their own health. Ultimately, we hope that it moves the industry one step closer towards a healthier and happier place for everyone to work in. As the late Frightened Rabbit singer and songwriter, Scott Hutchison once wrote, it all starts with "tiny changes".

Rhian and Lucy, October 2020

PART I:
NAVIGATING THE INDUSTRY

Welcome to the business section of this book. Having an educated grasp on the industry you're working in and how to grow and manage your career will mean you'll feel more empowered to prioritise your health. It's tricky to do that if you're spending time worrying about where the next paycheque is coming from, battling your way out of bad business deals, or working with the wrong people. It's also pretty hard to keep on top of your mental health while spending time arguing with someone online, allowing criticism and comparison to bring you down, feeling pressured by fans, or getting carried away with the emptier aspects of fame. Avoiding all of that is the focus of the following six chapters, which combine advice on business and health.

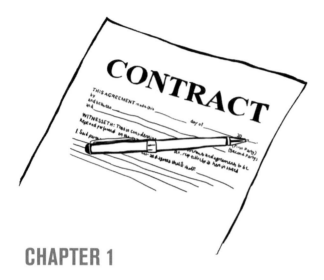

CHAPTER 1

BUSINESS BASICS

RESEARCH SUGGESTS THAT MONEY problems can be one of the biggest causes of stress for musicians,[1] whose incomes tend to be precarious due to the varied and unpredictable nature of the job. There's little knowing whether you'll end up flying around the world on private planes or pulling pints while struggling to make two gigs a week cover the rent. A well-paid project could be the most you'll earn all year or just the tip of a cash iceberg. So how do you create a level of security when there's often none to be found?

First of all, having a basic understanding of how the music business works gives you an idea of the different income streams out there, whether you can tap into them yourself, or who should be exploiting them for you (you'll hear the word 'exploit' a lot when it comes to deals, contracts and lawyers — don't be too put off by it because in most cases 'exploiting' something is just legal speak for 'making use of it'). The point is, if you enter the industry blind, decisions about who to work with and what steps you should be taking are literally a stab in the dark.

So over the next few pages, we'll paint a basic picture of the structure of the music business, including the main kinds of companies and artist team members and what they should be offering to the artist and when. We'll also cover a little bit about copyright and what to know when signing deals. What we're not going to do is delve into the ins and outs of the labyrinth that is the modern music business. Things move so fast these days that some advice would be out of date by the time you read it anyway. In any case, there are plenty of books out there for the nitty-gritty (you can find our list of recommendations at the end of this chapter).

Before we get started, here's one caveat — what you'd generally think of as the commercial music business is just one of the ways someone can make a living through music. There's also the corporate sector (doing private gigs for weddings and events), education (teaching), and health (like music therapy), as well as many music-related roles that can benefit from direct musical experience (you'll find more on this in the final section of this book). Since we're writing with those who work in the popular music industry in mind, the following mainly deals with the commercial business, but there's lots of information that will be helpful whichever path you choose to take. And it doesn't have to be *one* path — you might be surprised by how many people combine a few of those areas for a portfolio career where each strand involves a different aspect of the music business.

WHO MIGHT YOU BE WORKING WITH?

You might be wondering what comes first: a manager, publisher, record label, publicist, agent, or lawyer? Well, the not very helpful answer is any of them really, in any order. The ever-evolving nature of the music business has resulted in traditional roles merging. Investment and belief can come from one or a combination of those above, and there are DIY options, or talented friends, that can perform the role of a missing link. But it's helpful to know who specialises in what because depending on where you are in your career, one may prove more useful than another.

One example of how things can work: you've uploaded a track yourself (via a digital distribution company or directly onto a platform like YouTube or SoundCloud), it's picking up heat, and you ask a publicist to place a DIY video on a blog or website. This leads to a manager getting in touch; they help you record more music and then take you to labels. On the other hand, this might work instead: you get yourself a spot on a local open-mic night, a live promoter happens to catch your set and suggests you for a support slot the following month. The headlining act is already attracting label interest, so by accident, you find yourself in front of several label A&R scouts. Then there's this scenario: a self-released track ends up on a popular streaming playlist — two days later, your inbox is full of emails from managers... and A&Rs... and publicists and lawyers and... well, you get the idea. There's more than one way to get things moving these days.

HOW TO GET STARTED: AN OVERVIEW OF TEAM MEMBERS

The commercial music business consists of loads of different companies with loads of different interests, more often than not, staffed by music fans trying to do a good job. The key to working with these companies and people involves finding those who believe in what you do. Tim Ferrone, of artist services company Wrapped Up Music, explains:

"Try and find good, passionate people who can help you. Passion is an overused word in the corridors of the music business, but it's not a given. I've seen with my own eyes somebody who's working two artists at the same time:

one they're doing a good job for and are professionally obligated to deliver for, and one they love and are super passionate about. We're human beings at the end of the day and you can't help but be at least slightly emotionally led. The *passionate* people are going to go in deeper and give more than those who are simply *committed*."[2]

Before finding those champions, you first have to create your worth. More than ever, it's expected that artists get their careers started on their own before looking for people to help them. Fortunately, *also* more than ever, it's now possible to get things moving yourself. Twenty-five years ago, it might have cost hundreds of thousands of pounds to book studio time and record a demo; in 2020 you could get a track online and streaming for less than a tenner.

Regardless of when or whether you ultimately decide to look for a label deal, attention from those who work in the business is a sure sign that you're doing something right. A&Rs scour the internet constantly looking for new music and new artists, so you need to have a visible online presence and present it professionally.

If you're after a record deal, the advice from label A&R scouts as to how they like to be approached is usually this: "Don't approach." What they mean by this is that if you do good things, *they'll* find *you*. To be frank, this sort of advice is slightly disingenuous: some of them just want to keep their inboxes clear, and although it's not unheard of, it's relatively rare that a label will sign an artist who doesn't already have a **manager**. So while attracting label attention might seem like your goal, focusing on finding the right manager is usually a better early step. A decent manager will help you get ready to speak with labels, which may take months or even years, but as your Auntie Janet probably told you: "You don't get a second chance to make a first impression." (More on managers later in this chapter.)

In summary: if artists are signed to a **record label**, that company will help them earn money from their sound recordings by investing in development (which can include financial support for touring); making their music available to listen to and buy in various forms around the world; and marketing and promoting the music and artist with an international plan. If artists don't already have a team, they can provide a pretty robust one for you that includes people on the ground in all the major music markets worldwide. Labels can also help secure brand partnerships, get your music used in a film, advert, video game, or TV series (i.e. sync deals) and have contacts with places that will help to get your music heard, like streaming platforms, TV, radio, and press.

Publishers, meanwhile, will help songwriters, composers and producers earn money from their music by collecting income owed from those who have used the song (like radio broadcasters, streaming services, films, and TV programmes). In doing so, they protect the creator's rights by doing the administration that's required to ensure songs aren't being used without a license (and therefore remuneration) and that the royalty splits and information that identifies the song are listed correctly. They will also find further revenue earning opportunities for songs, which might include pitching them for sync deals or placing them with artists who might turn songs into smash hits by performing them. In addition, publishers can assist in talent development by facilitating collaboration with other writers and investing in new talent.

A BRIEF LESSON ON COPYRIGHT

A song has two separate sets of rights — the sound recording, and the musical composition. In the UK, the sound recording is usually owned by the person who produces it (or their record label if that person has signed away master rights) while the musical composition is usually held by the composer or writer of the song and managed by a publisher. Who earns money from what (and how much they earn) depends on individual deals, as well as who records, writes, and performs the song.

Confused? Don't worry, that's normal. Here's an onion analogy from digital media and music lawyer, Raffaella De Santis, that might help shed some light on the situation.

"The first thing you hear in a song is the sound recording itself, made in the studio by the producer and licensed by the label," De Santis says. Licensing, by the way, is an agreement that allows someone else, the licensee, to use copyrighted music — whether that's in a video game or movie, on a social network, or anywhere else you're likely to hear a song. De Santis continues: "But what you are listening to in that recording from a legal position is a bit like an onion — something which has many layers of rights within it. The recording contains the melody and the lyrics composed by the composer, and that composition exists separately from the recording, as a standalone right. That is where the analogy of the onion comes in because you have to peel away at the layers to get to all the rights embodied in the one song.

"Take the example of a film — you go and watch a film and you're watching the finished product, but the film contains many component parts, each of which have separate rights. A film is based upon a script and dialogue and an initial story concept, and that story concept gets built into the script, which is then performed by the actors, which is then filmed while the actors perform it to make the finished film. It's the same as a song — the music and lyrics are the concept and the script, the musicians are the performers, and the finished product is captured in the sound recording, each constituent part bound together in layers, like an onion."

Let's use Ed Sheeran's "Shape of You" as an example. The *sound recording* was made in the studio by producer

Steve Mac and Sheeran himself, who jointly own the sound recording copyright, which is licensed by Warner record label Atlantic. The *melody and lyrics* form the inside layers of that onion, which were written by Mac, Sheeran and Johnny McDaid, who jointly own the musical composition copyright. To throw another layer in there, three other musicians also own a share of the musical composition copyright — Kandi Burruss, Tameka Cottle and Kevin Briggs, who wrote '90s classic "No Scrubs" by TLC — because they asked for a share of the pie after hearing similarities between their hit and Sheeran's. Various percentages of the musical composition copyright are controlled by the different publishers who represent those six writers.

Alongside earning publishing income from the musical composition, songwriters, composers, producers, publishers, musicians, and performers are owed money from the performance of their songs. That revenue is collected and distributed by **collection societies**, such as PRS for Music, MCPS, and PPL in the UK. They pay music royalties (which mean payments to copyright holders for the use of intellectual property) to members when their work is performed, broadcast, streamed, downloaded, reproduced, played in public, or used in film and TV. PPL pays those who own or perform on the sound recording (i.e. the record labels and performers), whereas PRS and MCPS pay those who own the musical composition (i.e. the publishers, songwriters and composers).

As we mentioned before, these days the role of a label or publisher isn't only performed by what you might call 'traditional' labels and publishers — major companies (on the label side, Universal Music, Sony Music Entertainment, and Warner Music Group; the parent companies of which also own publishers) or independents (like labels: Young Turks, Domino, XL Recordings, and PIAS Recordings, and then BMG, which sits somewhere in between an independent and a major). There are also **label services companies or music**

partners (like AWAL, Wrapped Up Music, and Absolute) that offer various services (including distribution and promotion) without taking ownership of an artist's sound recording. With these deals, artists usually have more flexibility and can pick and choose what services they require. That said, it's worth noting that the 'traditional' players have responded to competition from label services companies, as well as growing power from artists in the age of social media, by increasingly entering into joint venture deals with artists and simply licensing their work, rather than outright owning it. This means that they're often 'rights partners' rather than 'rights owners'. (It's worth mentioning here though that a license agreement in perpetuity, i.e. forever, doesn't really offer the flexibility that the license part suggests. As music industry advisor Mike Burgess says, "any licence deal you do needs a termination clause. That is non-negotiable."[3])

The most basic route to market is through an **independent, self-serve distribution company** (like TuneCore, Amuse, DistroKid, CD Baby, and Ditto Music) which get music onto the various streaming platforms but usually don't offer a full, hands-on promotional package with digital marketing, radio and press placements. Songtrust and Sentric Music are equivalent examples of that for publishing — the companies will help collect royalties owed for a musical composition but won't offer much more than that as far as talent development and promotion are concerned. Those flexible tools are good for early on in a career when an artist isn't yet ready to approach the full-service companies, or if they've already built a strong team around them to fulfil the various functions those major companies offer in-house.

Which route you choose to pursue depends on the kind of career you want — there are independent success stories as well as major-label superstars, and it's possible for artists in either position to stay true to their artistic visions. But you'll also want to consider how much investment and support you need and how strong a negotiating position you're in when, and if, labels are interested. If your dream is to become the next Billie Eilish or Drake, you'll probably want the help of a major label machine behind you. If you'd prefer to run a cottage industry and have total autonomy over your career, it might be best to stick to the independent route. All labels, publishers, and similar companies have strengths and weaknesses, so it's essential to establish what's important to you, find those who can deliver when seeking deals, and to find people whose hands you feel wholly comfortable placing your career in. A good lawyer is also vital to have by your side when signing contracts (more on that later).

Wherever you might ultimately end up, one good reason to bite the bullet and get your music out there early is to get practice and receive valuable feedback. Islands Records US President, Darcus Beese, explains:

> "At the beginning, making music should never be overthought. To overthink stuff paralyses you and clouds your judgement. I love the people who work off naive beauty because they don't know what they are doing, but they're excited about it, and that counts for a lot. However unrefined your music is, it doesn't matter — put it up, because you need to get feedback. You'll get brutal feedback, [but] you'll also get good feedback, and that's what makes people what they are and refine what they are doing. There's no secret to success, it's just about putting music up and people enjoying it or not."

He adds that your response to that response could make the difference between success and oblivion. It's about "how you react to that feedback and how you get better and more laser-sighted, more refined about what you're offering to people; the visual, the music, and what you're trying to stand for."

LIFE ON THE ROAD

When it comes to playing live, a **booking agent** is the manager of an artist's career on the road who will find performance opportunities and negotiate fees. Like most other players, agents like to see a track record before getting involved, so lots and lots of practice is key.

Another vital role in the live music business is the **promoter**, who sells the tickets. They help plan shows or tours and can work directly with artists and managers during the early career stage and onwards. There's a multitude of roles beyond that — tour manager and creative director, to name a few, who will all come into play once a career is up and running.

Here's a story about Ed Sheeran to offer an example of how much practice it might take to reach a professional standard on stage. Sheeran spent much of his teenage years gigging in the sleepy countryside town of Framlingham in Suffolk, where, thanks to a population of around 2,000 people, he was a big fish in a small pond. At age 15, he played his first gig in London with musicians who had far more experience, then spent the next few years trawling the open mic circuit to reach the standard of competition in the capital.

Discussing his early career in music, Sheeran recalls: "My first gig was at Liberties in Camden, which is now called The Camden Head, and I was playing with five other singer/songwriters in their late 20s or early 30s, and they were all really fucking great. I remember going on after them and being so deflated. In my hometown, I was one of the only ones to write songs, and I came off stage with all these professional musicians who were so much better than me. I remember being like... 'I really need to get that good.'"[4]

His hard work in the ensuing years resulted in a support slot on a tour with Just Jack in 2009, which is how he met his now manager, Stuart Camp and booking agent, Jon Ollier. Ollier advised Sheeran to get paid gigs outside of London, and that's when he started earning a living from music. From his first London gig to making money, the process took around three years — and that's excluding the many years of practice in Framlingham. While lots of streams and views might feel like validation, if performing is part of your career, the true measure of value in what you're doing is on stage. Beese continues:

> "If you start uploading music, don't stop, because if you lose momentum, you'll lose those one or two people that come and go, 'I like what this person is doing.' Then at some point, someone says: 'I want to see you live.' You go and do your first live gig, and nobody turns up. You can check out, get a normal 9-5, or you go: 'Let's try this again.' And at some point, something happens, something clicks. You write a song; you get the feedback, you do a gig, the person that came before comes back with three friends. That starts a process that you build on. I always think that something is going to take two to three years from start to being tangible. Tangible is someone turning up and going: 'I fucking like that.' Anyone can email or put a nice comment on YouTube but buying a ticket and turning up is something completely different. Live is a really good measure of what you're doing."

Beese's advice regarding the live circuit might not apply to every type of artist, but the principle is sound: keep going, get better, build momentum and build a following.

MANAGEMENT AND MORE

For most artists, a good **manager** will be the most important piece of the puzzle. A manager is essentially your work parent who looks after your career (and most of the things covered in this chapter) while you get on with the serious business of actually making music. For this reason, it's essential to find one who knows what they are doing and has your back. Typically, a manager will take a percentage of an artist's total earnings — around 15% to 20% — and will get involved when they believe an artist is ready to start building a professional career. You'll probably get into arguments at some point but a good manager will accept that as part of the job — they'll be the 'shock absorber' who means you don't fall out with everyone *else* in your career. If you manage to keep your ego in check, get back on track and maintain an aligned vision, you could each secure a business partner for life.

Will Young worked with his manager, Faye Farmer, for fifteen years after winning *Pop Idol* in 2002 and he partly credits the longevity of his career to that partnership. But it wasn't always so rosy. Young explains:

> "Oh, we didn't get on at all at the beginning. We were in Cuba and I told her it wasn't going to work. She was the messenger for so much news like, 'Sorry you can't have that day off even though you've been working solidly for two months.' Then I had a crazy year during my third album. Thought I was really special, did a film, got a bit rude, got a bit insecure, so was then rude, fearful, and just wanted to be better. I wanted to do more. Faye said: 'You're being a dick and I'm going to leave you.'"

Decent managers specialise in tough love — and this was the tough love Young needed to hear.

> "And then I cried and once I'd finished the madness, we suddenly bedded in and we laughed the whole time. We didn't get stressed and haven't had a cross word since. She is a tour-de-force, that lady. I owe my career to her. There are people who have been with their managers for a long time and I always think that's quite telling because you bed in that relationship and you begin to know what each other is thinking. There are difficult moments, like when people are coming up and requesting things, and you just get a glance, and it's like boom, you know what to do."

When it comes to choosing a manager, composer, and producer Hannah Peel, who has gone through a grand total of four managers during her career — (that figure is correct at the time of going to press) — stresses the importance of shared vision and passion. She explains: "Find someone that respects and adores your music and loves what you create. If you have it in your mind that you want to sell a million records and be a pop star, you need to find a manager who supports that and will go with you on that journey. But if you are more compositional or producer-led, you need to find someone who is with you on the musical and creative output, no matter what journey that might end up being."

If you're entrepreneurially minded and willing to get stuck in to the business as well as music side of your career, it's perfectly reasonable to decide that you don't need a manager at all. Grammy Award-winner Imogen Heap, who has had record deals and a manager across her 20+ year career, offers an informed perspective. She says:

> "A lot of musicians assume that the path to success is to get a manager and get a record deal, but I prefer being able to be nimble and spread your net wide and have a community of people who you respect and share projects with, so you're not taking on the load all by yourself, and taking your risk with one person like a manager, which I think is quite an odd thing to do.
>
> "So many artists have chosen the wrong managers and that is the reason why they haven't succeeded. Maybe they've been held back by their manager or taken bad deals because the manager wanted the money, and that's not really talked about. Artists will take it very personally, 'Well it's because my songs aren't good enough or because I didn't give a good performance,' and the manager would probably make you believe that too because otherwise, you might want to sack them, so it always comes back to you."

Heap points to alternative career help like joining (or starting) a collective of artists who share knowledge and get the less exciting aspects of a career in music (like admin) done together. There's also an app she points to called Centralized, which helps self-managing artists project-manage their career bit by bit. It offers guidance on marketing, merchandise, recording, publishing, touring, and creative content and provides templates for emails and agreements, among other benefits.

Along with people who work in marketing and digital areas, a good **publicist** will manage the public image of an artist which will sometimes mean keeping them in the news (by arranging interviews, social media promo, track premieres and the like) but it'll sometimes mean the opposite: keeping artists *out* of the news when the going gets tough. Often the publicist or social team will be provided by a label (either in-house, or via an independent company), but if you're taking a DIY route, you can do your own research to find someone suitable (recommendations will help you here). While getting good music out into the world should be your priority in the first place, at some point, you might need someone to make sure it gets heard by a wider audience and that your artistic story and vision are communicated cohesively. There are thousands of new songs released every single day — the right team can help yours stand out from the rest.

LAWYERS AND SIGNING DEALS

Here's a fact that's not very rock-and-roll: **lawyers** have a pretty significant influence on the career of almost any artist. They're the ones who negotiate deal terms for every other member of the team. Once they're acting on your behalf, their legal obligation is to act in your interest — which is handy considering you'll quite understandably have very little idea how to protect yourself against bad deals and bad people, and might be better off staying away from the business entirely while you hone your talent and get a firm idea of who you do and don't want to be.

Liv Lyons, who was a musician before retraining as a lawyer, says the biggest law-related mistake she sees talent making is getting overly excited by a deal and signing on the dotted line before having a lawyer look over the contract. If you haven't had some expert advice, you're almost certain to be getting into an unfavourable deal, which might put others off working with you, as well as lock you into terms that are hard to get out of. A manager isn't going to be too enthused about taking on an artist (whose profits they take a cut from, remember) who is locked into a recording or publishing agreement that pays out less than market rate, for example. If you're in a bad arrangement, the result could be lack of proper payment while the companies you're working with happily profit from your work, which is naturally going to be demotivating and disheartening, and a state in which it will be tricky to reach your own full potential.

Music lawyers are quite a friendly bunch, says Lyons, and will often look over a deal either for free (they'll probably hope you'll recruit them formally as your career takes off) or for a small fee. The Musicians' Union has lawyers on hand who offer advice to members and can provide legal assistance for disputes where possible and The Incorporated Society of Musicians has an in-house legal team who can read over your contracts. If you're signing a proper lifelong record deal covering lots of albums, or a similar publishing arrangement, Lyons says that labels and publishers will usually offer to cover your legal fees anyway. So there is no excuse not to seek help.

One of the most important things to look out for in deal terms is the length. Lyons advises securing as short a deal as possible so conditions can be renegotiated as your career progresses, instead of being beholden to terms that were signed when needs were very different. "A five-album record deal sounds good, but you probably would benefit from just doing a two-album record deal because it means you get to the end of that deal much quicker, so you can renegotiate your royalties, all the advances, and have some leverage to get a better deal," she explains.

If you're stuck in a five-album deal, the five albums are the option of the label, not the artist — this means that they're not obliged to release all five albums. If they want to drop you after album one or two, they can, but if *you* want to drop *them*, you can't. Bizarrely,

Kanye West has a stipulation in his contract with publisher EMI that he must not retire or take an extended hiatus, ever.[5] That's on the extreme end of the unfavourable deal-terms scale, but a stark example of how long companies might try to retain ownership. In this case, less is truly more, and especially when considering protecting your overall wellbeing.

Another vital thing to keep in mind before tying the knot with anyone, in business terms, of course, is to make sure they understand the kind of artist you want to be. When singer and songwriter Tawiah signed to a major label and big management company, she had a bunch of musicians and a producer she enjoyed working with and had already released an EP. However, her new partners put her in the studio with different producers arriving on a metaphorical conveyor belt, which is a process she fast found didn't work for her. "I was in and out of loads of different studios, I'd meet somebody and be in the studio with them for two days then the next few days I'd be in with someone else," she says. "I found that quite a difficult process because you're not going to connect with everyone you meet. For me, music is such a personal thing and it's hard to be vulnerable and open up with a new stranger every couple of days." It was a vital learning process with a considerable cost. Tawiah spent the next five years trying to get out of her contracts and wasn't allowed to release any music of her own until she was legally free. Moral of the story: work out how you do and don't want to work and find partners that help facilitate that.

HEALTH

However a team is made up, every member has a responsibility to make sure the artist's health is of utmost priority, because if they get sick and can't work, neither can the rest of the team. That might mean that interviews, meet and greets, shows and tours need rearranging so the artist can have a break — and that's fine. Nick Shymansky, who managed the early career of Amy Winehouse (before she moved to another manager), explains this further: "When you become an absolute superstar there are so many requests, gigs, interviews, sponsorship deals, and private functions. So you have to have a team around you that can say, 'Absolutely not'."[6] As an artist, it might be tempting to continue running at full pelt while the momentum is there, but to do so while ignoring health issues is likely to cause more problems later down the line, as the Winehouse story so tragically told. The most important thing an artist can do is take their health seriously and be honest about when they need to stop. This might be difficult while working in an industry that encourages long working hours and has a highly competitive culture, but if you don't make time to look after your own health and happiness when you're busy, you'll be forced to make time for them when you inevitably become unwell.

Should an artist need healthcare or time off, those who are investing in their career have a responsibility to facilitate that and, if possible, help with any assistance that might be required. That's something the manager, or wider team, has a right to demand. Shymansky tells us: "During my tenure as Amy's manager, I took a protective stance and one of the ideas was to enrol her into a rehab clinic. Amy agreed to attend and as soon as I made it clear to the label that we'd require their financial assistance and general support, they instantly kicked in to gear. Unfortunately, Amy didn't see it through at that point, but the label was willing to back it. They spend a fortune on things like remixes, photoshoots and videos, and what business wouldn't want to sacrifice one of their videos or remix budgets to make sure that the whole prospect of the artist stays on track? But you have to be passionate and go in and fight for things in this business. None of us are professionals, it's all opinion, feeling, so you have to have a backbone and perhaps sacrifice some instant gratification if the artist isn't well, but in the long run you get a lot back."

Ultimately, Shymansky points to the responsibility of a manager in prioritising an artist's health. "In my opinion, it's a manager's job to galvanise opportunities and, more importantly, protection for the artist," he explains. "It's a manager's job to look out for the artist on every level."

DIVERSITY

Finally, when you're meeting any of the people we've mentioned above, it's likely going to be useful for you to know that the music business is, generally speaking, somewhat lacking in diversity (most notably in positions of power). In the UK, Black, Asian, and ethnic minority workers represent 22.3% of the British music industry, according to UK Music's 2020 report.[7] While that's higher than the 12.8% total representation for the UK population as a whole, it's significantly lower than the 30% of Black, Asian, and ethnic minority individuals who make up the workforce in London[8] — and though there are thriving local scenes in cities like Bristol, Birmingham, Manchester and Glasgow, London's simply where the majority of the music industry operates. In addition, while there's an equal gender split in the industry as a whole (49.1% people in the industry identify as female, according to UK Music), you'll still find a disproportionately large number of men in senior roles, resulting in an average gender pay gap of 29.6% across the three major record labels (Universal, Sony, and Warner) as of 2018,[9] and a 44.5% pay gap at major promoter Live Nation as of 2019.[10] (Only companies with 250 employees and over are required to report these figures, so we don't know how this looks across the wider business.)

Aspects of all this have been slowly moving in the right direction during the last twenty years, and that change has accelerated more recently as music companies have begun to accept responsibility for increasing diversity and representation. In addition to gender and ethnic diversity, there's also thought being given to neurodiversity — a term that applies to variations in thinking, like ADHD, autism and dyslexia, which is said to apply to 15% of the UK population.[11] Universal Music have led the charge here with their *Creative Differences* guide, offering individual insights and recommendations for change that aim to result in a more inclusive working environment that facilitates the creativity of those with alternative thinking (which applies to many artists too). UK Music stats suggest that just 6.4% of those working on the business side are affected by disability, so if you need special accommodations you may need to be vocal about these, and be clear about how people can support you. Despite this overall progress, very few people in the music industry would argue there isn't a lot of work still to be done.

On the artist side of things, female talent is less likely to have UK Top 40 chart success (three times as many male pop stars appeared on 2018's biggest hit singles[12]) and women are underrepresented at radio too (just 19% of the top 100 songs by British acts in the UK airplay chart from January to August 2020 were by solo female acts[13]). An analysis of the public-facing rosters of British music companies in 2019 found that just under 20% of artists signed to labels are female and just 14% of writers signed to publishers are female.[14] And as pointed out by singer and songwriter Ray BLK, her existence as one of three or four notable black female artists in the UK commercial music scene suggests there's an undercurrent of colourism in the industry. "It's not the fact that there aren't black or dark-skinned women available or talented enough, I meet them all the time. It's just that record labels, publishing companies and festival bookers don't think they deserve attention," she says.[15]

This lack of gender equality isn't just about equal opportunity and representation — there's also evidence to suggest the existence of widespread sexual harassment. Following the #MeToo movement, research by The Musicians' Union found that 48% of its members surveyed have been sexually harassed at work and 85% of those respondents said they did not report their experiences due to work culture and fear of losing work. In addition, 61% of musicians said they felt at greater risk of experiencing sexual harassment because of their freelance status.[16]

The LGTBQ+ community has historically been marginalised too, with dated ideas about public figures and sexuality and identity hindering musicians' ability to be open about their own and clearly express it in their art. With a few notable exceptions (like George Michael, Boy George, and David Bowie), it's only very recently that the music industry has started to actively promote anything other than heterosexual representation in music videos and song lyrics in the mainstream pop sphere. That's mainly thanks to a shift in culture that has resulted in an increasing awareness and visibility of LGTBQ+ artists and high profile names feeling able to be open about their own identity, like Lil Nas X, Sam Smith, Kae Tempest, Olly Alexander, SOPHIE, Kehlani, Frank Ocean, Jess Glynne, MNEK, Halsey, Laura Jane Grace, and Mykki Blanco. Still, as Pride in Music co-founder Guy Howes says, "as an industry, we still have so much to do to address LGBTQ+ stigmas and encourage more diversity in the workplace."[17]

There are also multiple barriers faced by disabled musicians and artists. A 2019 survey by music charity Attitude is Everything found that 70% of deaf and disabled musicians had kept their disability hidden because of worries it would damage a relationship with a venue, promoter or festival, while two-thirds said they have had to compromise their health or wellbeing to be able to perform live due to lack of accessibility accommodations.[18]

If you're in any of these under-represented categories, it may be harder to find people to work with who you feel truly relate to your vision, needs and particular background, and finding those who do might be the difference between fulfilling your dreams, or, just like Tawiah experienced, being stalled while directed onto a path that's not right for you. It can also result in a feeling of imposter syndrome, as artist, songwriter and producer MNEK has experienced. "My parents are Nigerian and British so I grew up in a black household, a black neighbourhood, I'm a black boy. When you get to any industry, you realise that in most places you are the only black person," he says. "I think I would have had a lot of comfort if I'd always had someone I could relate to culturally as part of my team from the start and I've often grasped for that over the years. When you're in a white industry as a person of colour, it's very daunting and you just don't feel like much is possible. It's nice to have people who uplift you and are in the fire with you."

So be aware of that, and take the time to consider what you need to be respected; mentally and physically healthy; and feel creatively fulfilled in a working environment so that you can articulate those needs clearly to whoever you might be working with and find situations that are conducive to that (we hope the rest of the book will help you to work this out). And like we've already mentioned and will delve into further, keep in mind that there are multiple ways to make a living and be successful in music. There's some great work being done by organisations like those mentioned above, so head to the resources section to find out where you can find support if you're experiencing discrimination, harassment, or just want a community of like-minded people to talk to.

We will end with another caveat. This chapter is, quite honestly, a bit optimistic. You could follow all of the above advice and still get nowhere in terms of reaching traditional commercial success. That's just the harsh reality of an industry that relies on talent, yes; but also on luck, timing, connections and favours. So please don't deem yourself some sort of failure if you haven't managed to get a manager, lawyer, record and publishing deal, and everything that comes with that. The truth is, that sort of complete set-up happens for the minority of those who pursue a career in music. Plus, it all looks shiny and glamorous on the outside, but that path comes with a lot of pressure and isn't going to be the happiest and most sustainable route for everyone. We'll delve more into this towards the latter part of this book.

To conclude, a professional career in music starts with:

- Releasing music and building a fanbase by yourself.
- Practising a lot and being open to receiving constructive feedback.
- Educating yourself about the structure of the business
- Working with people who love what you do and want to help.

The potential routes to market are:

- Doing it yourself, with the help of ad-hoc expertise as your career develops.
- Securing a label services style deal that allows you to keep hold of your master rights.
- Going the whole hog and signing a record label deal that might take ownership of your master rights but should offer a robust support and development package in return.

The various parties mentioned above are:

- **Managers** take care of an artist's overall career like the CEO of a company. That's a role that savvy artists (or smart friends) can also take on themselves.
- **Record labels** and **label services companies** look after the recorded music career of an artist and exploit the master rights for songs.
- **Publishers** take care of the musical composition copyright of a song and help further the careers of writers, composers, and producers.
- **Live agents** steer the live touring career of an act and **promoters** sell the tickets for gigs.
- **Publicists** act as a bridge between the artist and the media or public.
- **Lawyers** take care of negotiation when it comes to signing deals and can join a team at the early stages of talent development.

For far more in-depth reading on the music business, check out the most recent editions of:

- Donald Passman's *All You Need To Know About The Music Business* (there's an audio version of this too)
- *Music: The Business* by Ann Harrison
- Phil Taggart's highly readable *Slacker Guide to the Music Industry*

CHAPTER 2

MONEY MANAGEMENT

WE COVERED THE BASIC structure of the commercial music business in the previous chapter, and we're now going to offer some more practical advice about how to manage the money side of a career in music. It's great if you're one of the artists who already has a team to take care of the day-to-day stuff but if you're one of the many who don't, learning how to do it yourself will help to lessen the risk of money worries in the future. And even if you have a team, it's pretty vital that you understand your own financial situation. This can help to avoid being taken advantage of and ensures you're having an informed say in how your money is spent. We're not going to go too far into how to maximise the income you earn from music because that's another book for another time.

Instead, we'll cover accountancy, working for free, advances, and various sources of funding.

We understand that you might reflexively want to swerve this area. Partly because talking about finances can be boring and partly because you got into music *because you were into music*, not because you wanted to make money. We agree that money and artistry might best be kept separate in some respects — but you'll want to stay on top of both. If you want to engage with the music business, making money is a fundamental part of that (and if you're uncomfortable with making money from music, perhaps it's better kept as a hobby).

Because most musicians are self-employed, keeping track of finances is, unfortunately, a facet of freelance life that's just as vital as making music. If you're not receiving all the income that you could be and are struggling for cash, you're going to have less time and headspace to do the fun creative stuff. The average salary of a working musician in the UK was just over £23k in 2018,[1] which was around £10k less than the average salary for all full-time workers across the country.[2] That figure is going to fluctuate hugely depending on individual circumstances but it does offer a general marker that suggests musicians can't really afford to leave money on the table, and let's not forget that struggling for money is a major contributor to stress.

ACCOUNTANCY

Bringing structure to your finances is something a manager, bookkeeper, and/or accountant can help with but you can learn this yourself, and it doesn't have to be complicated. Composer and producer Hannah Peel keeps track of her incoming and outgoing money with a basic spreadsheet. "Because I've been running my own record label to release my records, you need to be so organised," she explains. "You need to have spreadsheets and know where that money is coming from and what's going out to keep an eye on it so that you're not missing an invoice to somebody, or you're not losing out on something." Whether self-releasing or not, keeping organised records is something Peel now does for every project she works on.

An income and expenditure spreadsheet usually looks like an Excel document for each tax year that lists invoices and other payments due, and whether they've been paid. A separate one covers business expenses like travel, accountancy, legal help, office costs — including a portion of bills if you work from home — and subscriptions for anything work-related like music streaming services and career-development apps. There are digital accountancy apps that offer pimped-out versions of this spreadsheet, like QuickBooks and Xero, both of which charge a fee for simple-to-use solutions that can make accounting less tedious.

A few tips:

- Have a **dedicated bank account** for your business money that's separate from your private account. It makes it easier to track what's going on and your annual tax return will be a lot less painful. Some of the new 'challenger banks' like Starling and Monzo make it really easy to set up business accounts that run alongside personal accounts. They all offer features that allow you to divide your balance into 'pots,' which is helpful when putting money aside for tax.

- If you can, **set around 20% of all earnings aside for tax as soon as the money arrives** so you're always able to cover the half-yearly bills from HM Revenue & Customs (HMRC). (If you unexpectedly end up with a 200m-stream mega-hit or Adidas decide they want to throw a load of money your way for a global ad campaign, bear in mind that you might end up in a higher tax bracket, so you'll need to set aside more than 20%.) Don't forget to factor in a student loan and national insurance.

- If it's your first time being self-employed, be aware that HMRC operate an eye-wateringly annoying system called payment on account which means **you're asked to pay half of *next* year's tax in advance**, based on your initial earnings. After the second year, it's easier to manage and can actually be quite helpful, but it can be a shock to people who are just starting out.

- Having a **good credit rating** is important for any borrowing you might need to do, as well as renting and buying properties and taking out a mobile phone contract. You can build this up by taking out a credit card and remembering to pay it off monthly (this could be used for business expenses).

- Seriously: remember to pay it off monthly.

- If you can spare a bit of cash every month, no matter how small, it's a good idea to **build up some sort of cushion fund** in case there's an unexpected expense, or you feel like a career pivot and have to take a cut in earnings for some time. This book was written during the coronavirus outbreak at the start of 2020 when the music industry was served a big blow thanks to the shutdown of live events and record stores. That resulted in many musicians (and other workers) being left out of pocket. You'd hope this sort of situation doesn't happen again (or not frequently, at least) but it's always worth preparing for unforeseen circumstances. It's not just about planning for disaster, though. If a track's picking up heat, you might suddenly find yourself in the position of wanting to hire a radio plugger or a publicist, or shoot a video, which you'll need spare cash for.

- The idea of **a pension** might seem a) boring and b) ridiculous to anyone far from retirement age, **but the earlier you start, the more you'll thank yourself when you're seventy** and feel like putting your feet up for a couple of years. As a bonus, you won't have to pay tax on any pension contributions you make, which is the closest you might ever get to free cash. Also, even if you're in your thirties, it's never too late: the best time to start might have been ten years ago, but the *second* best time to start is always right now. The Musicians' Union offers a scheme with Aviva and there are a lot of independent options out there too.

- Don't forget to sign up to PRS, MCPS, and PPL to receive income owed from the performance and reproduction of your songs. Both PRS (which MCPS operates under) and PPL have staff on hand to make sure works are registered correctly, so if in doubt, give them a call.

HIRING HELP

If you have some budget to spare, you might be thinking it could be a good idea to hire someone to help you with all of this. That person could be a **bookkeeper**, who will keep track of your incoming and outgoing financial records, or an **accountant**, who can take a more advisory approach. For the latter, it's especially important that you do your research first. History is littered with stories of dodgy accountants who at best are inept and at worst have taken advantage of musicians, siphoning off heaps of cash from their unknowing clients. This is why it's vital that artists, and their managers, know how to choose the right one. Like a lawyer, a great accountant is an essential part of an artist's team who will collect and control various income streams and make sure artists pay the right tax (and aren't caught unaware by a big bill from HMRC).

They might suggest you set yourself up as a limited company, which on the face of it might sound a bit 'Apprentice contestant' and can add an extra layer of complexity when it comes to accounting, but it may provide certain benefits such as more robust legal protection. They can also offer extended business management services that involve creating a money management plan to help alleviate financial worries and ensure smart and informed financial decisions, which is a large part of getting a successful career in music off the ground.

There might be times when your accountant tells you things you don't want to hear — but don't forget their job is all about seeing what's happening now, and trying to prepare for what might happen in the future; whether it's next year's tax bill or something further down the line. Nobody wants to be told: "You're spending too much on taxis." Equally, nobody wants to end up in a position where they can't even afford the bus. Also, if your accountant notices you hurling cash at cars and ludicrous holidays and doesn't at some point suggest you might instead consider putting down a deposit on your first flat, it might be a good idea to look for a different accountant.

When it comes to hiring an accountant, Nick Lawrence of Big Star Business Management says these are the vital things to keep in mind:

- Firstly, they would ideally be a **music business specialist**.
- Secondly, because of those horror stories mentioned above, they must offer **total transparency** when it comes to a client's accounts — you should always be able see how much money you have and how much you are owed.
- It's also pretty important that you **speak the same language** — bombarding you with jargon that you don't understand is pretty unhelpful (and if there *is* anything you don't understand, a good accountant won't think you're stupid for asking questions).
- Finally, when it comes to fees, **fixed costs** can help alleviate the scary prospect of surprise bills.

If you can't afford to pay anyone yet and don't have the headspace to do it yourself, The Incorporated Society of Musicians (ISM) offers discounted accountancy services and a tax helpline for members. Both ISM and The Musicians' Union (MU) have a wealth of money-related advice on their respective websites and offer membership packages with a variety of useful benefits. MU membership costs £227 annually and ISM charges £181 a year, with vastly reduced rates for students, those in the early stages of their career, new membership offers, and discounted rates for members of education unions including the National Education Union, the Educational Institute of Scotland and the University and College Union. If you're unsure, it's worth noting that MU and ISM benefits include instrument insurance, which can be around the same price as the annual membership fee.

CHASING MONEY

In theory, here's how getting paid for freelance services should work: you do some work (or agree to do some work) for someone else, and you send an invoice. Your invoice includes payment terms — thirty days is standard — and within thirty days, the cash appears in your account. In practice, things can be a little more complex and you may have to mildly harass your employer before getting paid. Whether you're owed £100 or £10k, you're entitled to your money, and who's to say £100 won't mean the difference between you being able to eat that week or not? It can feel pretty grotty pestering people for money (even when it's your money) but stick to your guns and make sure you get what you've earned.

If invoices are unpaid after some time, you're legally entitled to invoice again, charging a late payment fee and interest on what you're owed (Google 'statutory late payment' for more information on this). Escalating things further, you can even file a small claim — this involves the small claims court. We'd advise you use your judgment on whether either of these steps might burn bridges with future collaborators, but it's worth noting that with smaller companies, non-payment of an invoice may indicate a cash flow problem and it's easier to get money from a company while they're still operating than once they've gone bust.

When it comes to invoices, here's how to get paid fairly and promptly.

- Having the conversation about money with a client **upfront** makes it less awkward further down the line and allows you to make clear your terms, which should be when you're going to get paid, how much, and how.

- What to charge? That's difficult to answer because it depends on who you are and what you're providing, but remember that it's a **negotiation**, and set your fees according to what other people are asking for similar work. You can charge more than the average if there's a reason you or your offering are premium, or less to accommodate for lower budgets.

- While discussing the 'when', give a **deadline** that's reasonable but short — as we said, 30 days from completion of the work is fair — so that when you do send an invoice, it doesn't go to the bottom of the pile. Regarding the late payment fees we mentioned above, the magic words to place at the bottom of your invoice are: '*In order to avoid charges, please pay within 30 days of the date specified above.*' If it's a new client, consider asking for a deposit or to be paid in advance — some clients will be happy to pay half upfront and the rest on completion.

- Has someone failed to pay up? Don't let them forget about it. Make a note in your diary to contact them on the first day it's **overdue**. If that doesn't work, contact them weekly and then daily. Keep in mind that you have the right to use late payment legislation, which says that you, as a small business, need to be paid within 30 days unless agreed otherwise. The Musicians' Union and ISM will chase late payers on your behalf with their unpaid fee recovery service if you're a member.

WORKING FOR EXPOSURE

If you've already started a career in music, chances are you've come across this: being promised exciting 'exposure opportunities' that don't involve the sort of monetary excitement that allows you to pay your rent. "Oh that sounds good," you think. "Next time I'm in Sainsbury's I'll just pay for my weekly shop with 'exposure'. That'll go down a treat at the checkout."

Working for no pay is a tricky balance at the beginning of a career when experience and exposure actually *can* play a useful role, but there comes the point where your level of professionalism requires payment in cash and nothing else. It's all about weighing it up and deciding whether there's something in it for you, thinking about what kind of financial position the person asking you is in, and how much time it's going to take that could instead be used to get or do paid work. A local promoter who puts on a night as a labour of love genuinely might not be able to pay you anything more than petrol money — but you'll get a chance to hone your stagecraft and maybe shift a t-shirt or two. A multi-platinum artist looking for a support act on their arena tour is a whole different ballgame. Artists in this higher position should have the flexibility and budget to pay their support acts, but equally so, showcasing your work for tens of thousands of people might actually be worth doing so for free. Ultimately, the decision is highly personal to each individual artist: what are you financially able and emotionally willing to work for *right now*?

Hannah Peel, who has been asked to work for free several times, explains:

> "There's a point you get to where you don't want to do anything for exposure and you don't actually *need* the exposure. But when you're starting out, you can't be demanding fees because maybe you've only played two gigs and you're not going to bring an audience who'll pay on the door or pay for the beer to be drunk. It's a real balance but I think it's worth remembering that when you hit a certain point, you're like, 'No, this has to stop.' I was asked to do a [free gig] last year, and I just said a flat 'No, I'm not doing this unless I get paid.' And they came back and offered a fee."

When it comes to making music, there are other ways of asking for remuneration beyond a flat fee. Peel continues: "For example, if I'm asked to do a remix and the other artist doesn't have much money, there are ways around it. You can split the publishing or something that makes it feel palatable."

Working for no pay is something musician Imogen Heap has also grappled with throughout her career, particularly after having her daughter, Scout and finding that she was placing a higher value on her time. She explains:

> "Becoming a mother has helped me look after myself, put myself in the bigger picture and value myself more, and has actually brought me more money. Before I had Scout, I was used to working really long hours and being under incredible amounts of pressure so I would always say yes, even if it didn't pay. Since becoming a mother, I've been really amazing at saying no, and it's so easy because you just go, well, is that going to tire me out and how long am I going to have to be away from Scout?"

You don't have to wait until there's a bigger reason (or a little person) before you place boundaries on the time you give to others. Valuing yourself — and acknowledging your self-worth — is something anyone can do now.

ADVANCES

If you're lucky enough to sign a label and/or publishing deal and get a sizeable advance payment as part of the package, this section is for you. You may not even have to sign a major deal to get an advance – a number of distribution companies have started offering advances on future royalties in recent years, including TuneCore, Amuse and Stem. We'll mainly cover the more 'traditional' sources of advances here, but the principles of what we're saying are relevant to both. If you've had an advance from a distribution company, focus on the debt and planning part, not the bit about your creative freedom. A digital distributor won't be interfering with your creative decisions because their job is to simply deliver your music onto the relevant platforms.

Advances are exciting, aren't they? A big chunk of cash for you to do with as you so wish: absolutely ideal. Book that all-inclusive trip to Barbados; buy a car (in fact, make it two). Except: hold on a minute. Treating an advance as 'free cash' can be catastrophic for all your hopes and dreams. If you totally waste it, whoever has given it to you can't be expected to dish out again.

Here's how it all works.

Record label advances, for example, are usually made up of **a personal advance and some cash for recording and promotion**. The personal part of it is there to ensure that you are adequately funded as an individual to get you through the process of what the advance is given to you for in the first place. If you get an advance to help you deliver an album in nine months, you've got to make that cash last... well, nine months. At some point in those nine months, you'll hopefully be making live income but unless you've got financial support to cover the costs of touring (which could come from a record label or sponsorship deal), that income will need to be spent on covering your costs, so won't stay in your back pocket.

Advances vary hugely, and the amount you'll see will also vary depending on whether you're a solo artist/DJ or a member of a twelve-piece jazz ensemble, but it's important to remember that an exciting lump sum of (say) £15k might not actually be quite so exciting when you factor in how long it has to last and what it'll need to cover. If it's got to last you a year, you'll be on less than the national living wage.

Another thing worth bearing in mind with advances — and there's a clue in the name here — is **that they comprise money you're being *advanced* against future earnings**. If an advance has come from a recording deal or distribution company, an artist won't start generating income from their sound recordings until they've paid back (or, in contract terms, *recouped*) that advance from their share of royalties. While high advances from record labels are trumpeted in the press (and quite often exaggerated) as indicative of promise and success, lower is actually better in the long run because it means less debt, less pressure and more creative control. And you won't start making money as soon as your album's released — it can take weeks, months and even years for the advance to be recouped and for everything else to start trickling through.

Lawyer Liv Lyons is back to explain how this situation might work in a record label context:

> "The more debt you get into with a record company, the more the accountants and people at the top are going to go: 'This needs to be brilliant otherwise we are going to drop it.' They will then put pressure on the A&R and say, 'Well, you might be making nice music but that's not going to work for us — we are in too much debt for you to do what *you* want and you're going to have to create music that *we* want.'"

Before you know it, you're being cajoled into doing a collaboration with an artist whose music you couldn't care less about, tarnishing your vision and reputation before they have even had a chance to bloom.

It's also worth noting here that standard label deals are often made across multiple albums. So the '£1m contracts' we hear about might actually mean £200k for the first album, £300k for the second, then £500k for the third. All these figures will be subject to commission fees for your management, as well as myriad other costs. Those costs include cash spent on recording by the label (like studio time, travel, and equipment rental) which is added as expenses onto your overall debt, therefore increasing the time it's going to take for you to generate money from royalties.

If you're a songwriter and an artist, you might be able to combine a label advance with a second advance from a publisher. Again, this is the same deal as a label advance — you won't start generating publishing income until the money your songs have made from royalties and sync fees (and, to a lesser extent, sheet music exceeds the sum of the advance.

Whatever sort of advance you get, Nick Lawrence recommends working out a personal cash flow plan, whether on your own or with an accountant, which documents monthly spending and bills. Ideally, the sum of the advance will cover those costs for the time you need it to and a monthly allowance can then be paid into your personal bank account from the advance, which is kept in a separate account where it can't be withdrawn for fun and games. If additional cash comes in that does allow some freedom, and shouldn't be invested into something a musician needs, that can be paid as a bonus and spent on whatever you like (so, that's when you get the car or at least upgrade to quilted toilet paper).

When you do start earning cash, don't bank on it lasting. In an ideal world, success would snowball, automatically resulting in further success (financial and otherwise), but in the precarious world of music that's not necessarily a given. As ASCAP, BRIT, and Ivor Novello–Award winning songwriter, Wayne Hector, explains:

> "The most common mistake is the belief that because you started having a couple of hits, that it's going to continue. Being objective about it, most people have one or two hits in their entire career."

So instead of spending any first wins immediately with the assumption that there's more to come, it might be a good idea to put any surplus cash towards getting yourself into a stable financial position, no matter which way the wind blows. For Hector, that means buying a house. He says:

> "The hardest thing anybody ever does is finding a deposit to buy a home. I always say, if you were going to be really cold about it, money that you make from those first few songs, you should be able to invest that in [a deposit for] a home.

To me, that gives you a great start in life, and if you are lucky and it continues and you can pay off your home, that gets rid of the biggest problem you're ever going to have and it puts you in a position where maybe you'll be a little bit less stressed out and the creativity can continue."

A final word on advances: if you get dropped, or your music fails to generate enough money to pay it back, it shouldn't turn into personal debt. As Donald S. Passman writes in *All You Need To Know About The Music Business*, "**With very rare exceptions, advances are non-returnable, which means it's totally the record company's risk**. So if you don't sell any records, [the company] will never get back its advances."[3]

FUNDING

To offer an overview of the structure of the commercial music business, we've talked a lot about the traditional sources of investment. In reality, they are just some of many ways to get a music career off the ground. Beyond advances from a music company, there are lots of funding opportunities that can be used to further an aspect of a musician's career, whether that be for recording new music, going on tour, filming footage, staging an event, or doing some training and education.

Thanks to the digital revolution, artists now have loads of choices as to how they can earn money and build a fanbase and the number of successful DIY-ers is growing by the day. In 2019, Midia Research suggests that revenue generated by artists without record labels counted for 4.1% of the $21.5bn global recorded music market, generating over $873m in revenue — a figure which grew by 36% from 2018.[4] As we mentioned in Business Basics, outside of those who are defined as full-time recording artists, there are millions of musicians globally who have portfolio careers,[5] made up of performing, teaching, recording, touring, and whatever else they can do to make money.

Funding expert Remi Harris says **the most widely used sources of funding for musicians is money from friends and family, crowdfunding and then grants**. A loan from a supportive parent or wealthy relative is the easiest way to raise some cash, but if (like most of us) you don't have access to that kind of help or simply don't want to go down that route, crowdfunding and grants could be the way to go. Beyond that, there's the potential of investment from an investor or an investment scheme. There are also credit options that can be used for buying things you need, like Take it Away, which offers interest-free loans to buy musical instruments, equipment, software and tuition. Harris says it's best for musicians who are at an early career stage to focus on crowdfunding and grants, and that's what we'll delve into here.

Before we do that, it's worth noting that there is financial support out there for musicians who fall on hard times, for whatever reason that might be. Help Musicians offer financial aid for musicians in need, and the PRS Members Fund is there to support and provide advice to PRS members and their families, who may be struggling financially, physically, or emotionally. Don't hesitate to contact either of them.

CROWDFUNDING

There are generally two options for crowdfunding — sites like Kickstarter allow artists to raise funds for a project (like an album) by asking for various levels of donations from fans in exchange for access to the project once it's finished, plus higher-priced extras like limited edition releases, artwork, signed merch, tickets to launches/gigs, and an unlimited amount of creative options beyond this. Other sites, like Corite and Bumper Collective, offer fans the opportunity to buy a share of revenue in an artist's future work.

Ultimately, crowdfunding allows musicians to get financial support for their work from people who love what they do, directly, with no middlemen taking a cut (beyond whatever the crowdfunding platform charges) or making things unnecessarily complicated.

With that freedom comes the responsibility to deliver what's been promised and to put in the work it takes to run a successful campaign, which requires lots of time and preparation. Harris says that it's difficult to launch a crowdfunding campaign without an existing audience — which could be a supportive fanbase or friends and family — because none of us have much inclination to give money to people we don't already know, love, and trust, regardless of how great an idea is.

If you do have an audience and decide to launch a campaign, she advises to:

- **Set a funding target that's achievable and reasonable** for the work that you're offering.

- **Be proactive and committed**. "You should be continually posting on your campaign, so have media prepared before launch that you are going to use, like videos and posts." That regular communication goes for keeping in touch with the people who have pledged support, too.

- Try and drum up some sort of **outside publicity** to spread the word. Harris adds: "A good idea goes quite a long way. Because there will be other people out there doing something similar to you, it's helpful if you can think of a really interesting angle and have some kind of unique driving reason behind what you are doing that's going to connect to people."

We'll end this section with a word of warning. Crowdfunding platform PledgeMusic fell into administration in 2019, reportedly owing artists and bands a sum estimated to be between $1m and $3m.[6] That money had been raised from fans in order to fund projects. Many artists awaiting payout from successful campaigns at the time of PledgeMusic's demise had to kiss goodbye to cash they were expecting to receive, and were given the difficult choice of either leaving fans disappointed (potentially breaking the all-important bond of trust) or funding projects through other means. We mention this story not to put you off crowdfunding entirely — there are lots of other platforms out there that will have longevity — but as an example of how precarious it can be to place your career (and your fans' trust) in the hands of just one platform that's potentially insecure. Which isn't to say that judging a platform's level of security is easy, and those who were impacted by the PledgeMusic story had no clue as to what was to come, but exercising caution and reading the small print is always a good idea.

Iain Baker of the band Jesus Jones, who lost £5k as a result of the demise of Pledge, urges anyone doing any sort of crowdfunding project to check the small-print scrupulously on contracts signed with platforms — especially those that are fairly new and funded by venture-capital money — and to see exactly what levels of security are connected to any funds that people may put into a crowdfunding project. He explains: "Try and leave your money in a location that is as secure as perhaps it could be. So much of the tech industry is underpinned by waves of investor money — venture capitalists are putting money into companies saying, 'Well it doesn't matter if Spotify, for example, doesn't turn a profit on my $20bn investment now, because we hope we are in this for the long run and will turn it into $100bn in 10 years' time.' But if global events change, people can catch a cold fairly quickly. These venture capitalists can suddenly sour on a project and the huge sums of money which underpin a lot of these modern sites could vanish overnight. If it does, what happens to the money that they are supposedly looking after for you? People need to look at how secure the financial foundations of crowdfunding sites that we wish to become involved with are."

Perhaps a less risky route is to ask fans to support your music through a platform like Patreon. It offers creators a way to set up a recurring revenue stream from those who want to support their work. An artist could have several price tiers ranging from £5 to £50 a month, all of which offer varying levels of value. US duo Pomplamoose (Jack Conte and Nataly Dawn), for example, charge $5 a month for a new song download every week, a say in what songs are recorded next, and access to a community chatroom. For $10 a month, fellow creators get instrumentals and stems for all their songs, original demos, musical charts, and everything in the previous tier. The $50 a month tier includes all of the above, plus the contributor's name in the end credits of every video they support and a personalised thank you video from Conte and Dawn.

Virtual tipping is another way musicians can directly earn money from their fanbase, which is something that's gained real traction in China through streaming services like QQ Music, Kugou, and Kuwo and karaoke app WeSing and TikTok app Douyin. Through those platforms, fans can choose to pay extra for music and merch and send live streamers virtual gifts which can be converted into cash by the recipient. During the coronavirus pandemic in 2020, virtual tipping entered the Western markets too. Spotify introduced a feature which allows artists to link to their personal Venmo, Cash App, or PayPal accounts on their profiles, while SoundCloud launched a Direct Support Link to allow fans the opportunity to support musicians during a financially tough time (some musicians also put a tipping option on their own websites). Beyond tipping, there's Bandcamp, which offers various payment models, including fixed prices for projects and subscriptions, and a pay-what-you-want option where fans decide how much they want to pay for whatever an artist is selling. As you can see, there are a lot of ways to get paid for creative work in the digital age.

GRANTS

If crowdfunding's not for you, or if you don't want to develop your work in the full glare of expectant friends and fans, grants might be the better option. In the UK, you'll find that most of these are offered by PRS Foundation, Help Musicians and the Arts Council.

Your first task here is to work out which grants might be relevant to your specific situation because the main funders offer lots of different types. PRS Foundation, for example, has funds that support artists at the beginning of their careers, those at a crucial tipping point, artists looking for international opportunities and a female-focused development programme. Help Musicians runs postgraduate awards, a professional development fund, one for independent music creators and another that focuses on supporting multi-disciplinary projects. Keep in mind that a funding application can be quite a taxing (translation: incredibly dull) process, so don't use a scatter-gun approach and apply for lots in a short space of time (PRS Foundation CEO Joe Frankland recommends a maximum of three per year). Do some research and speak to the funder to find out which one might be relevant to you, and focus on one application at a time.

Funders generally like to see a track record, so evidence of creating and performing music for a decent amount of time, which could be released music that's gained some traction and perhaps a team member or two. Knock-backs are never easy to take so make sure you're really ready before putting in the time and effort required to write an application to ensure the highest chance of success. Competition is fierce — PRS Foundation funds around 10% to 15% of applicants per year — but there are ways to make yourself stand out from the crowd.

Found the fund that's right for you? Here, Remi Harris explains how to start an application.

- **Stage one: preparation**. "Sign up to the funder's online portal if there is one, download the application questions and guidelines. Check the deadline and what you need to gather together before you apply. Ideally, chat to someone from the funder and check you're eligible for the fund you're applying to."

- **Stage two: project concept and budget**. "Start developing your concept and the budget before jumping into answering the questions. Write a paragraph or bullet points on what your

Hannah Peel has received funding from PRS Foundation as well as the Arts Council, and previously curated events in Liverpool for which she went through many a funding application. Her top tip for applicants is to drill down into the budget and take it from there. She explains: "Look at the budget straight off, work out exactly what income you have and what expenditure you have. Look at what is and isn't needed and really hone those numbers down to a T — get quotes from people, put everything in, make sure you include the VAT. Be really meticulous. Once you know the budget, you can formulate your plan and everything else around that so the team you are going to have is informed by the quotes you get and the prices you need, and forms the plan of the calendar as well. Going straight to the numbers might seem ridiculous because you want to be creative, but that's what it all comes back to."

project is and what you are hoping to achieve, and how much funding you'd need to deliver that. Think about where you can get money from, including your own resources and any favours you can pull in plus any ability to charge a ticket fee for a gig or for a recording. Then look at the shortfall, which is how much money you need."

- **Stage three: revise the budget.** "Sometimes the funding people want to apply for is well below the costs of doing the project and they can't raise enough money elsewhere. That's when they have to either whittle down their project so that it's a bit more achievable using the subsidy from that funder or they have to really prioritise what they want to do. All of that is part of the planning before you submit your application — are you going to make it a big massive project and do a huge bit of fundraising because you want it to be that big, or are you going to scale it down and get most of what you want to get done achieved? From there, you can start to have serious conversations with funders or just go ahead and prepare an application."

When putting your budget together, don't always assume prices you're quoted for services are the prices you need to pay. One photographer might quote you a thousand quid for some press shots while another might do it for £250. Mind you, didn't your mate from college just get herself a DSLR? Keep an eye out for insider guides on how to keep costs down — music publishers Sentric, for instance, occasionally call on their contacts to advise new artists on how best to spend £1000,[7] which throws up some interesting ideas (this doesn't just apply to funding budgets, of course, it's also going to help your bank balance to be resourceful and creative when it comes to spending money on your career generally).

Did you apply and have no luck? Don't get disheartened, the decision isn't necessarily reflective of your talent and potential, it could just be a case of bad timing. Get some feedback from the funder, use that to make your application stronger and re-apply, either elsewhere or next time that specific fund opens for applicants again.

BURNOUT

As we said at the beginning of this chapter, most musicians are freelancers, which means they are often juggling myriad demands and jobs at any one time. Managing this, alongside a culture of pressure, tough global touring schedules, and the 24/7 nature of the music industry can result in reaching a place of total and utter physical and mental exhaustion, which we know as 'burnout'. Beyond the money-related stuff, this is why there's another essential component to managing a career in music — and it's to do with maintaining a reasonable workload and taking time out to preserve your health.

As of 2019, burnout has been recognised by the World Health Organization as an 'occupational phenomenon' and is described "as resulting from chronic workplace stress that has not been successfully managed".[8] It is characterised by three things:

- Feelings of **energy depletion** or **exhaustion**
- **Increased mental distance** from one's job or feelings of **negativity** or **cynicism** related to one's job
- **Reduced professional efficacy**

The key takeaway from WHO's definition is the concept of **unmanaged chronic workplace stress being the root of burnout.** As we suggested earlier, there's evidence to suggest that the pressure and long working hours that come with working in the music industry aren't exactly helpful in this regard. In a recent study of health and wellbeing in music, one participant was asked if he got weekends off: "No, it's literally all the time," he answered. "It's not like 9-5, it's like 9 to just whenever... It just consumes us."[9]

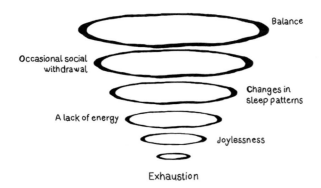

The diagram above shows how burnout can take hold and suggests behaviours that might signify things are starting to slide downhill. As workloads increase, it can be tempting to work longer hours to clear the backlog, cancel the drink with a friend to squeeze in the meeting, and stop exercising and eating well to get things done. But it's in these moments that we gradually stop doing the things that bring us balance, joy and connection, and in doing so, move one step closer to exhaustion and burnout.

It's not something that strikes overnight: the danger is that it's so gradual you might not even notice it happening.

Beyond maintaining an awareness around what causes burnout, and how you can try and maintain balance to prevent it from happening, there has been research that suggests the power of Acceptance and Commitment Therapy (ACT) for treatment[10] which encourages living a values-based life. Ultimately, if the symptoms in WHO's description above resonate with you, speak to your GP or seek professional therapeutic support.

To conclude this chapter:

- Create a **structural approach to keeping on top of your finances**. You can do that on your own, with the help of an app or a professional bookkeeper or accountant.

- Keep an open mind to working for free during the early stages of your career but **be wary of the fine line between exposure and exploitation** as your professionalism develops.

- If you ever get your hands on an **advance, spend and save it wisely**.

- Consider the **various ways of making money and raising funding** for your work and pursue, in a considered and strategic manner, whatever makes the most sense for where you're at in your career.

- **Don't work yourself into the ground**, learn your limits and take time out often to rest and enjoy life outside of music.

CHAPTER 3

CRITICISM AND OPINIONS

AS A CREATIVE PERSON, it's inevitable that you'll want to put your work out into the world and that at some point you'll receive criticism. With any luck, you'll receive praise too, and that can bring its own unique complications, but for most people, it's negative feedback that's the hardest to navigate.

The further your work travels, the more people it'll reach, and the higher the chance of hearing negative feedback. As anyone with a social media account will be aware, it's never been easier to receive people's opinions thanks to myriad online communication channels (as we'll discuss further in the next chapter on social media). Closing your apps won't necessarily silence the noise because you'll also hear thoughts from any number of industry execs, journalists, peers, friends, family members, taxi drivers, shop keepers... the list goes on. As a musician, you'll likely feel that your work is an extension of yourself, so you'll probably take criticism personally. But it's also important to understand that negative feedback is not always a reflection of the quality of your work and may be more to do with that critic's specific taste or limited vision.

Human beings are, to put it politely, a complex set of creatures with very individual experiences and tastes and it's impossible to please them all. Indeed, you've probably seen or heard musicians who've tried to please everyone and you've probably noticed that such an approach isn't exactly conducive to great art.

Here's a story to illustrate that point. Before The 1975 became the worldwide sensation they are today, with three No.1 albums and BRIT Awards to their name, they got turned down by every major record label and were rather boldly declared the worst band in the world at the NME Awards in 2014.[1] After honing their hybrid sound, which was like nothing else that was around at the time, the group and their manager, Jamie Oborne, were rebuffed at every door they knocked upon. According to frontman Matty Healy, the band were told by labels that they "were confused" because their songs didn't have a uniform sound.

Naturally, Healy and the band were upset. As he explains: "Because our band wasn't this frivolous, fun hobby of ours, it was very much our identity and who we were. So by the time we'd gotten to where all these grown-ups were who we'd been told held the key to our success, and they were telling us that we weren't good enough, it really, really hurt. It was the fact that all of our songs sounded slightly different, which they probably thought came from some contrived concept of trying to sound like a million things. They thought that we were overthinking it... it was like, no *you're* overthinking it, we're just making music."[2] So they continued making their style of music, which was released through their manager's record label, and ended up being the band that everyone wished they'd signed (and receiving a 5* review[3] and album of the year plaudit from their new fans at NME[4]).

Equally though, we need to state that not all negative feedback should be ignored. For every band like The 1975 who've managed to make sense of a 'confusing' vision, there are dozens of bands whose work *does* need refining or whose ideas *will* benefit from further clarification. For those bands, negative feedback could actually provide them with the information they need to become more compelling artists. More on that later.

CHALLENGING THE STATUS QUO

Receiving criticism is especially likely if you're offering something new or different — which is precisely what The 1975 were doing at a time when 'guitar bands' weren't the flavour of the month. DJ, broadcaster and journalist Mary Anne Hobbs has observed that trend throughout her career, championing music that sits outside the mainstream. She explains:

> "**If you do anything progressive, modern and distinctive, you are going to divide opinion**. I think that has happened historically all of the time. If you look at the history of classical composers, jazz musicians, hip hop MCs and the grime community, even if you look at people like [legendary BBC broadcaster] John Peel and [Glastonbury organiser] Emily Eavis — every time she announces, let's say, Stormzy as a headliner over and above Oasis, she'll get a barrage of criticism."[5]

Peel, who was a long-standing BBC Radio 1 DJ for nearly forty years until he passed away in 2004, often had to fight for what he believed in. Hobbs continues: "John went through many struggles at the BBC. They decided to ban punk at one point, and he continued to play it because he believed it would become culturally significant and of course history has recorded that he was right. He used to put a Sex Pistols single on and announce it as 'The Pink Fairies' on the radio!"

It's not just left-field choices that are criticised and questioned. Ed Sheeran had to fight with his record label for his ode to an Irish flame "Galway Girl" to be included on his album *Divide*[6] and it turned out to be one of the most popular songs on the record. As well as an army of critics on social media, James Blunt has been panned by Noel Gallagher, Damon Albarn, and Paul Weller,[7] but has one of the biggest-selling albums in UK chart history. And in an audition for the BBC during his early career, David Bowie was declared an "amateur-sounding vocalist" who was "devoid of personality."[8]

Those stories don't take away from the fact that getting panned feels mortifying in the moment but Hobbs urges creators to see it as something to identify with positively. "Generally it means that what you're doing is moving forward," she says. "Reflect upon the fact that it isn't just you who's subject to this experience, it's generations of artists, thinkers, and musicians, and probably scientists as well." The only thing you can do as a creator to keep that track moving is to drown out the noise and follow your instincts. She continues: "When you are inside the moment, you can't really quantify the value of something, you just have to respond incredibly instinctively to it. It's only over time that things develop historical significance and you and the rest of the world can reflect differently. You just have to do what you believe is the right thing."

Again, however, it falls to us to suggest you're pragmatic when dealing with feedback because some criticism really is constructive. It can be hard to accept that you might have made a mistake, but if every radio plugger tells you your song's poorly mixed and isn't ready for airplay, or if every publicist notes that calling your band Two Dimension might be unimaginative, or if your manager suggests a new song called "I Love You" might be a bit clichéd, take a moment to ask yourself if they might have a point.

NAVIGATING A CRISIS OF CONFIDENCE

If you have had some 'challenging' feedback, commentary or been on the receiving end of unflattering press coverage, untangling and improving the way you experience any negative thoughts that you have as a result might help you to navigate a crisis of confidence. The first step is to **be honest about how you're feeling.** Psychotherapist Helen Brice, who specialises in working with performers and writers, explains: "The first thing is to be aware that this is what you're experiencing, this lack of confidence. That's the hard thing — the acceptance that things aren't going as well as they could be. When you can accept it, and that doesn't mean approving of it or being okay with it, then you've got a choice of staying like that or changing."

Then, Brice says it's important to **limit how much you look at, how much you listen to, and to take control of how you experience your own thought patterns.** "It's about developing a filter for caring less about some of the critical stuff and getting over your own judgment of yourself," she explains. "We all judge; the idea is to judge and get over it, [and] don't keep beating yourself up with these harsh judgments."

Mindfulness can help to develop that awareness and filter. Brice continues: "I would usually encourage people to [engage] with a practical mindfulness exercise, which is called the Awareness Continuum, a term coined by Professor Tom Lynch. I view mindfulness, which is a bit of a buzz word, as simply awareness. Not necessarily a meditation, and definitely not a relaxation exercise, but a description of what you're sensing, feeling, thinking, or an image or memory that comes to mind. It seems counterintuitive, but naming the unwanted experience reduces its intensity by at least 20%."

The Awareness Continuum uses short sentences to describe the experiences that are happening inside and outside of us, which can help to separate and avoid confusing our feelings with the reality of a situation. Brice explains what it might sound like:

- Start by saying the word 'I' followed by 'am aware of'.
- Next, name a sensation, emotion, urge, image, or thought. It's

important to keep the phrases short and don't clump your different experiences together. For example, I am aware of the thought 'I am hurt' or 'I've received negative feedback'; I am aware of the emotion of anxiety; I am aware of seeing a mean comment about me. I am aware of the urge to cry; I am aware of the emotion of anger; I am aware of the thought 'I'm not posting on social media again' or 'Don't be silly' and so on.

- Practise this for a few minutes, silently to yourself or out loud.

This exercise is best practised in a neutral situation to hone your awareness so that when you require some distance from an adverse experience, the skill has become second nature. This can help you avoid giving a knee-jerk reaction that you might regret later, or from feeling paralysed and unable to respond in a careful and considered manner, and to be better able to ignore anything unhelpful and move on.

There's a physical component to feeling less energy about criticism, too. "When we're anxious or nervous or frightened, our face becomes very flat," Brice says. "Our muscles become very tense and this intensifies our feeling of threat, so we have to get the muscles moving to turn our threat system off and our safety system on. There are various things to do like raising your eyebrows, having a closed mouth smile so that your smile lines are visible around your eyes, and leaning back in that rest and digest mode. So move your body, own more space, slouch a bit more, and breathe from the diaphragm and through your nose. That can be done daily or as often as possible to get used to it for when you need it, and you repeat it during an interaction. Whether it be in person with someone or if you're looking at difficult stuff that you're reading online, you switch your safety system on by changing your physiology in those ways."

Diaphragmatic nasal breathing is a form of deep breathing that slows the heartbeat and can lower or stabilise blood pressure. Here's how to practise it:

- Whilst sitting on a sofa or in an armchair, lean back.
- Drape your arm(s) over the back of the chair, slouch a little.
- Deliberately breathe more deeply and slowly through your nose; use long, slow exhalations, also through the nose. Purposely exhale through the nose longer than normal.
- Slow your rate of breathing to six breaths per minute. On an in-breath, focus on raising the stomach, not the chest.

You can practise this alone, but Brice recommends that you also practise this during neutral interactions and build up to more difficult interactions where you might receive disconfirming feedback, criticism, or even intimidation. "Your stress will be reduced if you also do this before and during reading those unwanted comments," she says.

Aside from resulting in a potentially unhealthy state of mind, it's also helpful to remember that it's bad business sense to spend time listening to and engaging with those who don't know you and don't love what you do. Singer, songwriter and performance artist Amanda Palmer realised this during a "come-to-Jesus" moment after taking her career into her own hands, splitting with her label and using Kickstarter to fund her second album. She says:

> "I found myself [thinking], **if I spent my artistic time and energy defending myself** on Twitter for six weeks, **what am I not going to be doing? What am I not going to be making, and who do I want to give my time and energy?** Do I want to give it to these music industry people who think I'm terrible, these trolly people who think I'm a bad feminist? Do I want to give it to these sexist people who think this is all happening just because I'm Neil Gaimon's wife, or do I want to spend that time and energy on the community who gets me and make meaningful art for them, for me, for whoever is going to show up? It will be a net negative if I spend my life and artistic energy in defensive mode instead of in open-hearted mode. I'm just going to have to accept that it's going to be hard and constantly tempting to go explain myself and

defend myself, and I have to remind myself every day that is not your job. You're an artist."[9]

PERSONAL CRITICISM

You'll quickly find that there are two types of criticism: one which centres on your art and one which centres on *you as a human being*. The latter can be particularly hard to accept. We've all heard horror stories about labels and managers telling their artists to lose weight, for instance, and we've all read people in the media (and on social media) being critical of an artist's appearance and behaviour (which is often dramatised for effect). Lily Allen has borne the brunt of this unwelcome commentary since being used as frequent tabloid fodder in her early career and onwards. As she explains in her memoir *My Thoughts Exactly*, the 'cartoon' version of herself created by tabloids has even impacted her own sense of reality. "Public Lily, the Lily in the media, the Lily that most people saw or read about became *so* distorted that even I had trouble reconciling her with the original cast from whence she came. It was confusing. Who was in charge of who? Who was real? The quiet person who felt alone inside or the noisy one that everyone listened to, but who seemed unable to control what she was saying?"[10]

The British tabloid newspapers and gossip magazines are particularly experienced in tearing down people who are in the public eye — we saw this when Amy Winehouse was clearly struggling with health and substance use issues. Pictures of her were splashed across the news alongside insensitive and sensationalist editorials. Similarly, Allen has been painted as a terrible mother with a severe drug and party problem. She explains: "Cartoon Lily was successful in terms of her career, but she was a mess as a person. She took too many drugs, got drunk, didn't mind her manners, said what she thought, didn't watch her back, and was loose with money and sex. Her weight fluctuated. Her hair changed colour. She wasn't bad-looking and she could clean up all right, but you could get photos of her looking rough as shit. She was a tabloid editor's dream."[11] Once the tabloids started reporting on Allen, the carousel didn't seem to stop. "I'd do or say one thing, whether good or bad, and the tabloids would write whatever they wanted, create whatever story they had decided to run in order to perpetuate whatever narrative they'd decided to create."

While the tabloids have this morally questionable reporting method finely honed, there's lots of opportunity beyond that for commentary on who you are and the opinions you might put out into the world. Matty Healy from The 1975, for example, isn't afraid to offer his perspective on as many subjects he can get his hands on. As a result, he's been branded as both "a shamanic figure who stands apart from artists afraid to speak their mind" and "a preening pseudo-intellectual speaking from a soapbox carved out of privilege and narcissism."[12] As you can see, public opinions and those of the media can be extreme and don't tend to allow much for the variety of traits (both good and bad) that generally make up one human being. So be mindful of that, and take time to consider the kind of person you're comfortable putting out into the world before the decision's made for you by someone else with a different agenda.

Be careful of what you're saying to journalists, who may seem nice as pie in person but distort your words into a headline that shifts copies and gets clicks once they get back to the office. As Allen writes: "Basically, it doesn't matter how a journalist gets their copy, as long as they're not making something up, and what you've said is on record. There's no point feeling hard done by. Instead, you learn that all that matters — for the little life of that little piece over which they have control — is what you've said. You learn not to say stuff or how to say it more carefully. You learn to be more guarded. It took me a long time to learn those lessons."[13] Those lessons can be learned with the help of a public relations person, and perhaps some media training too.

You could also take the lead of New Wave pioneer Gary Numan, who simply doesn't read any sort of feedback, whatsoever. He explains:

"If I do a Tweet and loads of people make a comment, I'll never know what they say. I avoid it because it does bother you, **you can read a thousand lovely things and one nasty one, and it's the nasty one you'll be thinking about when you go to sleep**. Don't look for praise because if you go looking for praise, you're going to find the other stuff as well. The problem with the internet is that it's given everyone a voice and it seems to me that so few people know how to be respectful of that voice. You've now got an opportunity to say what you think and so many of them come out with this vicious, vitriolic nonsense. I'm not going to read that, I've only got a few years left, I'm not going to waste it! I'm sure some people like what I do, some people don't, and I'm all right with that."[14]

USEFUL CRITICISM

As we mentioned, not all criticism should be ignored, and as Darcus Beese says in the Business Basics chapter, feedback is one of the things that will help you improve. Everyone is pretty terrible at the beginning of whatever creative endeavour they have chosen to pursue and it takes lots of practice, time, and recalibration to reach full potential. But during that process, there is a difference between nasty feedback from people who don't want you to succeed, and constructive critique from those who do.

Mary Anne Hobbs concludes:

"We live in an environment at the moment which I suppose is unlike any other environment that we've ever lived in as human beings, where we are criticised almost constantly via social media, which can be incredibly destructive. So there is a real distinction between taking on incredibly valuable criticism and trying to switch off the barracking of trolls on social media. Those two things are entirely separate. If you listen to constructive criticism from people who love and care about you, even if that criticism is harsh, it's probably really valuable because those people want you to succeed. The criticism of people who want you to be successful is really important, the criticism of people who want you to fail is not."

When it comes to criticism from fans, that distinction between those who want you to win and those who don't can be a tricky one to navigate. Because fans love you, right? Well, it's not that simple. Going back to the example of David Bowie, one wonders what his career might have looked like if he'd only ever made music to please fans who'd bought early releases like *The Laughing Gnome*.

Equally, how many times has a band or artist been branded a "sell-out" by fans because they didn't like the direction of their new music? Bring Me The Horizon's sixth studio album *Amo* was less 'heavy metal' than their previous releases and the experimental sound was widely praised by reviewers. Some fans and peers who preferred the band's heavier stuff weren't so complimentary. Frontman Oli Sykes explains: "We're not a band like Radiohead where, whatever they do, you're already geared up to say 'that's cool'. People accept them as artists so they can do things without any fear. With rock and metal, I think a lot of people connect with the lyrics because they feel like they don't fit in. Now, maybe the people who made fun of our early fans at school are also coming to our shows, and they don't like that."[15] But with any fans BMTH might have lost, they will have gained a whole new set who really like the new music. Some fans do want you to win, whatever that might mean, but others want you to stay exactly where you are so they can continue to feel part of an exclusive world.

In short, fans can be fickle, and it's important to understand the context from which their opinions are coming. Additionally, basing your life on other people's expectations of who they think you should be is a fairly sure route to misery.

It's essential when taking on criticism to consider:

- Where it's coming from — **does that person have a level of expertise required to offer a sound judgement** on what you're doing?
- Is it being **delivered constructively**?
- Does the person **genuinely understand what *you're* doing** or are they basing their thoughts on what *they* would be doing?
- Does it involve **tips on how you can improve** in a way that feels true to who you are?
- Is the critic part of an **inner circle of trusted confidants** who only want the best for you?

If none of the above is true, it's probably best to ignore the criticism and move on. If any of it is, it might help to set aside your ego for a moment and consider whether there's something useful you could take on board in order to reach your full potential.

CHAPTER 4

SOCIAL MEDIA

YOU DON'T NEED US to tell you that social media is a double-edged sword for musicians. On the one hand, it offers direct access to those who love what you do, along with inspiration and support from like-minded people around the world, and the occasional whimsical animal meme. On the other, it's engineered to be addictive, seems to be full of people doing better than you, feels like spinning plates when you feel you need to be active on ten platforms at once, and to top it all off, it's an endless cesspool of bullying, hate, comparison, and resentment.

If you're still picturing a double-edged sword, you're probably thinking of one where one edge is a lot bigger and much sharper than the other and that sounds about right. Research has suggested a strong link between high social media use and mental health difficulties[1]. When you consider that musicians are more susceptible to mental health problems than the general population,[2] it's clear this is an area where you should proceed with caution. Navigating these murky waters is not exactly plain sailing and requires strategies and boundaries to avoid being negatively affected by the online world.

Before we delve into all that, we want to make clear that there *are* lots of benefits to social media if you're an artist. It's easy to find articles and opinions that paint social media as a wholly destructive thing that harms mental health, self-confidence and productivity, but that's not the whole story. One huge plus is the fact that it facilitates the relationship an artist has with their fans, which can be really powerful. In a recent research project, artists highlighted how a strong connection with fans gave them a great sense of meaning in their work and contributed to their overall levels of wellbeing.[3] A lot of that connection came from fans getting in touch on social media and telling artists how much their music means to them or how it had helped them get through a difficult time.

Also, as Stephen Buckley from mental health charity Mind points out, social media can give people a voice. He explains: "Social media has been incredibly powerful for some people with mental health problems to talk about their experience in a way that makes sense to them. It enables people to connect with other people with very similar and shared experiences and overcome the stigma and isolation that many people feel. On a practical level, it's a great place that you can ask for and find support."[4]

Indeed, by being open on social media, beatboxer, SK Shlomo, received a listening ear when he needed it most: "If it hadn't have been for social media, I wouldn't have had that moment where I was in a really bad place and my phone pinged with someone saying, 'Hey, are you okay? I know things are hard at the moment.'

If I hadn't already used social media to express the fact that I was at risk, then that wouldn't have happened."[5]

Social media is neither good nor bad in and of itself, but it's your individual relationship with it that matters. So as with many things, practise moderation, be mindful of how you use it and if you find yourself experiencing mental health issues like anxiety and depression, seek professional help.

WHAT TO POST?

Let's take a look at the kind of messages artists might want to post online. The first thing to consider when thinking about what to share is your legacy. **What is it that you want to be known for?** Is it music and creativity? Or how great you look in a selfie living your best life? Some artists manage to pull off both — but however you really want to be remembered (or even considered in the here and now), that should be what you're mainly posting about online.

You'll often find value in sharing shots from the studio, lyrics, videos of the creative process, collaborators, updates while on tour and anything that gives fans insight into the thing they love you for. If there are particular interests, causes, or campaigns you want to align yourself with, that's cool too. If you have some great jokes, even better. Ben Anderson, who spent five years building up Rudimental's social media presence and is now Social Media Health Specialist at coaching collective Your Green Room, believes posts should focus on three central pillars, which are:

- Your identity as an artist
- The world (or scene) you're relevant to or operating in
- What you're promoting

Anderson suggests that before you start posting anything, the first step is to define those three pillars so that your public persona is clear from the get go. That will make what you're about easy to understand and support for the fans you want to find. He explains: "If you have really strong foundations around who you are as an artist and you also have an understanding of who your extended world is — and that could be your scene, genre, or target audience — you can start thinking about social media strategically by building that image of yourself. After a little while, you build this persona, image or style guide of what you stand for, and at every point, everything is built around those core beliefs and underlying values."

That artist identity can be wholly linked to your personal identity and constructed by thinking about your own values and interests. What are your passions? What do you support and value? What don't you like? For Rudimental, Anderson helped them construct an artist proposition that displayed the multi-cultural nature of the four members and their shared values, which were unity, freedom and love. Then, each member's individual interests — spanning musical influences, vinyl, and football — were used to showcase their personalities across their personal accounts. Lewis Capaldi, meanwhile, expertly showcases his self-deprecating sense of humour alongside promo, while Jessie Ware's interests are clearly centred around family, cooking, and friends (which, incidentally, is the theme of her podcast *Table Manners*). Ellie Goulding posts messages about fitness and the environment alongside music-related news and Matty Healy from The 1975 often uses his platform to champion upcoming artists (whose careers he's sometimes directly involved in via his label Dirty Hit).

Your own interests will appeal to like-minded people who are part of the world or scene you're operating in and working out who those people are will help you decipher what sort of language they might respond to. Part of that world might be other collaborators or known people who you share interests with, so post about who you're with, too. What you're promoting should be pretty clear, whether it's music releases, gigs, collaborations or merchandise, but don't go overboard with the sales posts or your feed will look like one big #sponfest and fans will switch off. Aim for about 10 to 20% sales-related posts and the rest should be the contextual stuff.

SHARE WITH CARE

You can approach social media in various ways as an individual, but as a musician, social media is there so you can engage a fanbase. That might mean thinking carefully about how much personal information you want to share. Anderson, for example, advises clients to try and "be as real as possible but without giving out your most precious and valuable parts of yourself." For some, holding something back and maintaining an air of mystery online leaves people wanting to find out more, which in turn fuels demand. For others, there might be solidarity to be found in being (or, from a self-preservation standpoint, appearing to be) totally open and sharing challenges, vulnerabilities, and difficulties to help others.

That's the approach SK Shlomo takes. He explains: "[It might be tempting] to only show real positivity or real success. [But] I stopped posting a picture of me in front of a massive crowd and saying how great it was, and started posting a picture of me in front of a massive crowd and saying how I was grateful for it happening but also these are some of the things that I found really hard about it. We lost an unborn child a while back and I had a really hard time trying to perform through that experience." In being honest about his own struggles, SK has encouraged a more honest and open dialogue about mental health with his fans. He continues:

> "A lot of times I get asked, 'How can I start to be more supportive to the people around me who are struggling with their mental health but they're not talking about it?' I always say that if you talk vulnerably about what you're going through, that sends a very clear signal to the people who are listening that you are okay with it. You aren't going to judge, dismiss, or minimise someone else's problems if you're showing that you're happy to talk about your own. That makes you appear stronger, not weaker. If you're able to be vulnerable, it makes you seem approachable, and human, and not someone who's going to hide behind a mask."

Whichever way you decide to approach your online presence, it's wise to maintain healthy boundaries. You may choose to share a personal story online or it may be something that you just save for friends and family. Social scientist and vulnerability researcher, Brené Brown, is a big proponent of how connection thrives with vulnerability, but warns that "when we're looking for compassion, we need someone who is deeply rooted, is able to bend and, most of all, embraces us for our strengths and struggles. We need to honour our struggle by sharing it with someone who has *earned the right to hear it*. When we're looking for compassion, it's about connecting with the right person at the right time about the right issue."[6]

It's also important to consider that context and meaning might get lost in translation online. Author Matt Haig, who has written two books about his own struggles with mental health, writes in *Notes on a Nervous Planet* that he once found himself in a Twitter storm after posting 'Anxiety is my superpower'.[7] His intention was to communicate his feeling that while anxiety isn't a good thing for those who suffer from an angst-infused life, it does, very occasionally, have a silver lining. For Haig, that silver lining is that it forced him to stop smoking and get physically healthy, made him work out what was good for him and who cared for him and didn't, and ultimately made him extraordinarily rich through writing about it. Lots of people interpreted the post as him downplaying the downsides of what can be a debilitating mental illness, prompting tens of thousands of outraged replies. Naturally, that made Haig feel quite anxious.

As he explains in the book, when hit with anger it's quite easy to hit back *with* anger — in fact, it's actually a neurological reaction called 'mirroring' — but as anyone who's ever followed Wiley on Twitter will be well aware, all that does is fuel the fire. It's far simpler to avoid the storm altogether and keep some thoughts to yourself or present them later when the context is clear and your mind is calm. Closing the app and venting to a friend instead is also a good way of making your point without involving thousands of others!

Anderson summarises: "It's about understanding that what you're posting is potentially going out to different people with different frames of reference, different windows on the world, and they might not take it in the way that it was intended. Context gets a bit wishy-washy online." He suggests veering away from anything that might be divisive or could alienate someone or a group of people, so nothing that could be taken as sexist, racist, or homophobic, for example. Anderson adds: "Once you get into the world of being 'that shock value person' that stuff is there forever. Even though I believe in freedom of speech, on a moral level, it's just not good to post anything that might hurt someone else."

COMPARE AND DESPAIR

What could be more relaxing than kicking back after a long day and scrolling through hundreds of people doing exciting and cool things with their lives while your own life seems comparatively boring and full of failure? About three million things, to be frank! It's all well and good to suggest you rise above it, that you be happy for other people, that you count your blessings and are grateful for what you've got. But in truth, it's tough to do that when a band or artist you see as a peer is doing all the things you want to be doing, or is getting all the reviews you think you should be getting, or has been added to New Music Friday playlists when you haven't.

Compare and despair can be an easy pattern to fall into when using social media, as the BRIT Award-winning singer and songwriter Mabel discovered at the beginning of her career. "I was in quite a destructive phase [with social media] when I was really addicted to it," is her recollection.[8] "'This artist is doing that, she's wearing this, she played that show.' It was really holding me back from being the best I could be because I was focused on other people's journeys and not my own."

But as fellow singer and songwriter Nina Nesbitt points out, it's important to remember that everyone is probably going through the same thing and yes, that means even those who look like they're hashtag-winning. "I think sitting on Instagram looking at other artists is very tempting, what are they up to, what have they done? But at the end of the day, I hang out with a lot of these artists and they're all thinking the same thing, like how to break through or is the music I'm putting out good enough, is it getting enough streams? Everyone's facing the same thing. So try and not get carried away with what you see online and just work hard and love what you do."[9]

No matter what level you're at, there's always going to be another mountain. As Miley Cyrus once noted: it's the climb.

Unless you've got a Buddhist level of enlightenment — unlikely unless you were practising as a very advanced and spiritual child — one solution is to simply avoid looking. Just don't follow people whose posts result in negative feelings of comparison. If it's awkward not to follow them, there are ways of muting or removing them from your feed, depending on the platform. (Don't accidentally block them though — that could cause untold drama.) Composer and producer Hannah Peel has the 'ignorance is bliss' mode finely honed. She says:

> "I sometimes don't even look at my social media feed because it can affect your ability to create, how you feel, or your self-worth when you see all these amazing things. One of the phrases that should be implanted in everyone's minds somehow is '**all that glitters is not gold**'. Behind every tweet that says, 'Hey, I've got a gig or have composed this', is probably 50 hours of work and people don't see that side of things. It just looks like someone is doing really well or they are really beautiful but have actually been transformed by an app!"

If unfollowing or muting doesn't work for you, another option is to put the more superficial solution to one side and dig deeper: to go to the root of the problem and to work out what it is that's causing those negative feelings. Using that information, you can take action that may be more meaningful and more helpful in the long run.

Comparison coach Lucy Sheridan, who helps people get out of the compare and despair pattern, takes a different approach. She says the jealousy and envy that sometimes arise as a result of scrolling through social media are signals that perhaps you have an unmet need you can take steps to address. "I try and manage my way through it," she says of her social media strategy.[10] "What is this trying to tell me? Because yes, I can be jealous of seeing someone checking into a departure lounge because they are going on holiday again and maybe I haven't had any time off in months and months. I can keep feeding this beast within me that will never actually feel full or I can follow it through and say to myself with kindness: 'Well, so what?' What are those holiday pictures telling you about something you can do in support of yourself? So what I know it's telling me is: 'Okay Lucy, book a holiday, no one is going to give you a medal if you work another Saturday.'

"It's like a puzzle — go in, get your information and then get out of there and do something with it. When we are in those moments of feeling down, these horrible friends of social media comparison come into play like envy and jealousy. There is nothing wrong with any of that, because they are our feelings and they are valid, but instead of it taking us ten feet down, it can take us seven and a half feet down and we can come back up again. Things can feel very different there."

Beyond that, try to understand that what you see online is not real life. Like Peel said, images are airbrushed and filtered, years of work and disappointment may have gone into that one exciting announcement, and it's impossible to gauge whether emojis are genuinely representative of how that person is feeling at the time. Mabel continues:

> "You have to remember that it's the highlights we're seeing. On my page if you looked at it you'd be like, she just did a big awards show, she smashed it, but you wouldn't know that two days before I was crying about it, or stressed about it, or all the dramas about my outfit. It's so important to remind

ourselves that what we are looking at are the highlights of somebody's life and we don't see the fact that maybe they woke up feeling another type of way today."[11]

Ben Anderson agrees that awareness regarding the lack of reality on social media is imperative if you want to get out of that comparative mindset. He explains:

> "**Social media is like an advert — so look at it actively rather than passively.** Someone on social media might be objectively one of the most beautiful people in the world but even they have to airbrush their image to make themselves look more beautiful or to present this image of perfection. If they can't maintain that then how are you expected to, and is that even what you want? When you are consuming stuff, if you understand that it's not real, it's a fake perception of reality and those people are ideal selves, they are projections, you can kind of disengage with it a little bit. You might as well be looking at a cartoon! Also, the stronger those foundations are of who you are, who you want to be and what you stand for, the easier it is for you to protect yourself."

If you find yourself getting into the habit of comparison, try and find clarity in the knowledge that your life is the only one you can live. Whichever struggles you're facing, yours is a completely unique journey that's probably being coveted by others too. It's also worth remembering that studies have shown again and again that once we have our basic needs met, along with a certain level of income, it's the things we can't buy that make us happy. According to the Harvard Study on Adult Development, which tracked 724 adults over 75 years, good quality close relationships are the crux of what keep us happier, healthier, and living for longer.[12] So it's going to pay off massively in the long run to invest your energy into positive relationships in the real world, instead of working on increasing your follower count in the online world and dealing with negative feelings that arise as a result of scrolling through Instagram.

Finding it difficult to watch endless highlight reels? Instead of following peers, perhaps **curate your feed like it's a magazine designed especially for you.** Follow the people who inspire you, accounts posting motivational quotes, funny memes, beautiful pictures, great recipes, cute animals, or whatever else sparks positivity.

HOW MUCH IS TOO MUCH?

As has been widely discussed in recent years, social media platforms have been engineered by smart people in Silicon Valley to be highly attractive to our primal need for acceptance and validation. That's to make sure that we spend as much time as possible on them, meaning in turn that advertisers spend more money. We see a like or a follow, a red heart or a thumbs-up, and our brain gets a dopamine boost that's associated with pleasure and social acceptance.[13] The same thing happens for other addictive stuff like drugs, alcohol and cigarettes, which is why it's quite easy to waste hours stuck in an online feedback loop searching for those little hits of satisfaction. That's largely a total waste of time, distracts us from the thing that actually makes us happy — real-life human connection — and shifts focus from what's going to result in a long and sustainable career and personal fulfilment: in this case, making good music. As singer, songwriter and BRIT-winner Ella Eyre puts it: "I think for me a lot of my stress [with social media] is built up by having to be creative on another platform that actually doesn't really help me financially. We put a lot of time and pressure on ourselves to make our social media the best it can be, but at the end of the day, it's a vanity project."

So how much time online is *too* much time online? According to GlobalWebIndex,[14] the global average time spent on social media per day, per person, is two hours and 24 minutes. The point at which that time can have a negative impact on mental wellbeing is between the two and three-hour mark, as revealed in a study by researchers at the University of Oxford in 2017.[15] Another research project by academics at the University of Pennsylvania suggested that keeping use down to 30 minutes a day can lead to better mental health outcomes and a reduction in loneliness, depression, anxiety, and the less clinically recognised, but nonetheless very real condition of FOMO (fear of missing out).[16] Those recommendations are a loose guide that depend on the quality of time spent online — an hour spent messaging friends on Instagram is unlikely to be as detrimental as five minutes arguing with a racist on Twitter or ten minutes investigating an ex's new partner. But it's clear that there is such a thing as too much, which is why it's important to check in with how something is making you feel while you're using it. Stephen Buckley from Mind says red flags to look out for include "disconnecting from relationships with your friends, family members, or colleagues" and "sleep and rest being impacted as a result of spending too much time looking at a screen."

Some of that advice can apply to anyone, regardless of job — but it's more complicated for musicians for whom social media is now part of the job. That said, there are still ways to limit the time you spend on socials and creating a manageable relationship with your online profiles will allow you to get on with being creative elsewhere. Working smart and approaching social media as a task to complete in a limited amount of time as part of your working day can help avoid wasting hours in an online loop. So have a daily plan of what you want to do on there, perhaps focusing posts on those three pillars that Anderson outlined earlier — your identity as an artist, the world/scene you're relevant to or operating in, and what you're promoting.

Then, have a weekly check-in to sit down and think about whether that plan is working for you and tweak it accordingly. Do you find it easier to get social media out of the way first thing in the morning, for example? Or is it best to split up one hour into twenty minutes at the beginning, middle, and end of the day? Do you prefer to store up a bank of content to post as you go about the rest of your work? Is it possible to dedicate a day to filming and photographing in various places to then post over the coming weeks? Before you go to an event or gig, is there a specific post you want to get out of that experience? That could be a shot of you performing, or with someone you admire, or a live behind-the-scenes video. Having an organised schedule and focused strategy about what sort of thing you're publishing can also avoid that all too common procrastination due to being indecisive over what to post.

Moreover, if you've finely honed your online voice, it's easier to hand over your account to be managed by someone else without losing authenticity (which may well sound absurd — but you might be surprised to find out how many of the artists you're following on social media have already taken that leap).

Ella Eyre is one such artist and finds that having a plan and people to help facilitate that has helped her manage the pressure that she feels to be 'always on'. She explains:

> "I've found that having a plan in place that's focused on a schedule works. So if I'm in the middle of releasing [new music], which makes life a lot easier because there is a point to posts, it's about having a team of people around you who are helping. They make sure that the engagement and posts and content are there whether or not I'm 100% there. It's helped me have a much more positive and relaxed relationship with social media because I'm not panicking and stressing about it all the time. It's not just me having to come up with a caption that engages well and has a point to it and hopefully promotes me in some way."

A word of warning: if you do hand your accounts over to someone else to manage, make sure they are linked to your email address and that you have all the passwords. If they are registered with someone you work with, and that business relationship sours, you could lose all the hard work that's been put into building your fanbase online.

For Eyre, having a posting plan for the coming week helps her focus her creative efforts elsewhere, and that's something anyone can do whether they have a team or not. She continues: "It really helps to know what's going to happen that week before the week has started. Then I can focus on the part of my job which is being creative in the studio or being on stage, as opposed to worrying about how many likes my gif has got from the video."

If you're frequently finding yourself stuck in that online loop, take a break. Go cold turkey and delete the apps from your phone. The world isn't going to stop turning and your career will go on if you're not posting for a week or two. It might be difficult at first, but if you can move past the initial FOMO, tranquillity *will* eventually arrive. There are some great apps out there like Buffer that can queue up posts to be published throughout the day. You can log in first thing in the morning, create a few posts for that day or week, and leave it to do its thing while you get on with life in the real world. If you do need to be on social media every day, carve out specific times to do that work, then close the apps and move onto something else. Some artists find that removing apps from their phone and only using socials on a laptop, or moving them into a folder three home screens deep, reduces temptation.

DEALING WITH TROLLS

In the online world, it's very easy for people to project whatever pain they might be going through onto others. Obviously there's an argument to be made that some people are simply, if you'll excuse our French, arseholes. But the fact is that if someone walks down the street shouting abuse at people, there's a threat of confrontation, violence, and rejection from society. On the internet, they can be as anonymous as they like and receive no retribution for saying horrible things.

As we touched upon in the previous chapter, it's a sad truth that anyone who puts themselves out there creatively is at risk of negative comments — so how can they be dealt with most effectively? Firstly, it's worth remembering that the person trolling you doesn't know you and whatever they've said doesn't therefore really have a lot to do with you — it's more about them. Secondly, don't engage. There's no reasoning with the unreasonable — and thirdly, if you need to, block (some particularly ludicrous individuals do see being blocked as a somewhat ropey badge of honour, so muting may achieve similar results without giving them the satisfaction of knowing they've riled you). You could also take the lead from Taylor Swift, who says that one of the lessons she learned before her 30th birthday was to switch off comments from her social media posts. That doesn't work on all social networks but the point is that nobody needs negativity from strangers in their lives. Swift explains:

"I learned to block some of the noise. Social media can be great, but it can also inundate your brain with images of what you aren't, how you're failing, or who is in a cooler locale than you at any given moment. One thing I do to lessen this weird insecurity laser beam is to turn off comments. Yes, I keep comments off my posts. That way, I'm showing my friends and fans updates on my life, but I'm training my brain to not need the validation of someone telling me that I look 🔥🔥🔥. I'm also blocking out anyone who might feel the need to tell me to "go die in a hole ho" while I'm having my coffee at nine in the morning. **I think it's healthy for your self-esteem to need less internet praise to appease it**, especially when three comments down you could unwittingly see someone telling you that you look like a weasel that got hit by a truck and stitched back together by a drunk taxidermist. An actual comment I received once."[17]

Turning off comments, removing yourself from platforms entirely or getting someone else to manage your account can be useful strategies for groups who are disproportionately targeted by trolls. This is particularly true for Twitter, where there's ample evidence to suggest that women and members of ethnic minority groups bear the brunt of much abuse.[18] As detailed in BBC Three's documentary *Odd One Out*, Little Mix member Jesy Nelson has been a victim of this dark side of internet culture. Cyberbullies targeted her when she was just 20-years-old, following her band's *X Factor* win in

2011. Spiteful comments about her appearance had a significant impact on her self-confidence, body image, and mental health and eventually led to a suicide attempt. "All the other girls [in the group] were living their dream and I was living my worst nightmare. I felt like the whole world hated me," she says.[19] Being on the receiving end of abuse is going to be tough for anyone but it can have a particularly negative impact on young people like Nelson and plenty of other artists who start their career in their teens and early '20s, who may not have had the time to develop the life experience and self confidence that could help them deal with it.

Self-care and body image therapist Liz Ritchie, who spoke to Nelson in the documentary, explains: "Someone like Jesy was thrown into the public at [a young age] and with no experience of how to promote herself and what her identity is. I think Jesy didn't at that time have the sophisticated psychological tools, which most young people at that age don't have, to be able to deal with any kind of bullying, trolling online, or negative comments."

Ritchie rightly points to the responsibility of a social media platform in safeguarding its users. Nelson, who wasn't active on Twitter at the time of writing, suggests trying to spend more time with loved ones and encourages anyone on the receiving end of abuse to seek help. "I think we are all so obsessed with looking at images, reading comments and trying to live up to what society wants us to be. Just be with your friends and family more, engage with people more and try not to become so obsessed with your phone and social media. If you are struggling with it, tell someone because it does help." Like Nelson says, if you are on the receiving end of abuse and find that it's impacting you and your mental health, it's vital to find support. Friends, family and team members are the first points of call, and helplines like the National Bullying Helpline, and Childline for those aged 19 and under, can provide a valuable listening ear. The police can also get involved for cases that are considered a criminal offence.

Beyond that, Ben Anderson suggests that the more magnanimous among us might be able to try feeling some sympathy for the trolls, or even empathy. He explains:

> "Trolls can drive people to terrible feelings if you feed or engage with them and actually take what they are saying to heart. But instead, they could be seen as victims of the world or people who have been alienated themselves. You see that bully in school as the person who caused you a lot of pain, but at the same time you look at their life and they have been projecting over to you because of the stuff they have been feeling. I'm not saying that everyone who has trolled someone is a victim but I think it helps to take a viewpoint that's a bit more bigger picture."

So dealing with negativity can involve avoiding seeing it, asking for help if you are on the receiving end of bullying, and trying to understand the people who are offering it and what their motives are. Then, without feeding it, finding a way to cope with it without taking it to heart. It can't be personal if the person who's posting doesn't know you, truly. In most cases, giving into that 'mirroring' reflex and biting back to a troll or a negative comment is only going to cause more anger and upset than if you were to brush it off or engage with it in a lighthearted way. While certainly not for everyone, James Blunt has his troll strategy well-honed — his Twitter timeline is full of re-tweeted insults from trolls framed by his own witty comebacks.

Ultimately, Anderson says that building those foundations mentioned earlier in this chapter of who you are as an artist and what you stand for will help make any insults slide: "Once you know that you're conducting yourself as part of your build as an artist, you can detach from the deeper feelings around it and understand that people like different things and you are never going to please everyone."

SILENCE THE NOISE

It can be difficult to remember this when certain gatekeepers require you to have a following in order to offer support, but history has shown that good music travels, especially in the age of internet-enabled virality. Take 2019 summer smash "Dance Monkey", which set the internet alight despite the fact it was only the second single from then fairly unknown artist Tones & I. That's how Lorde's career kickstarted too, with "Royals", which people went wild for after discovering it on SoundCloud. There are countless more examples throughout history. That's not to say that it's easy for a track to go viral or that promoting it requires little effort — lots of work and support helped those two examples behind the scenes — but their success wasn't down to large followings on social media.

It's also worth noting that some of the biggest stars in the world take a minimalist approach to social media — Adele, Chris Martin of Coldplay, Frank Ocean, Drake, and Ed Sheeran are among many artists who don't appear to spend a lot of time online (or if they do, it's using alt accounts). A successful career in music always comes back to the quality of the music and how compelling an artist's world is, and those things are achieved through lots of time spent perfecting your craft and building relationships, not obsessing about how many humans have clicked a button.

Hannah Peel has been in positions where her track is being considered for a radio playlist but has been denied by gatekeepers due to her 'not having enough' followers on social media. But it doesn't really matter — with a 10-year career in music behind her, both as a soloist and part of group The Magnetic North, she's independently sustainable. That's thanks to healthy income from sync, two successful funding applications, compositions for TV and film (including her first-feature length film score for the Emmy-nominated *Game of Thrones* documentary). Oh, and she splits her time between the bright lights of London and living by the sea in Northern Ireland, which sounds idyllic. Peel has got around any lack of interest at radio by forming relationships with potential supporters by getting to know them and personally sending them her music. "So they've been on a journey with me from the beginning," she explains. "My opportunities have not come from bots or people at the top looking at a number, they've come from people starting to respect me for what I do."

Finally, here's the sage advice that British A&R Alec Boateng, who has worked with artists including Jess Glynne and Stormzy, told the audience at Urban Development's Industry Takeover day in 2019:

> "I always say to an artist when they are doing something that is about to be public facing, why do you want people to stay with you? Why do you want them to come back? **Whatever you want people to know you for in 10 years' time should be your focus, everything else is a side dish.** If social media brings numbers to that, cool, but as an artist, if you are focused on knowing why you are bringing people to you, that will allow you to make the right or better decisions as to how you handle social media so you don't focus on it as much, you're not looking at things that haven't got as many likes and think that it affects your album or this or that.

> "Please, **just focus on being good at what you do, growing your art or nurturing your own talent.** With a lot of artists I work with, when they are saying something that has been directly affected by opinion [on social media], I say, 'You're just letting the noise in.' Just be cool, make an incredible album, because that's the focus that's going to change everything for you. People who pour themselves into their careers and music protect themselves from the noise, or they have teams that do, and I think that's a really important thing."

To summarise:

- Social media is a tool that can be used to build a fanbase and share your work. Use it **strategically** and **think carefully** about what's most useful to post about in that context.

- Consider how open you're comfortable being and **what boundaries you might need to set** to preserve your mental health.

- If you fall into a pattern of comparison, remember that **what you see online is often not the whole, or most authentic, picture**. Avoid following (or seeing) accounts that cause negative feelings and if you see something that does, digging deep to find the reason behind that might help you realise an unmet need. Ultimately, **focus on your own path**.

- Try not to **spend more than two to three hours per day** on social media. Consider keeping use down to 30 minutes a day when you can and taking days off from it entirely (especially when you're not working). Organisation and planning will help you here, as will apps like Buffer, or, if it's available to you, handing over the responsibility to someone else.

- When you are online, **think about the quality of what you're doing**. Being productive at work or chatting with friends is likely to leave you in a positive and motivated mindset, whereas comparing yourself to others and getting into arguments will bring you down.

- If you're receiving negative comments online, **consider blocking, reporting or muting users and turning off comments on your posts** (where possible). If you are a victim of bullying, make sure you tell someone as soon as possible.

- Remember that **social media is not the be-all and the end-all** — focus on your music and building positive relationships in the real world, and **learn to engage with it in a healthy way**.

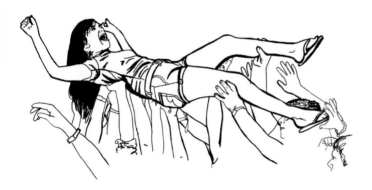

CHAPTER 5

FANS AND BOUNDARIES

IN TIMES GONE BY, artists were generally elusive beings not of the ordinary world. Fans discussed their shared adoration of these gods with fellow fans in online forums or, going back even further, on the phone or by post. Glimpses of the artist would be gifted at shows and in rare interviews but it was quite tricky to properly see if there was a human behind the facade, which only added to the allure and intrigue. As we discussed in the previous chapter, that's largely gone down the tubes in recent years. Musicians are expected to be present on multiple communication channels to advance their careers and for that reason, their relationship with fans has never been more direct.

Managing the pressures and demands of a fanbase who have direct access to a person they adore and might think they know personally, or would quite like to get to know, can, at times, be exhausting. It is, as summarised by Nancy Baym in her book *Playing to the Crowd*, **relational labour**, which requires "each person to find a tolerable balance between being interactive and being autonomous, being open and showing restraint, day after day, on platform after platform."[1]

It sounds like an awful lot of work. But it's work that's necessary and can give more than it takes. Much as creativity is often its own reward, we all want to feel like we're doing something that matters and is being appreciated by others. Music fans offer that validation and recognition in spades. They also offer tangible recognition in the form of ticket sales, merch purchases and, to a somewhat more debatable degree, streaming.

BUILDING A FANBASE

Before we go into how to manage the demands of a fanbase, you've got to build one. That requires time, patience and a less-is-more approach (at least at the very beginning). The first people to focus on are those within your extended network who support and appreciate what you do. So perhaps, like singer and songwriter Phoebe Green, your fans start as online friends with shared interests. She explains: "I've had Twitter since I was about 12 and was always tweeting. I was a massive fan when I was younger, one of those proper dedicated fans to everyone, and I made quite a lot of online friends through that at an early stage. Once I started making music myself, they all became fans of me as well as my friends."

Green made an EP while at school and put it on Bandcamp, and by the time she released her debut album aged 19, *2AM*, there was a strong foundation of core fans that has continued to grow. "When I released *2AM* I already had this small but dedicated fanbase," she explains. "Even though I hadn't met half of them, I felt like they were my friends because they'd known about me from about the age of 13. When I released my album, I had a lot of support, and then because of playlists and stuff like that, the fanbase grew. With streaming, everything has done well since because I had that foundation from so early on."

The key to creating a fanbase that allows you to have a long and sustainable career is not expressed in the number of people who follow you on social media — it's about how engaged those people truly are. Someone could have fifty-thousand Instagram followers and millions of streams on Spotify, but the true measure of success will centre on the few thousand who'll buy something to support the artist, whether that be a gig ticket, merchandise, or vinyl. This is why chasing after hundreds of thousands of followers, instead of focusing on those core real world people who will pay to support you (as well as liking what's posted on social media), is a pretty futile effort. Getting a million streams on Spotify could be worth a few thousand pounds (shared amongst whoever requires a cut — don't buy a car just yet) but selling 500 t-shirts you designed yourself or 500 limited edition EPs on CD or vinyl could bring in more revenue.

Of her many thousand social media followers, Green estimates that around one thousand of those are core fans who will support her no matter what. In the beginning, focus on the first five, ten, fifty, or a hundred fans who will show up to gigs because they believe in you or have a personal connection with your music. They are also the ones who will help expand your fanbase further. Music marketing expert, Darren Hemmings, explains:

> "People like to say they were there first, so when they discover an act and understand that the act is relatively unknown, they do become quite vocal supporters. It's a kudos thing. If I was banging on to you about the next big group before anyone else was, I get the bragging rights, I was there first. **The people who are 'early investors' in music groups get behind them passionately,** so those first one

thousand fans you make are often the ones who will go a real distance in banging the drum and spreading the word. If you get 100 fans and they all tell 100 people, there are not many steps to go from being a very small band to a very big one."

Rather than trying to reach 5,000 people, why not impress 1,000 people enough that they'll each tell four friends? Focusing on a small number of avid fans, instead of trying to get a large number of disengaged internet likes, will also make it easier to reach those fans. Social media websites have a habit of punishing pages that have a low level of engagement, so if the amount of likes far outstrips the number of people who are regularly checking in with what you do, there's a high possibility that anything you post won't be seen by those who matter.

Hemmings says that while this does vary, the generally accepted standard of reach on social media is five to seven per cent, meaning that for every 100 followers, anything that's posted might show up in the feeds of as few as five. Social media platforms are, quite frankly "a nice term for advertising platforms," Hemmings explains. "They are simply ad platforms with a front end built onto them that indulges our ego! They are not there to reach people for free, they are there to take your data and sell it, which is a whole other area of debate. So if you do want to reach these people, you have to pay. If it sounds too good to be true, i.e. I can reach a million people for free, it probably is."

Apart from paying for advertising, which can be costly, the way around limited reach would be to build a network independently around a dedicated personal website and email database. Run The Jewels are an example of an act who've got their fanbase in a place where they are guaranteed to be able to contact them directly. Thanks to the fact they gave away an album for free in exchange for email addresses, the group has a large email database of fans to whom they can send messages without fear of being replaced by a paid advert. A monthly newsletter is sent out containing updates on what they are up to, written in a personal and funny way, which has an open rate of over 50%. According to stats from email marketing company MailChimp, the average open rate for music-related newsletters is just over 20%,[2] and while that's not as impressive as Run The Jewels' stats, it's a lot better than most artists' social media reach.

So how do you create an engaged fanbase? It starts with honing your artist proposition — which is what social media expert Ben Anderson says in the Social Media chapter about who you are and what you stand for. Then, consistently writing, releasing, and gigging for the few in your network who chime with what you do. In *Tribes*, author Seth Godin writes about human beings' innate desire to belong to a group, which is said to stem from a survival mechanism that helped protect us from predators when we were living in the wild.[3] Today, tribes continue to be formed around shared interests, a way to communicate, and some sort of leadership. That can be seen throughout history in music — One Direction led their tribe of Directioners, Taylor Swift has her Swifties, and Ed Sheeran is followed by a load of Sheerios (it's worth noting that most truly engaged fandoms will name *themselves* — it's one example of how important it can be for fans to take a kind of ownership of their favourite artists). Providing you're doing everything right, your tribe should slowly grow with other people who have a similar mindset. They could be friends or family members of those who've already signed up to the fan club, as well as people you reach by being present and active.

UNDER PRESSURE AND BOUNDARIES

So you've started to get fans, who can be lovely and great, but they can also be quite demanding. It's nice to be stanned but that excitement can feel like pressure from behind a screen. Especially when you're busy or stressed, or in the middle of a tough creative process and just can't think about the result yet and someone's yelling "COME TO BRAZIL" at you on Twitter. Fans in 2020 are increasingly well-acquainted with the mental demands they can place on their favourite artists, but it comes with the territory that they might also assume you're some superhuman with endless energy, sipping a cocktail by the pool in your penthouse villa (this is particularly likely if all you post on your Insta are pictures of yourself, well, sipping cocktails by the pool in your penthouse villa). The thing is, if they are a proper fan, they won't ever go away, so there is no pressure to try and meet every demanding request. Everyone works at their own pace and good work is rarely rushed. If that open line of communication gets a bit much, log off.

It's also important to realise that pressure and demand prove that you're doing something right. Ben Anderson is back to explain: "You want fans to be asking you when the music is coming out or when you're playing the next show because it means they are following you and are eager. If you've got music coming out and no one is asking you for it, it's a bit of a problem!" So approach demands with the mindset of running a small business that's providing something there's an appetite for, rather than taking pressure personally. Anderson continues: "Treat it like a game and build that suspense up to a point where you are always leaving them wanting more and excited." That goes with handling disappointments too — if you've had to cancel a gig and let people down, the reaction isn't going to be one of joy. The only way to deal with that is to be communicative, apologise, and, if possible, promise to make it up to them. Sometimes life brings about situations beyond our control — it happens to all of us, but of course it's harder to deal with when it means letting lots of people down. When the storm is over, re-engage with them and move on. And try and remember how brilliant it is that there's such a strong appetite for what you do.

The relationship today's direct lines of communication create also puts artists at a greater risk of being in contact with people who may overstep the line and might even put the artist and those around them in danger. Singer and songwriter Lauren Aquilina has someone who harassed and stalked her, as well as her friends and family, online. She dealt with it by blocking that person before getting the police involved. American singer Lucy Dacus had to issue some rules on Twitter after becoming spooked from past experiences with fans, which were: "Please don't come to the stage door when we're loading in or out, don't try to enter the green room, don't wait by our van, and do not follow me to places. Even if you're the absolute nicest person with the best and kindest intentions, it still feels like an invasion."[4]

Fans might also get in touch with personal problems they are looking for help with, which Aquilina deals with in a similarly sensible way. She explains: "I get the occasional thing where people will tell me about their life problems and expect me to be an agony aunt. If I do get someone who is being too forward or personal, I know how to call them out on it in a nice way. It depends on the message, but usually, I'll be like, 'I appreciate your message but I think this is something you should talk to your family or a close friend about, probably not me because we don't know each other. But I hope everything is okay.'" In extreme circumstances, such as when you fear a fan might be in danger, you might feel more comfortable passing messages on to a manager or someone in your team to avoid shouldering alone the problems of other people, which can be dangerous for them and draining for you.

While it's important to remember that making time for selfies when you're out and about is pretty much part of the job, creating boundaries doesn't make you heartless, uncaring, or a diva (as feared by Dacus). It's only by creating a healthy distance between yourself and your fans that you'll be able to have enough energy to be the most energetic, kind, and compassionate version of yourself in all areas of your life. That has been demonstrated through research by social scientist Brené Brown, whose studies have shown that the shared quality amongst the most compassionate people is boundaries of steel.[5] When you think about that, it makes sense — how can you be kind to others if you're not being kind and nurturing to yourself? American singer and songwriter Lauv puts it like this:

"I need to first and foremost look after myself: I can't help other people if I'm not in a good place. When I feel like I'm in a good place I do my best to be active and connected. But I've also got better, when I need space, at just hopping off and not being online."[6]

Psychotherapist Jodi Milstein, who was a music industry executive for two decades before retraining, says that the definition of healthy boundaries is "somebody who is looking after themselves". She continues: "It's kind of like in relationships, we have to be taking care of ourselves in a relationship and then we also have to nurture the relationship itself. In business and with musicians, they have to take care of themselves and then they also have to nurture the band and this machine that they've created. To do that, you have to have some sort of balance in your life and you have to be able to set certain boundaries and stick to them. Healthy boundaries are whatever someone is establishing to preserve their emotional, mental and physical wellbeing, and, as they get older, perhaps that of their family too."

Here's what healthy boundaries should allow you to do:

- Have high **self-esteem** and **self-respect.**
- **Share personal information gradually**, in a mutually sharing and trusting relationship.
- **Protect physical and emotional space** from intrusion.
- **Be assertive** — confidently and truthfully say 'yes' or 'no' and be okay when others say 'no' to you.
- **Separate your needs, thoughts, feelings and desires from others** — recognise that your boundaries and needs are different from those of others.
- **Empower yourself** to make healthy choices and **take responsibility** for yourself.[7]

The result of not setting boundaries? Research has suggested that poor boundaries can result in resentment, anger, burnout,[8] stress, financial burdens, wasted time, and relationship issues, which can cause mental distress.[9] Obviously, we'd all quite like to avoid all of the above, and setting personal boundaries between you and your fans, but also anyone else you spend time with in and outside of work, is integral to doing that. Knowing where those lines are drawn will be different for everyone so spending some time thinking about where yours are is essential. Then it's about finding your voice and articulating your needs. Milstein continues:

> "So often we are taught to just be quiet and okay, listen to those people who are telling you what you should do and if something is bothering you, brush it under the rug and just don't let it bother you. But we know that when that happens, it builds and gets bigger and bigger and when there is something that has built up over time, it gets more and more difficult to diffuse. **Communication is a key part of setting boundaries and a key part of mental health.**"

It's not only about what you say, it's also about how you say it — communicating your needs positively can be the difference between receiving a positive, understanding response and causing conflict. Milstein tries to help musicians "learn to speak up for themselves in a way that is not demanding because if you are demanding something then you are not necessarily going to be received as well and then you become 'that person'," she says. "So it's also about learning communication skills, especially if we didn't come from positive communication skills in our family of origin, because we then carry that on to our adult lives and working and intimate relationships."

Unhealthy boundaries are characterised by:

- **Sharing too much too soon** or, at the other end of the spectrum, closing yourself off and **not expressing your need and wants.**
- **Feeling responsible for others'** happiness.
- Inability to say "no" for **fear of rejection or abandonment.**
- **Weak sense of your own identity**: you base how you feel about yourself on how others treat you.
- **Disempowerment**: you allow others to make decisions for you;

consequently, you feel powerless and do not take responsibility for your own life.[10]

Generally speaking, when you feel anger or resentment about doing something or find yourself complaining, that might be a sign that you need to set a boundary. Justin Bieber ended up cancelling all future meet and greets because he felt "drained and unhappy" afterwards, as he explained in 2016: "[I] want to make people smile and happy but not at my expense. And I always leave feeling mentally and emotionally exhausted to the point of depression. [I] never want to disappoint but I feel I would rather give you guys the show and my albums as promised... I want to stay in the healthy mindset I'm in to give you the best show you have ever seen."[11] That's a clear example of someone realising that a boundary needed to be set and firmly setting it.

For others, the close interaction of meet and greets might be motivating and exciting — you need to work out which one is you. Similarly, do you enjoy replying to emails from fans or does it feel draining? If it's the latter, make a blanket rule of not communicating with fans over email or ask someone else to do it on your behalf. Do you feel weird about publicly sharing personal things about your private life or are you a completely open book who enjoys sharing with others (within reason, as we've discussed in Social Media)? If it's the former, set a boundary about not doing it and stick to it. When you get back from tour, do you need a certain amount of time off to readjust? If so, be clear about that. There are many ways you can set boundaries in your personal life too. Again, saying no to people is not mean or selfish, it's making sure that when you do spend time and communicate with others, they are getting the best version of you. If anyone accuses you of being attention-seeking or self-indulgent for setting a boundary, perhaps that's a sign that person (or fan) doesn't have your best interests at heart.

When it comes to defining and setting boundaries, it can be helpful to make a short list describing areas in your life where boundaries are being crossed. For example: someone is asking to interview you the day after you get back from tour when you're going to be exhausted and would like to have some time off work. Then, you define the action you're going to take, which could be: I'm going to set a blanket rule of always having one week (or whatever you need) completely free of any sort of work each time I return from tour. That can be difficult to do, especially in the early stages of a career when it can pay off to strike while the iron's hot, but once there's some momentum, it gets easier to pick and choose what you do. Milstein adds:

> "It's also about figuring out what you can do to get more bang for your buck. You have to take care of your fans, that is important, but if there's a way to do get-togethers before a show, and have groups of people instead of one at a time, then you are making more use of your time. It's about finding that balance of who is important to interview with and which shows are important to do and trying to be nice all the way around so that you don't get a bad reputation. That's where having management who can help you balance that is important, and if you're in a band, working as a team is even more important now because there are so many social media outlets that one person can't do it all."

Here are some tips for setting healthy boundaries:

- When you identify the need to set a boundary, do it **clearly, calmly, firmly, respectfully**, and in as few words as possible.
- **Do not justify, get angry, or apologise** for the boundary you are setting.
- You are not responsible for another person's reaction to the boundary you are setting. **You are only responsible for respectfully communicating your boundary**. If it upsets them, that's their problem.
- Remember, **your behaviour must match the boundaries you are setting** — you can't successfully establish a clear boundary if you send mixed messages by being all apologetic.

- At first, you might feel selfish, guilty, or embarrassed when you set a boundary. Do it anyway and **remind yourself you have a right to self-care**. Setting boundaries takes time, practice, and determination. Don't let anxiety, fear, or guilt prevent you from taking care of yourself.
- **Develop a support system of people**, both in your professional and private life, who respect your right to set boundaries.[12]

Sometimes, enacting boundaries is simply about learning how to say no. While it wasn't the case at the beginning of her career, this is something 15x Grammy-winner Alicia Keys has now learned to do. She says:

> "I didn't have any boundaries. I didn't know how to put them in place. In fact, I gave them away willingly, happily, gratefully just to hopefully go to the next step, to what I thought was closer to what I was hoping for or what I thought would make doors open or possibilities come regarding my career as an artist. I didn't even understand that you could say no. It took me so long to actually know that on tour, I could say, 'This is my someone special to me's birthday, let's make sure that I'm not working on that day.' I didn't even know how to do that. I didn't even realise that I could."[13]

When it comes to making choices, it's common for artists (and people generally) to make them by committee, soliciting and listening to multiple opinions which can cloud their own. Your intuition is there to help you make the right one but it's not always easy to access. Keys continues: "I was so inundated with everybody else's opinion, especially because I started creating music so young at 14-years-old in this crazy, scary industry that wants to tell everybody what to do, especially women. I got very habitual about always asking other people what they thought I should do, assuming they knew more than I did. That started to become a habit in my life and for quite a long time, I couldn't access my own opinion because I wasn't exercising it."

That habit, alongside the arrival of success, resulted in Keys moving further and further away from herself. "At the very beginning of my career, I knew what I wanted, I knew what I wanted to do and I had the support to do it. Enter success, enter this whole different perspective and parameter and people having access to their opinion of you and you suddenly realising, 'Wow, all these people like what I do, are they going to like when I do this?' I started to get into a mind frame where, as opposed to just doing what I felt was 100% right, I started to think about it more as a business or more in the capacity of: 'Will people respond?' I never thought of that before because I didn't have anybody to think about responding to it for. That is when there was a shift and that's when I started to get more outside of myself.'"

It's not just Alicia Keys-level of success that can cloud your intuition, which might be tricky to find as a result of insecurity, lack of knowing yourself, and like we said earlier, placing too much importance on other people's opinions. Today, thanks to some high-profile advice, when faced with a choice, Keys waits for a 'resounding yes' before agreeing to anything and gives herself more time to think if it's not there straight away. She also recognises that when she's doing something she truly wants to do, she feels energised, while feeling drained might be an indicator that a wrong choice was made. She explains:

> "**You feel good when you are doing something that you really want to do and when you are actually listening to yourself.** I would be so overwhelmed or overworked, I would just be saying yes to everything and then I'd be exhausted. A big lesson that Ms. Oprah shared with me is that she said she had also experienced that — she was also always looking outside of herself for the answer and she finally realised that she was the only one that really knows herself. We're the only ones that truly know what's good for us and only us. So she said, 'You know what a resounding yes feels like.' Today that sounds so obvious but in that moment, no-one had ever explained it so simply to me. It means

that if someone presents you with a question, you know right away when it's like, 'Hell yeah, I'm dropping everything and I'm doing that.'"

If your response is not a 'resounding yes' then it's a no, at least until it is, as Keys further explains: "It doesn't mean that you're not thinking about it, it doesn't mean that you might not need to get more information about it, maybe you want to ask a few opinions, but as long as it's a maybe, it's technically a no until it's the resounding yes."

What about if it feels impossible to say no and take a break? "Sometimes you have to take that mental health break and take care of yourself," Milstein says. "Those who say, 'Oh, I can't get off of this conveyor belt' have to think: 'Well, what would be the consequences if I don't?'"

We'll leave it to Nancy Baym to have the final word in this chapter:

> "Ultimately, we need to become **conscious** of our own needs and **identify** our own limits. We need to be **attentive** to our experience and **reflective**, observing ourselves so that we can **learn what works for us and what doesn't**. Know that **your limits will change over time**, sometimes by the hour. And remember, **restraint is also a virtue**."[14]

To conclude:

- When building a fanbase, **prioritise creating engagement with the first few who love what you do** over getting lots of disengaged social media followers.

- **Have strategies in place** for any pressure fans might put on you. Remember that you're a business that requires demand to survive and **communicate clearly** if you need to let them down.

- Enact boundaries to **protect both yourself and others**.

- Make sure you're **looking after your own needs first and foremost,** and communicate those needs positively.

CHAPTER 6

FAME

FAME'S SO INGRAINED in the way we view the world that we rarely pause to consider it objectively. But imagine explaining to a space alien that here on Earth certain people are worshipped — but also despised — by legions with whom they've never even shared a room. Imagine explaining that certain people are endlessly analysed on websites and in magazines, simply because of a particular facial expression they happened to pull in Pret, or that the same person might be paid a million quid to wear a branded shoe in a photograph. The alien might just hop back in their spaceship and fly off again. Or, if the alien race in question was anything like the human race, they might say: "That sounds ridiculous, also where can I buy a copy of *Heat* magazine?"

In the book *Fame: The Psychology of Stardom,* authors Andrew Evans and Glenn Wilson point out that the phenomenon of fame has changed considerably through the ages[1]. It was once something bestowed upon heroes and spiritual leaders, or explorers and inventors, which is quite different to, say, becoming TikTok famous for throwing a piece of ham at someone's head. The rise of social media has only furthered the ease with which people can find an audience, with 3.8bn people — nearly half the world's population — active on social media as of January 2020.[2] Fame can happen quickly with a viral hit or stream of funny tweets when suddenly an 'overnight sensation' (who may well have been posting daily for years) finds themselves the focus of multiple lenses, with little or no training in how to deal with the bizarre situation they find themselves in.

Fame is often thought of as something to be chased, largely because it's seen as the ultimate sign of success, with less consideration being given to the fact that the challenges that come with being in the limelight make some of those who found it wish they never had. Some of the most successful musicians to have reached that pinnacle of fame haven't held back when describing the downsides of their public lifestyles. Billie Eilish says that fame from age 13 means she lost out on a lot of the fun aspects of being a teenager because she was working, and that her life is 50% horrible thanks to the "trash" of fame.[3] It's not all bad of course — Eilish also enjoys a 50% "unbelievably amazing and completely priceless" life thanks to the music and performance side of her career.

Justin Bieber has described the loneliness and isolation of a famous lifestyle. He explains: "You're in your hotel room and there are fans all around, paparazzi following you everywhere, and it gets intense. When you can't go anywhere or do anything alone, you get depressed. I would not wish this upon anyone."[4] Lady Gaga also weighs in: "As soon as I go out into the world, I belong, in a way, to everyone else. It's legal to follow me, it's legal to stalk me at the beach, I can't call the police or ask them to leave. I miss people. I miss going anywhere and meeting a random person and saying 'Hi' and having a conversation about life."[5]

Closer to home, Lucy Spraggan, who became famous overnight after appearing on *The X Factor* in 2012, shares some educated insight:

> "**Fame is the weirdest thing anyone could ever go through**. I think **the pressure it has on the normal person's identity, physically, mentally, everything, is unprecedented**, and I don't think you can compare it with many things. I've always been of the mindset that people who go on [talent shows] know what they are getting into, but fame is not what you'd think it is. Fame is never being able to go anywhere without makeup on ever again. Fame is becoming so paranoid that when somebody is texting on their phone, you wonder if they are recording or taking a picture. Fame is meeting someone at a party and having to work out whether they are a journalist or not. It's pretty mad."

While all of the above would be difficult for anyone to handle, there's evidence to suggest that musicians might find the nature of a public life particularly challenging. The 'sensitive musician' is a well-worn cliché but scientific evidence backs it up. While rock stars might exude utter confidence onstage, when psychologist Jennifer Grimes interviewed 21 of them backstage at three major metal tours, she found that most displayed contradictory traits of openness and sensitivity, as well as introversion, and extraversion.[6] Back in 2002, a team of researchers from Heidelberg University in Germany found that musicians have bigger and more sensitive brains than people who do not play instruments[7]. Meanwhile, researchers at Northwestern University have found that the more years of musical experience a musician possesses, and the earlier the age at which they began studying music, the better their nervous systems are at interpreting the emotional content of sound.[8]

When faced with fame and all that comes with it, it's not hard to imagine how someone with traits of sensitivity, introversion and emotional intelligence is likely to find the pressure immensely challenging and stressful. And it's important to remember that Bieber-level fame, with paps and gossip columnists chasing you, isn't the only type you might experience. A new singer playing 200-capacity venues and with relatively few Instagram followers could feel many of the same pressures. They may experience similar feelings of 'what do these people really want?' if they're cornered by a handful of fans after a show or find their inboxes deluged with requests and 'fanmail'.

Attention and opinion aren't the only challenges that come with fame, of course — there's a wealth of potential stressors beyond that. The Holmes and Rahe scale, which has been used as a measure of stress since the late '60s, offers some insight into how fame can affect stress levels. On the scale, life changes are assigned a number based on their level of impact on the human psyche (higher for most impactful, lower for the less). Psychiatrists Thomas Holmes and Richard Rahe used that to determine the correlation between stressful events and illness by studying the records of over 5,000 medical patients who were asked to tally up their score on the scale based on 43 life events. The results were quite stark — half of the participants whose life changes accumulated a score of between 200 and 300 in one year were found to show health problems the following year. In the box on the next page, taken from Evans and Wilson's book on fame,[9] you can see which of those 43 life events might be experienced alongside fame.

Marital separation may not seem like an obvious one, but as suggested by clinical psychologist Donna Rockwell, who specialises in helping celebrities cope with fame and successfully navigate celebrity life, the stress that comes with fame is often transferred onto the friends and family of the famous person and relationship breakdowns can happen as a result. "Fame doesn't only impact the famous person but the whole of the family — the spouse, the children, everybody pays in some way for all of that public scrutiny and attention," she explains. "How do you bring up children around that so that they don't feel less than, for example? The family is something a musician or famous person should care the most about but relationships often break up due to a lack of care."

Life event	Life change value
Marital separation	63
Business readjustment	39
Change in financial state	38
Change to a different line of work	36
Change in responsibilities at work	29
Outstanding personal achievement	28
Change in living conditions	25
Revision of personal habits	24
Change in residence	20
Change in social activities	18
Total: 322	

Overall, the total score of the list of life events someone newly famous might experience is 322, which according to Holmes and Rahe's findings, would suggest famous people should keep an eye on their health. Add those factors to loss of privacy, potential isolation from friends and family (some of whom might distance themselves due to lack of understanding), and the risk of being taken advantage of thanks to business affairs being handed over to others, and it's a potential disaster health-wise. Especially if the right people aren't there to support someone through the process.

DEALING WITH FAME

When it comes to dealing with fame, the first thing to consider is that while you might see it as proof that you're doing well artistically or commercially, you shouldn't really be chasing fame for fame itself. For most, the goal of a career in music shouldn't be to become famous (or rich), which would be a bit like winning the lottery. How many musicians can you think of who reach world superstar status, like Adele or Beyoncé? How many *X Factor* contestants, however famous they may have been during the Saturday night live finals, became bonafide superstars? The reality is very few. Most musicians fall under the public radar and exist as cottage industries or run portfolio careers — and do very well creatively, mentally, and even financially. This is why chasing fame is, more often than not, a futile and frustrating process. Having fame as a goal is also a motivation that deserves some interrogation. Do you think it will meet some unmet desire within you? To get a bit spiritual about it, we have all we need to find happiness and peace within ourselves, and no amount of outward success (as long as your basic needs are being met) can replace the job of digging until we find that peace. Or in the words of the late, great, David Bowie: "Fame itself, of course, doesn't really afford you anything more than a good seat in a restaurant."[10]

If fame does find you, Rockwell says the experience requires training and understanding. Her advice for dealing with the constant attention is to truly educate yourself about what's going on, to "understand Celebrity Worship Syndrome and what fandom is, become a PhD of the psychology of fame and celebrity so you can withstand it for yourself." That sort of education is what we will attempt to offer a lite version of here.

The developmental process of fame according to Rockwell's research starts with becoming famous and loving it (because of all the ego-stroking), before it becomes too much, resulting in a love/hate relationship with fame, and then an addiction to it.[11] Rockwell explains: "This thing that you had no awareness of and then are thrown into, you start craving and becoming addicted to the 'temptational' aspects of the fame experience. What that does neurologically is that your brain starts expecting that level of excitation in your neurological pathways, so that's the admiration, adulation and attention — people getting excited at the sight of you." After that comes a rocky period of trying to adapt to the new level of attention that inhibits everyday life, and finally, acceptance of the new way of being arrives.

So if you're famous, and assuming you're not *actually* The Chosen One, you might wonder: why are so many people acting like you are? Celebrity Worship Syndrome is an obsessive-addictive disorder where someone can become obsessed with the details of the personal life of a celebrity. In varying degrees of intensity, it's said to affect a surprisingly large section of the population – around one-third, according to research on the phenomenon.[12] Less dramatically, an oft-cited theory is that celebrity obsession is an evolutionary trait – on a basic level, it makes sense to pay attention to people at the top of a hierarchy to learn the behaviours and achievements of something (or someone) you aspire to be. Knowing what's going on in the lives of high-status individuals also makes it easier to navigate the social scene.[13]

Neurobiologist Michael Platt attempted to display just how ingrained that urge might be with a study using twelve thirsty adult male monkeys.[14] The monkeys were offered the choice between their favourite beverage (a Juicy Juice cherry drink) or the opportunity to stare at the dominant 'celebrity' monkey of their pack on a computer. In every case, they chose to look at the picture but opted for the juice when the alternative on the computer was simply one of their fellow subordinate monkeys. The celeb monkeys, meanwhile, were just as interested in their fellow celebrities. Human beings are also prone to gossip, which is said to have started as a tribal protection mechanism to weed out selfish people who might put the others in danger.[15] So chatting about annoying colleagues, for instance, could be for the same underlying reason, and it's worth wondering if the way certain news outlets print gossip stories about certain celebrities is a similar attempt to protect some notion of a status quo.

According to Rockwell, when a person becomes celebrated, 'normal' people tend to enjoy being in the presence of that person because it makes them feel famous and therefore special too. In her research, she calls that 'reflected glory'. Rockwell explains: "You could say their mirror neurons get lit up when they are a friend of the celebrity in some context, the trainer of a celebrity, or [their] hairdresser. There is some neurological charge from that proximity."

PERSONALITY PROBLEMS

So famous people start getting a lot of attention from lots of people who want to bathe in their extra special light. Why is that an issue? Well, as well as resulting in a social bubble where 'friends' aren't necessarily actual friends, it runs the risk of creating, quite understandably, a rather large head. Rockwell continues:

> "There is a term coined by [US physician] Robert Millman, who was a consultant to major league baseball, called 'acquired situational narcissism'. What that means is that **even if someone hasn't had early life experiences of parental deficit, with lack of early life mirroring that would lead to more traditional cases of narcissism, just being in the public eye is enough to mimic that for us** internally and neurologically so that we can start taking on the attributes of narcissism."

Narcissism is a particularly undesirable personality disorder that creates self-centred and arrogant thinking and behaviour, and a lack of empathy and consideration for others. The good news is that research suggests musicians are the least narcissistic celebrity group when compared to reality TV personalities, comedians, and actors.[16]

Whether someone develops full-blown narcissism or not, if attention is on them all of the time, it's not hard to see how that could create a kind of selfish nature and a big ego. In fact, we'd suggest that for most people it's a perfectly natural response to a perfectly unnatural situation. Equally, though, neither of those qualities are conducive to having healthy and positive relationships — some of the things that keep a famous person grounded, and any person happy. Rockwell adds: "All this attention is coming in and if that happens long enough, just like any physical change at the gym on a muscle, the brain muscle also changes, so it just has the expectation of incoming and it forgets how to adequately do outgoing."

As pointed out by Justin Bieber and Lady Gaga, being adulated can also result in a special sort of loneliness, which can be caused by a depersonalisation. In Rockwell's research, participants reported feeling like a 'thing' — or a commodity — rather than a human person of unique character. That's why Lady Gaga "took a long hard look at that property line" she mentioned in her earlier quote and found one place she can still truly be herself. "I said well, if I can't be free out there, I'm going to be free in here [pointing to her heart]."

To cope with that sense of loss of self, a 'character splitting' might occur to manage the distinction between the famous person and the core human being. It's unlikely that David Bowie was in full Ziggy Stardust garb when sitting down to have Christmas dinner, while Beyoncé has Sasha Fierce and Stefani Germanotta is Lady Gaga, and, well, maybe Ed Sheeran has a different selection of t-shirts for home wear. George Barnett is George Ezra, and he finds having a distinction between his artist and 'real world' self valuable when transitioning back into home life after the end of an album cycle. "Say the record lasts 18 months, I'm introduced to people more as George Ezra in [that time] and it does become a bit of an identity thing of, 'I can't remember the last time I was George Barnett.' That's partly why I love and sink back into home life so easily."[17] We'll go into this idea of alter-egos further in the Stage Strategies chapter.

Most of us display slightly different behaviour tailored to the specific social situations we find ourselves in, but for famous people, that's taken to a whole other level. The 'character splitting' is then a mechanism used to manage a public or professional personality while still retaining a private self, saved for only the closest relationships. As stated in Rockwell's study by an anonymous participant: "The only way I think you can really handle

[fame] is to say, 'That's not really me... it's this working part of me or the celebrity part of me.'... So, I am a toy in a shop window."

Having an artist moniker or band name that isn't your real name can also make it easier to navigate career struggles. Nina Nesbitt, whose artist name is her real name, found it particularly challenging to deal with being dropped from her label as 'herself' and advises younger artists to create a professional persona in order to take it less personally when the going gets tough. She says:

> "I look back now to when I started and wished that I'd created a name for myself so I could learn to separate it. I would definitely recommend younger artists to think about doing that because when things are going great, you feel on top of the world because you're like, 'everyone loves me and my music and this feels great, I've written these great songs and people want to be friends with me.' When things are going bad, you're like, 'oh my God, people hate me and my music.' It's very hard to separate it. I just felt like an embarrassment and a failure, personally and professionally."[18]

GROUNDING STRATEGIES

There are four themes that participants in Rockwell's research reported as helping them deal with challenging aspects of fame, while still being able to enjoy spoils like access, wealth, and gratification. Firstly, they found it important to **cherish and nurture trusting relationships with friends and family** who would be there regardless of the fame. It's not hard to see how someone with notoriety and money might attract people with disingenuous intentions, but you want people in your life who will deliver some home truths when you need them, be there for you no matter what, without judgement, and stick around when the going gets tough. Having an honest support network is something top songwriter Wayne Hector wholly endorses:

"When I started having success, maybe I got a little bit of an ego going and my friends sat me down and said, 'You need to fix up,' and that's why I still have the same friends. I think that's what friends should be — the uncomfortable truth and people that are willing to tell you something that you don't want to hear, even at the risk of that friendship."

Rockwell continues: "Have a supportive family and friend structure where you keep yourself open to truth when you hear it. To stay humble is the aspiration and to stay curious and open to what loved ones have to say." Fame is unlikely to last forever, so it's also important to have a support structure if there's ever an opportunity to 'transition' back into everyday life.

Secondly, Rockwell says that **learning mindfulness** (as Helen Brice mentioned in the exercise for the Criticism and Opinion chapter) helps people stay grounded, understanding and less overwhelmed by the life of a celebrity. "It slows everything down, and you are able to see things more clearly," she explains. Mindfulness means paying total attention to what's happening in the present moment and acting, well, mindfully. This is the opposite of behaving reactively without much thought and making the assumption that all the attention you're getting is thoroughly justifiable and reflective of a higher status. Think of it like having a kind but firm voice in your head that's always trying to steer you on the healthiest path.

In *Mindfulness for Dummies*, the definition of mindfulness is:

- **Paying attention** to whatever you chose to attend to.
- **Being in the present moment** and accepting it for the way it is.
- **Avoiding reactive behaviour** according to past conditioning, and replacing it with a deliberate and considered response.
- **Letting go of judgements** (rating experiences as good or bad, or things as like or dislike) in order to see things as they are rather than through the filter of your personal judgements based on past conditioning.

- **Behaving open-heartedly** by bringing a quality of kindness, compassion, warmth and friendliness to your experience.[19]

For example, a mindful celebrity would understand the psychology behind the interactions they have with fawning fans and that it's essential for their own sanity to avoid getting carried away with it all by having some strategies in place. One anonymous example from Rockwell's research is someone who turns the attention he gets from fans back onto them by asking a few questions to find out a bit more about who *they* might be (also known as 'good manners'). Others might use religion or spirituality to stay grounded or simply have a personal checklist to make sure their actions and words align with their personal values. That list could include what matters to you, who you care about, what you want your life to stand for, and what you want people to say about you after you're gone. Which one is it going to be? Kind, grounded, and connected? Or disconnected, egocentric, and lonely? As stated by one of Rockwell's research participants: "You constantly have to reassess who you are, take [the fame] off of you and make sure that you are centred as a person."

Thirdly, among those who tend to have a healthier relationship with fame, Rockwell identifies a theme of **philanthropy and giving back**. She explains: "The people that fare the best with fame are people who can interpret and see fame as currency, as something they've been paid that they can spend in making the world a better place." A prime example of that from the music world is Stormzy, who has pledged £10m over a decade to organisations that help fight racial inequality in the UK. Dua Lipa meanwhile has set up the Sunny Hill Foundation to help underprivileged people in Kosovo (where her parents are from), U2 frontman Bono has been very public about his philanthropy, Elton John has his AIDS Foundation, and no-one who witnessed it will ever forget Bob Geldof's passionate pleas of "GIVE US YER MONEY" during Live Aid in 1985 (it's on YouTube). Rockwell continues:

"It's **the people who can see themselves in the context of a larger whole and what they can do with what they've been given to do their small part in making the world a better place**. They **immediately transcend the pathological aspects of the fame experience** and are able to dedicate their energies to something larger than this iconic archetype, this representation, this reduction of themselves to the rockstar, the governor, the actor. They can be John and Mary and Sue and feel engagement with the living process of self by using their fame and celebrity to help someone else, to feed someone else, to put a smile on someone else's face, a pair of glasses on a child who can now see. These are the activities that famous people can use to transcend the downsides of fame and grow into their full potential as a human being."

And finally, if it's available to you, it can be helpful to find a professional who can help you through the process. "Don't expect to be able to do it alone," Rockwell concludes. "Just like you would get a trainer to go to the gym, you should have a trainer to help you through the experience of being famous and celebrated. They should be there from the beginning, continuing to remind you **that fame is impermanent, it can't last forever, and what do you want to do with your life that's larger than that?**"

To conclude:

- For all its spoils, be aware that **fame has many downsides and should not be a reason for pursuing a career in music** (the statistics suggest you're going to be disappointed so it's probably a futile endeavour anyway).

- If fame does get bestowed upon you, **learn about it so you can manage the experience in a healthy way**. Be aware of the developmental process of loving it, hating it, and then becoming addicted to it.

- **Keep your ego in check by staying grounded** through healthy and positive relationships, learning mindfulness, practising your personal values, and giving back.

PART 2:
SUPPORTING HEALTH

Over the last few chapters, you've hopefully gained an understanding of the industry and how you can manage your health in that context. We'll now look in more detail at the common health issues musicians face and some of the challenges of the environments they work in, such as on tour. There'll be self-care tips to manage your health generally, guidance from experts and organisations and signposts to tailored support for more complex issues. Before delving into this section, we want to make something clear. We are not health professionals or medical specialists. None of this is a substitute for medical intervention or advice in the case of mental or physical illness. These chapters are not a guide to diagnosis, nor a cure-all to replace treatment. If you are experiencing health issues, please see a qualified health professional (you'll find lots of ideas of who to contact in the resources section at the end of this book). If, however, you are after general information about the health issues musicians face and how to manage them, read on!

CHAPTER 7

TOURING

WHEN ALL THE HARD WORK in the studio is done, going on tour, sharing your music with audiences in person, and having people singing the songs that you've written back to you can be incredibly rewarding. Musicians have said that the experience of performing is one of the most enjoyable facets of their career[1] and may be one of the reasons so many can justify spending time away from their families and friends as they take their music to far-flung places.

But despite the highs, it's on tour that things can, and often do, start to go wrong. **Touring can be physically and mentally challenging,** with many musicians reporting they get ill due to a lack of healthy food and proper rest.[2] Exhaustion from little sleep and constant travelling can result in breakdowns in communication and relationships, not to mention mental breakdowns when it all gets too much. With friends and family being so far away, support systems can be hard to find when problems arise. Psychotherapist Tamsin Embleton, who spent 10 years working in the live music industry before retraining, explains: "Emotions are amplified and you're away from support networks, self-care routines, and all the things that help to make you feel grounded."[3]

One of the phrases that crops up time and time again when musicians talk about the challenges of touring is that of **the 'highs and lows'** they experience regularly. Playing in a packed venue full of fans is swiftly followed by a night alone in an empty hotel room or crammed into a tour bus or van. Days are spent travelling, being bored and killing time, before arriving at the venue ready for another high. Idles drummer Jon Beavis explains: "Being on tour with a band is the ultimate high but it can also mean ultimate lows. It's very tough when you're in the back of a van for three months, or even three weeks. Everyone's tired because we put in so much for all the gigs and you've then got to do all the merchandise, load out, drive to the next hotel or the next place to just park your car and sleep in the van. It's insanely tiring."

Singer and songwriter Nina Nesbitt adds: "You have to hype yourself up to go on stage every night, even if you're knackered, and the adrenalin gets you through. But after that, you get a crash, and sometimes you can't sleep because you're buzzing from playing the gig. It's a weird mental space you have to get yourself into." These frequent rushes of adrenaline that Nesbitt refers to can make it difficult to maintain a balanced mental and physical state, even when you're not on stage. Embleton further explains: "Performances can be euphoric but they also involve a lot of adrenalin and cortisol flooding the nervous system, which can make it hard to regulate emotions and bodily states. Artists who have underlying issues may find that those issues are exacerbated if they don't have good support networks and routines that help them to wind down and recover from events or periods of stress."

There's also the **high of touring for three months, then a low of coming home back to reality,** sometimes having forgotten how to look after yourself. This might sound ridiculous but if you've spent three months with managers, tour managers, and other crew members taking responsibility for everything from passports to whether or not your preferred flavour of Pringles are on the rider, it can be hard to adjust to not having an itinerary when you wake up in the morning. One participant in a recent study on touring said "the void" that touring leaves "is actually more dangerous than the activity itself".[4] Trying to manage these feelings alone can lead to alcohol and drug use, as the study further described.

Nutritionist and tour manager Suzi Green, who has worked with artists including PJ Harvey, Marina Diamandis and The Chemical Brothers, says **common health problems she sees on the road include addiction in various forms, substance misuse, exhaustion and burnout.** She says:

> "I don't think many people on tour manage to get eight hours' sleep more than once a week if they are lucky. Moving is inherently stressful and there's a lack of consistency in your surroundings, which on its own puts your body under quite a lot of stress. Also, the trouble with touring or travelling is that unless you are at a certain level and touring with a certain amount of budget, you don't always have a hell of a lot of control over what you eat, where you eat or if there's even any time to eat. Personally, I think food and sleep underpin everything. If those two go out the window then you are a bit like water on a tray — it's harder to keep your equilibrium. You might get away with it for a short time, especially if you're younger, but you definitely won't get away with it for long or when you're older."

In years gone by, unhealthy lifestyles on tour were almost seen as badges of honour. David Bowie was rumoured to exist on milk, peppers, and cocaine during his Thin White Duke period,[5] while Keith Richards has said that the Rolling Stones' 1975 tour was fuelled by a rule of 'one song, one bump' of cocaine — lines of which were strategically hidden behind the speakers on stage.[6] Many more examples of the self-destructive excesses of major touring musicians can be found within films, books, and documentaries. However, as the music industry increasingly relies on touring for the bulk of its income, unreliable musicians are no longer tolerated. Dave Webster, who is the National Organiser of Live Performance for the Musicians' Union, says: "The drunk touring band is a cliché, especially with the strict driving rules now in place. The raised awareness regarding fitness, good diet and the effects of drugs and alcohol are something people take far more seriously these days."[7]

Tour manager Erica Leite, who's been on the road with Dua Lipa and Bastille, agrees. "I think touring is so different now than it was even ten, fifteen, twenty years ago," she says. "Back then you were doing loads of drugs and drinking all the time. Now it's like, 'Would you like a bottle of water and a banana?' Everyone is way more health-conscious." There's another reason why it makes sense to keep in shape — as Webster says, increased competition and scrutiny in today's music business means that there is no room for error in performance, which will be negatively impacted by ill-health. "Delivering consistent performance is so important," he explains. "Especially with the growth in social media, which now dictates that a poor performance on one night can influence subsequent performances and future sales." When there's a venue full of smartphones pointed at your performance, capturing each moment for later review, the line between 'rock and roll' and 'total shambles' disappears — and it's fair to say the ruse of nipping behind a speaker stack for a 'livener' like Richards did would now be quickly rumbled by Twitter detectives.

Support is increasingly in place to better help musicians with some of the aforementioned challenges, and that's what we'll delve into over the coming pages. It'd be impossible to cover everything here, and musicians at different career stages or working in different genres will encounter different experiences, but we offer an overview, and hopefully provide food for thought on how to prepare yourself or those you perform with. Read on for more information on key issues you might face in advance and how to prevent them, alongside strategies to stay healthy on tour and when you return home.

DIET

For many musicians, **access to good food on tour is one of the biggest challenges to their overall health**. Being on the road often means service station food, and sometimes when you want a hot meal, junk food is the easiest option — not to mention the cheapest. Money can be tight for those who don't have the luxury of catering, and on a limited budget it's easy to rule out £5 salads when you hear the siren call of two cheeseburgers for £1.98. One study of 35 musicians found that although touring musicians and singers had positive attitudes regarding healthy foods, the stressful demands of touring impacted their food choices, leading to detrimental effects on health and performance.[8] As we all know, good food plays a vital role in keeping us healthy, both physically and mentally, and sourcing the right nutrition has to be a priority if you want to avoid becoming ill.

Additionally, **musicians have a very physical job to do onstage and it's vital that they have the energy they need** to get themselves through that activity, night after night. You also want to make sure you play the best you can, which is almost impossible if you're starving or coming down from a sugar high. Diane Widdison, who is the Musicians' Union's National Organiser for Education and Training, says it's crucial to think of yourself as a musical 'athlete'. She explains:

> "More musicians are looking at the research that has been done into the importance of nutrition for athletes and realising that there are many similarities in what the body

needs for optimal performance. Food is fuel for the human body and therefore what we eat and drink really impacts the way we feel. The musician's life can often be hectic and chaotic, but time invested in eating healthily will be rewarded by improvements in physical performance and mental wellbeing."[9]

We're not saying the occasional Bargain Bucket is going to wreck your career but general healthy eating is important, both to fuel your way through a performance and to keep you going for the long-haul in your career. When it comes to thinking about what to eat, BAPAM's Sensible Eating for Performers factsheet[10] includes the following advice:

A **balanced diet** is not just about cutting out those foods that are bad for you; you may need to add foods that are lacking. Your diet should contain the following:

- meat, fish, eggs, beans (main source of protein)
- fruit and veg (five a day)
- grains (rice, wheat, pasta, plus potatoes)
- milk and dairy
- fatty and sugary food (puddings and chocolate – as a treat!)

Broadly speaking, a balanced diet means eating something from the main five groups at every meal, or over the course of a day. These five groups are:

- carbohydrates
- proteins
- fats
- vitamins
- minerals
- in addition, you should make sure you drink enough water

You might be thinking that this advice is all well and good for someone who doesn't spend months on end travelling, but amid the turmoil of touring, **there *are* ways you can be organised and source the right nutrition**. Nutritional therapist Caroline Davies suggests stocking up in advance "on healthy snacks to avoid giving in to temptation at service stations, such as unsalted nuts and seeds, fresh and dried fruit, and protein bars."[11] She continues: "If you have a fridge, keep it stocked with carrots and cucumber to snack on, adding hummus or nut butter to make for a more filling snack." Suzi Green agrees that preparation is key:

> "If we're on a bus, I'll fill up the fridge and get loads of decent snacks, like unsalted nuts and crudités. It's about trying to make things appetising and interesting so people will actually pick at them. I even know a guy who carries his own portable slow cooker that he makes soup in — it's an electric thing that he plugs in and throws vegetables and water in, simmers it and makes soup. He's a crew guy in his '50s who has done the rock and roll thing and now he looks after himself."

Green also suggests taking a portable blender like a Nutribullet on tour, to make healthy smoothies and cold soups with while on the go. "Nutribullets are good because they are quite small and fit in your hand luggage," she adds. "They are really high-powered blenders so you can do an awful lot of stuff with them. If you've got something like that with you, it's really easy to carry packets of protein powder, superfoods or greens powders that can be combined with fruit and vegetables on your rider."

For artists with a high profile, most large venues offer catering where there are healthy choices available or you may find that the tour manager arranges a rider, which artists can help design. Tour manager Ben Perry, who has been on the road with musician This Is The Kit and her band, says they stay healthy on tour by requesting the money that might have been spent on providing catering so they can buy their own food instead. "Most of the time now when I do the advancing, I generally say to people, 'You've put aside a hundred quid catering budget, give us a hundred quid, don't get us anything,'" he explains. "With This Is The Kit, we don't use plastics or anything else, so we've all got water bottles, and we literally don't need anything other than the kettle and a space. We sort ourselves out and no-one has to worry about what they've got to buy and things getting wasted."[12]

It's worth noting here, that any sort of restrictive eating runs the risk of creating an energy deficit and being malnourished as a result, leading to a host of health issues. And as Taylor Swift points out, inadequate nutrition could have a big impact on performance ability and energy levels afterwards. "I thought that I was supposed to feel like I was going to pass out at the end of a show, or in the middle of it," she says. "Now I realise, no, if you eat food, have energy, get stronger, you can do all these shows and not feel [exhausted]."[13]

For some, the advice of eating healthily isn't quite as simple as we're making it out to be here, and they may need to seek professional help. If diet is an issue for you, take a look at the Disordered Eating and Body Image chapter if you haven't already and head to the resources section at the back of this book to find signposts to professional help.

DRUGS AND ALCOHOL

It's relatively easy for life on tour to turn into one big party. On the road, there's often a constant supply of alcohol, perhaps drugs too, and lots of opportunities to indulge after gigs or when bored while travelling. It might sound like an absolute dream scenario but it can all go downhill pretty quickly if you're not careful. As Erica Leite explains: "**Limiting and learning how to drink responsibly and in moderation is hugely important**, and that's something people really struggle with."

Making sensible choices can be particularly challenging to manage if you know you have a problem, or you are choosing to be healthy and those around you are making different lifestyle choices. Green says:

"I think the most difficult thing for an artist is if they are quite healthy and their band isn't, or maybe they've gone through some issue and become much healthier than they used to be while everyone else is still partying. That's the hardest situation for all concerned. I think your way through that is you need some likeminded people around you."

That could mean choosing a crew or band members who are a little bit more sedate (if that's within your power) or perhaps taking a friend or family member on the road with you for support. And it's a choice you *can* make. One young solo artist we spoke with said that on his first tour, the crew who'd been chosen for him were partying hard and encouraging his participation; it wasn't his bag and he found the entire tour incredibly uncomfortable. On the advice of a more experienced artist, he chose a different crew for his second tour — they still stayed up late, but were playing video games instead of taking drugs, and he enjoyed the experience a lot more.

Amid all the temptations, **it can be hard to remember that you have a job to do.** Ben Perry's advice is to not let yourself "fall into the usual traps of just getting wasted every night, waking up hungover, eating trash." He continues: "It's so easy to do because it's so exciting. You have to remember you're working as well." Caroline Davies says the impact this lifestyle has affects "performance and energy levels" and it can be wise to try to have some alcohol-free days if you don't want to cut it out entirely. "Dehydration will reduce focus so carry refillable water bottles," she adds. "Herbal teabags will help as an alternative to conventional tea and coffee too."[14]

There is lots of evidence to suggest that while it might be hard at the beginning, the benefits of cutting down on substances or abstaining entirely is worth it. When multi-talented musician Imogen Heap realised it was possible to simply decide not to have a drink (thanks to inspiration from a friend), avoiding alcohol had a positive impact on her ability to think clearly, which is a fairly important life skill whether you're on the road or not. "It was this real wake up call," she remembers. "I'd been living in a haze and was waking up with hangovers but didn't really know because it just felt normal… but why was I a bit sluggish? Then [when I stopped drinking] everything started making a bit more sense because I was a bit more lucid. I started having some clear thoughts about things, and clarity in the mind is a hard thing to obtain so perhaps there was a shift in my consciousness around taking more control."

Leite points out that drugs can also be used as a way to cope with the energetic fluctuations on tour, which is a slippery slope. She says:

> "I think one of the fears I have is that when people aren't eating well and aren't sleeping well, drugs come into play. 'I've got to take an 'x' to get going again, and I've got to take a sleeping pill to get down, and can't sleep and then I've got to wake up again' — that freaks me out. I've seen too many people lose their life from going up and down and up and down and up and down."

For those who might have a problematic relationship with substances, we cover this topic in more detail in the Substance Use chapter. For the rest of you, remember that moderation in this area is key and you've got a job to do. Every night is party night on tour for someone and if you're that way inclined, you'll always find someone to party with you.

EXERCISE

Exercise is good for your mental and physical health, it helps you sleep better, it keeps you in shape and it's great for your wellbeing. Finding a gym and fitting it into a busy schedule on tour can be challenging but there are some other solutions. Green points out how easy it is to go for a run during breaks or practice a few downward dogs. "I started running when I started touring again because all you need is a pair of shoes and not much else. I can just open the door and go," she explains. "Quite a lot of people do yoga as well because you can pack a really thin portable mat. Yoga and running are the easiest things because you can pretty much do them anywhere." Leite also incorporates exercise into her artists' routines. While on tour with Bastille, every day "we find where gyms, boxing clubs and rock climbing gyms are," she says. "We have a running club, and we block out time every morning or afternoon for people to make sure they get a couple of hours of exercise in."

Both Leite and Green talk about how exercising with others can hold you accountable and make it easier to do, so think about anyone on your team who might want to do some exercise with you and make it a priority.

If your experience of touring consists of nothing but hotel rooms, backstage areas and the back of a van, simply getting out of the venue and going for a walk can make a massive difference. And if there's a chance to get out into nature while doing so, even better — lots of research suggests that spending time in nature significantly boosts health and wellbeing. An extensive study by the University of Exeter in 2019 found that those who spent two hours in nature every week had significantly higher levels of good health and life satisfaction versus those who didn't.[15] In addition, Jonathan Higgs from Everything Everything finds that getting out and exercising, where possible, helps him and his bandmates steer clear of alcohol. He says:

> "We try and get out and about in the day — I'm not very good at it but the other guys are. If we're in a city they go and walk around it and don't just sit in the dressing room or on the bus. We exercise, go for a run or a swim, do anything except vegetate and wait until it's drinking o'clock because it creeps down in the day — it's 5pm, then 4pm, and suddenly you are drinking at midday and it's like, what the hell are you doing? Every day is not Christmas day!"

SLEEP

As Green mentioned earlier, **good-quality sleep is so important for all musicians and for singers in particular**. It's equally vital for smaller bands where one of the members is the driver, especially for long journeys. Getting enough sleep isn't just about being able to do your job well — it also has a lot to do with maintaining good health generally and living longer. Matthew Walker, author of *Why We Sleep*, describes its benefits: "Scientists have discovered a revolutionary new treatment that makes you live longer. It enhances your memory and makes you more attractive. It keeps you slim and lowers food cravings. It protects you from cancer and dementia. It wards off colds and flu. It lowers your risk of heart attacks and stroke, not to mention diabetes. You'll even feel happier, less depressed and less anxious. Are you interested?"[16] Of course you are.

The World Health Organization recommends an average of eight hours of sleep per night for adults, and as Walker describes in his book, routinely sleeping less than six or seven hours a night over a long period of time can result in a host of health problems. Even in the short-term it can have some pretty undesirable knock-on effects for your system. "Inadequate sleep — even moderate reductions for just one week — disrupts blood sugar levels so profoundly that you would be classified as pre-diabetic," he writes. As well as helping to avoid health issues, getting enough good quality sleep refreshes our ability to make and save new memories, which aids learning, clears useless information to make way for the useful stuff, and facilitates creativity,[17] which are all pretty vital for musicians.

Nina Nesbitt says lack of sleep is "the main source" of all her mental health struggles on tour. She explains:

> "It's just exhaustion. I toured America for the first time two years ago and I had absolutely no idea how hard that was going to be. It was incredible to see America but the first tour

we did, we couldn't afford to have a tour bus so we drove around with four of us in a car in between big merchandise boxes. We'd have to drive seven hours a day, get to the venue, do a meet and great, do the show, get straight into the car, pack up all the gear and drive another two to three hours to make up the journey to the next place. We'd then crash in a motel that's pretty dodgy for four hours and get up again and repeat it. As much as you love playing the shows and doing what you're doing, it's hard."

As Nesbitt's story describes, getting enough sleep might be tricky for artists who are at a mid-level career stage and can't yet afford a tour bus and nice hotels but still have a fairly busy schedule. However, as all the evidence we've mentioned so far confirms, it's vital to do what you can to get as much sleep as possible. That might include having a say in a travelling schedule and designing it to be as pro-sleep as possible (an understanding manager and agent will help you here). You could also take some comforts from home like a pillow (you can get special ones that help you sleep while upright and travelling) and a blanket, use an eye mask and ear plugs, and agree a lights off and noise curfew with bandmates.

Speaking of light: endlessly scrolling Instagram isn't a great way to relax your brain before bed, so plugging in your phone on the other side of the room or turning it off while travelling is a good method for removing temptation. Plenty of people swear by white noise or even drifting off to an audiobook — in both cases you'll find that most apps have timer functions. Avoid caffeine close to bedtimes and remember that contrary to popular opinion, alcohol does not help you to sleep. For more tips on how to get a good night's sleep, head to the resources section where we've included a link to top tips from DJ and sleep science coach, Tom Middleton.

RELATIONSHIPS

When you're on tour, it can feel like you're in a bubble and the only world that exists is the one you're currently in. Crew and bandmates feel like family and professional boundaries between colleagues and friends become blurred. There's a sense of a shared mission and the camaraderie can be fantastic. But things can go wrong, too. **Relationships break down, tensions arise, and you may need to rely on your real family and friends at home**. If you've cut yourself off for months on end, relying solely on the people around you, it may be feel difficult to reach out to those at home so it's vitally important to stay in touch with loved ones when you're on the road. As Ed Sheeran points out, those people back home are the ones who should be there for you if you just need to offload. He explains:

> "When I'm on tour, I'm with my touring team and then I'm hanging out with other artists. That's super cool but I think it's important sometimes just to sit down and complain and you never have that kind of conversation when you've just met someone because you're not meant to complain. On the first song on *Divide* I had a line where I say, 'nobody wants to see you down in the dumps because you're living the dream, this shit should be fun'. But sometimes you're just pissed off and want to have a rant, and if you're having a rant to someone you don't really know and they are like, 'Why the fuck are you complaining?' that's not what you want to hear in that state. You just want to shout at someone for an hour, even if they don't agree with it, and that's what friends do."[18]

If you're lucky enough to be able to do so, **you can take someone close with you on the road**, as singer and songwriter Lauren Aquilina did on her recent US tour. "The last tour I did in the US was the longest tour I've ever done and I was nervous about it because I haven't really enjoyed touring that much in the past," she says. "But I took my boyfriend with me as my guitarist and I think that really helped, just to have someone there that I really trusted and was familiar with."

For some people, the touring experience can be very isolating, particularly if you are a solo artist and rely purely on yourself for backing or if you've hired a band you don't necessarily get on with. If that's the case for you, how do you avoid feeling isolated? What can you do in advance to make sure that family and friends understand the challenges you're going to face? Sometimes just telling them can be enough. People who don't work in music often don't fully understand some of the tougher aspects of this job and imagine that when you're on tour, you'll be partying every night and won't want to be bothered. Letting them know what you find challenging can help them to help you, and it could make a massive difference to your overall levels of enjoyment and wellbeing.

When it comes to relationship breakdowns within the touring team, Ben Perry finds that some of the problems that face bands as their profile grows can be helped if they are sorted early on. "If there are little things that you don't deal with, they just grow and magnify as the whole process grows," he says.[19] Some bands find it helpful to have therapy when things go wrong, which can happen over Skype anywhere in the world, and others take their therapist on the road with them. Jon Beavis says Idles have had "countless fallouts" due to exhaustion while on tour, but time alone, being mindful, and talking openly helps heal wounds. He explains:

> "Everyone has got their own tactic — if I've got a spare half an hour and it's been a tough day, I'll just go off on my own for a walk, and [band mates] Joe and Lee go for coffee a lot. We are all very mindful — everyone knows when someone is feeling down and everyone now knows how we can help them, and that everyone has a different way of being helped."

POST-TOUR RECOVERY

Towards the end of a long tour, you might find that you're desperate to go home and yet when you actually get there, you miss being on the road or feel really unsettled for a while. Living in transit for so long can take its toll and after a prolonged intense, emotional experience like touring, where, for some, people are taking care of your every need, **returning to the mundane minutiae of everyday life can be tough**. Suzi Green explains:

> "Everybody feels really weird when they come off tour and go home. You almost need to have a 24 to 48-hour incubation period of returning to normal. You go home to your partner and they look at you and go, 'Who are you?' and you are like, 'Oh, I don't know how to talk to you.' You've been so used to being with this group of people, whether you like them or not."

Sam Parker, who is a mental health and wellbeing consultant and partner of an artist, says touring can be particularly taxing on relationships. She explains: "The continuous cycle of break and repair in the 'intimacy field' over medium and long periods of time can be difficult to navigate and manage successfully." As the partner left at home, she says she often feels resentment and jealousy, which can be hard to work through together remotely. Parker continues:

> "In the touring setting, these issues can end up being dealt with during snatched conversations potentially in different time zones with heavy duty 'having fun' noises from the band dressing room in the background or a tour manager chivvying your partner along. After all, it's day-off night and they are all going out to let off the steam and tension of the previous five show days. The adult in you is glad they are having fun and a break, but the child in you feels angry and envious and left to get on with the adult responsibilities of your lives together. And when there are children at home too, you can multiply all this by ten."

According to Parker, the way this is dealt with depends on an individual's 'attachment style' — a term coined by psychologist John Bowlby in the '60s which links the quality of care experienced by a child with how they navigate relationships as an adult. Parker says she has an 'anxious avoidant attachment' style which means she withdraws "into an 'I don't need you' stance." She continues: "I protect myself from pain, loneliness and rejection by pretending I don't need my partner. The flip side of this strategy is that I will then find myself crying and feeling a heavy loneliness on a random Wednesday night. It's not a conscious decision but an unconscious one." On the other hand, Parker says her partner has an 'anxious attachment' style. "That means that to protect himself from pain, loneliness and rejection, he has a tendency to do the opposite – cling and/or control," she says. "Or weirdly, in the pre-touring situation, detach completely, acting as if I don't exist around about two weeks before he's due to go."

We are not all built the same and different attachment styles will result in different responses to touring schedules, whether you are the one on the road or left at home. To learn more about this, we've linked to a quiz that will help identify your tendencies in the resources section. According to Parker, attachment styles can be changed, and she suggests individual or couples therapy from an experienced therapist for anyone navigating difficulties. She concludes: "One of the first lessons learned by military spouses during a long separation is that **coming home and being one-half of a couple again takes some getting used to**. I find it interesting how pertinent this is to my experience of touring life." We've linked to some tips from Mental Health America on how to get through this process in the resources section.

Along with re-establishing relationships, when you have to open the bills that have been piling up, deal with life admin, and sort out any health issues that may have cropped up on tour, real life comes crashing back into view. You may find that being away from family responsibilities has been a welcome relief and returning to them can be a bit of a shock. All of this is totally normal. Green deals with it by being aware of the inevitable. "I don't know if there is any special technique other than knowing I'm going to feel a bit weird for a day or two before I land," she explains. "Also, if you've been on quite a long adrenalin run, some people hit depressions, which is a natural thing that is going to happen — if you've been living it up here you are going to fall off a cliff a bit. I think there is a lot of comfort to be taken in knowing that actually everyone feels this and it's normal."

Green suggests that just as deep-sea divers need a decompression chamber when they emerge from the ocean's depths, getting on the phone with someone you've been on tour with to find comfort in solidarity and shared experience can ease you back into normal life. She adds: "I always thought someone should start a leaving tour rehab where you go and spend two days with blackout curtains, a good coffee machine and Netflix before you go home to your family, to normalise!"

Ben Perry says that having a bigger picture plan can help too. "I think the biggest issue for people, especially musicians, is if you finish a tour and you've got nothing else booked. Certainly if you're younger, you've finally done that big tour, you're really excited, then you come home and it's been great and all you want to do is the next one or get back into the studio. I think having a longer-term plan really, really helps."[20]

That plan could include some **decent time off** to recoup and then getting back to a day job and/or plotting your next career move if there isn't anything already in the diary. There can be a feeling of intense loneliness at this stage, which is why it's important to **make sure you stay in touch with loved ones and friends** while you're on tour and arrange to meet up when you get back so you can reintegrate more easily back into normal life. If **therapy** is something that works for you, arrange a session in advance for when you return home and try and give yourself lots of time and patience to properly make the transition back into the 'real world'. As Green points out, it's not a good idea to come back off tour and then go straight into promo or more travelling for work: she says it's "about **having enough time to stop, recalibrate, then start the next thing**".

POST-TOUR REVIEW

Once you've taken some time to decompress and readjust back to reality, it can be worth reviewing how the tour went. **What worked well? Why? What didn't work so well, and again, why?** It's easy to make the same mistakes over and over again without taking the time to work out why things went wrong and what could be done about it next time. For some, the answers to these questions may involve feeding back to management (if you have it) about how things could be done differently next time. Or it could be that you need to be more organised — perhaps there was an extra piece of gear that could have been helpful. Whatever it is, take a bit of time to review when you're in a neutral headspace and chances are things will improve next time.

SUMMARY

As we said at the beginning of this chapter, the experience of touring is going to be different for every musician reading this book, depending on your career point, musical genre, and specific health needs. However, there are some overarching topics that affect everyone and are worth thinking about. It's also important to note that you could follow all of the advice above and still experience health problems, which is a very valid reaction to the extreme toll touring can take on the body and mind, even if you're 'living the dream'. Writer, producer and musician Catherine Anne Davies, who performs as The Anchoress, spent four years on the road with Simple Minds, did all the 'right things' and still had difficulties. She says that was due to regularly experiencing the extreme highs and lows that we mentioned at the beginning of this chapter.

> "What I am testament to is the fact that even if you don't drink, don't do drugs and you're super healthy — and I'm a yoga and healthy eating nut — you know you're really mental health aware, you've got a support network around you and you went in to therapy, even that does not guarantee

that you are not going to have problems. I had a set of rules about how you look after mental health — just don't drink too much, everything in moderation and exercise. I did all of those things and found that does not immunise your brain against the effects of the chemical rollercoaster that is touring. We're not supposed to get these massive adrenaline highs and then also isolation and loneliness. If you do that every day for four years, that's what's going to mess up the chemical balance in your head."

This is where sensible decisions about scheduling can help, which can be hard in today's global music industry where most tours are worldwide, but regular nights off can be the difference between a career stalling or not. "**If you can be in control of how you tour, I'd say make scheduling your priority**," Davies concludes. Green reiterates this advice and says the key is to plan ahead. She explains:

> "**Decide what kind of tour you want to have ideally during planning stages**, if you have the power to do so, but definitely before you hit the road. **Set some goals** — to leave the venue every day for a walk, exercise three times a week, or have two days alcohol-free, for example. Whatever you feel you need to do. If you decide your parameters ahead, you'll be more likely to stay on track."

When on tour, the intense workload, lack of connection to friends and family, and time away from home can also take its toll on all members of the touring team. Your tour manager or sound engineer is just as much at risk of problems as you are, so it's essential for everyone on the touring team to recognise this and look after each other.

If there is one takeaway from this chapter, it should be **to know what you need and to ask for it**. This applies to management and other team members too — when people ask how artists could be better supported, the answer is always to ask the artist in question what they need (and give them time to think about the answer before they respond). It's all very well for managers to arrange massages and smoothies at every venue (wouldn't that be nice), but it may not be what their particular artist needs.

From a business perspective, it makes total sense to make sure an artist is healthy, happy, and supported, even if this means sacrificing a bit of budget to allow for ample time off, both between shows and after coming home. Green continues:

> "From a management point of view, if they are always looking at the bottom line or budget, you are going to get more shows and better shows out of someone who is healthy and happy on tour. I do think you can only sustain a party lifestyle or a gruelling experience like being on tour maybe through your '20s, if you're lucky, but if you have an artist with any longevity, it's going to get a hell of a lot harder as you get older to be able to do that. So I think the way of keeping some sense of wellbeing is at the very least coming off tour and having decent time off and some sort of redress to balance. If your pendulum is swung one way on living a very hardcore life, then you've really got to put in the complete opposite to come back to the middle and have a little bit of balance."

To conclude, if you have a management team, make sure they know exactly what you need — it's in their interests to look after you as well as yours. And if you don't have management, it's up to you to be your best manager and make the right decisions to prioritise your health. That all begins with self-knowledge and finding out what works for you.

Finally, for further reading, have a look at the Healthy Touring Checklist and rider created by BAPAM which is linked in the resources section. Also look out for the *Mental Health and Touring Manual,* created by Tamsin Embleton, which is due for publication in 2021.

- **The touring lifestyle is tough on mental and physical health** due to the highs and lows that musicians regularly experience, lack of sleep and access to healthy food, constant travelling, and being away from support networks.

- Despite this, **there are ways of looking after yourself while on the road**; the basic tenets of which centre on doing your best to maintain a balanced diet; limiting drugs and alcohol; and getting regular exercise and good quality sleep.

- It's important to **keep in touch with friends and family at home** so they can provide a listening ear when you need it and help you reintegrate back into 'normal' life when home.

- When you return from tour, **there's likely to be a recovery period that feels unsettling**. Be aware of that and do what you need to ease yourself back into your home life and rebuild intimate relationships.

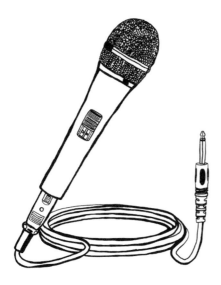

CHAPTER 8

VOCAL HEALTH

IF YOU'RE A SINGER – and unless you've taken the rather unorthodox step of getting someone else to sing your songs while you lipsync your way to the top – and people have won Grammy awards by doing just that – you'll know your voice is the most important element of your career. So it might strike you as odd that vocal health isn't really a subject that gets much attention when you're starting out.

Maybe vocal nodules, polyps, and gastric reflux just aren't as sexy as learning about the craft of songwriting, how to find fans, earn more money, or navigating the trials and tribulations of touring life. But without a healthy and well-cared-for voice, singers have nothing — **if the voice doesn't work, the singer doesn't work, and if singers don't work, they don't get paid**. That's a pretty undesirable scenario for anyone at any level of their career — and depending on the extent of the damage that's been done, poor vocal health may even be career-limiting. Even in less extreme cases, severe vocal issues can result in cancelled shows, which are costly and risk disappointing fans.

The mental impact of poor vocal health can be just as profound, with loss of voice having an impact on a person's identity and wellbeing. Hit singer and songwriter Shakira describes just how lost she felt after suffering a haemorrhage in her vocal cords in 2017: "I always thought there were going to be things in my life that would go away, like beauty, youth, all of that stuff," she says, "but I never thought that my voice would leave me because it's so inherent to my nature. It was my identity. So when I couldn't sing, that was unbearable. There were times I couldn't even get out of bed – I was so depressed."[1]

The good news about vocal health is that problems don't need to be career-ending. Recent coverage of surgical procedures faced by stars such as Adele and Sam Smith has shown that issues of this kind can be common for professional singers, and they can still enjoy huge professional achievements post-surgery.[2] The even better news is that the *majority* of vocal problems are preventable, and there are simple things you can do to make sure your career won't be negatively impacted.

When vocal health starts to falter, artists or members of their team might turn to Google for solutions, where they'll find an endless amount of advice, some of which isn't based on science and could do more harm than good in the long run. So, in this chapter, we're going to give you research-based information from organisations such as the British Voice Association (BVA), interviews with leading voice experts, as well as referencing key studies on vocal health. We'll look at the key things you should consider to look after your voice: what to avoid, what to do, and where to go if problems occur. Vocal health doesn't need to cause any anxiety — if you have the right information and know that what you're doing works, you can enjoy singing without any worry.

PREVENTING ISSUES

Let's start with the most important question — how do you prevent problems from happening? If you're serious about looking after your voice, vocal rehabilitation coach Dane Chalfin says the best way to protect it is to **invest in some singing lessons**. He explains: "A professional athlete invests in his training, a lawyer goes to a law school, a doctor goes to med school, and most professional musicians will invest in some kind of training at some point." Chalfin continues:

> "I believe that investment in your instrument, particularly as a voice user, is the most important thing you can do for it. If you want to do it for real and you want to be in a position where you're not ending up treating a disorder later, start investing early. Like any athletic machine, this mechanism is made of muscles, cartilages, ligaments, connective tissue and it all ties into the postural system, our respiratory system, the vocal mechanism itself, emotion and communication. It's linked to so many different places that every one of those elements are important. If one gets out of balance, the whole system starts to collapse. You have to invest."

We'll go into more detail on how to find a good vocal coach later on, but for now, just be aware that all the vocal health information below will count for very little if you have an inadequate technique. Some vocalists worry that a vocal tutor will iron out (or steamroller!) vocal uniqueness or any of the brilliant idiosyncrasies that give their vocals personality, but a good teacher will be skilled at retaining all those qualities while making sure they're presented in the healthiest and best possible light. It's much harder to sort problems further down the line, so it's worth investing in lessons early on. Chalfin continues:

"I'd like to see people reconnect with the value of training, time, investment, growth, and development at a pace that works for the human body and the human brain that transcends this idea that we can, in commercial music, become famous overnight without having invested in any work. Because the problem is, you always have to pay the ferryman and **the artists that I work with who have had a meteoric rise to fame, without any preparation, have paid for it**. They started to try to learn how to build their instrument while simultaneously having to play it in front of a lot of people, and that creates its own unique set of challenges."

Somewhat unexpectedly, Chalfin points to a quote from Italian philosopher Machiavelli to hammer home his point: "He who has not first laid his foundations may be able with great ability to lay them afterwards, but they will be laid with trouble to the architect and danger to the builder." He concludes: "That probably sums up 90% of my professional life — helping people put foundations in after they're successful."

This is something that Paloma Faith experienced — she didn't start singing lessons until after releasing her debut album, when she kept losing her voice on tour. She explains:

"I was doing singing as a sideline to more arty performance, then someone was like, 'I like your voice and think you're cool' and [becoming a singer] happened like that. My first record went out and I went on my first tour and kept losing my voice because I hadn't had any proper training. I was like: 'I want to be amazing and perform to all these people who have bought tickets.' I thought I'd better learn to sing if this is going to be my life."[3]

In order to try and avoid a similar situation, take Chalfin's advice and invest in some lessons early on.

VOCAL HEALTH BASICS

Once you have a good vocal coach, there are some really important vocal health basics that you need to know as a singer. These are:

- Hydration
- Rest
- Diet
- Exercise

Pretty boring, but pretty simple, right? And yet, absolutely vital. As we described earlier, your body is your instrument and that's why it's so important to look after your general health.

HYDRATION

When we talk about hydration, we're talking about drinking water and lots of it, throughout the day and **ideally four hours before you start singing**. It really does take that long for your body to process the water so that your vocal folds are properly hydrated. Necking a bottle of water just before you go onstage doesn't do much, apart from perhaps bringing about the urge to go to the bathroom halfway through your set. Chalfin says the amount of water you need depends on your size and level of physical activity. He explains:

> "Sip water based on your physical activity levels – the old 'two litres a day' idea is rubbish because it depends on your size and activity level. Someone small might drown themselves in six litres of water, whereas someone large who is doing extremely high effort levels of physical activity might be okay with that."

The key is to find out what's right for you. If you regularly suffer with a dry throat or just want to up your vocal fold hydration levels overall, you can also **buy a steamer**. It's basically a pot that comes in different sizes. You pour boiling water in it, wait for a couple of minutes, and then inhale the steam that comes out for approximately three to five minutes, which hydrates your vocal folds directly. This is a great tool that can be taken on tour to make sure your voice stays in the best condition possible. The Dr Nelson's Inhalers are some of the best and can be easily found online for between £30 and £45, depending on the size. You'll also be able to find electric versions online. Just make sure they have an adjustable heat setting as you don't want the steam to be too hot.

A couple of important points to mention about steamers:

- Use pure boiled water — don't put any drops of essential oils in as they can irritate your throat.
- Once you've steamed, stay quiet for fifteen minutes or so to give your vocal folds proper rest.
- When this time is over, do a gentle siren to loosen things up a bit and prepare your voice for speaking again.
- If in doubt, consult a voice specialist about the ideal steaming setup for you.
- Finally, considering it's going in your mouth, don't forget to practise good hygiene with the steamer — keep it clean and it might be a good idea to stock up on replacement mouthpieces.

REST

It's vital that singers protect their sleep and get good quality rest because not doing so really affects the voice. Jet lag can also prove problematic for singers on international tours crossing different time zones, with the effect on the body similar to that of insomnia (for more on this, we covered good sleep hygiene advice in the Touring chapter).

Also, **vocal rest** (simply not speaking, singing, or using the voice at all) can be an easy and effective way to give the voice a break before a gig, if you're having problems. There are badges you can get (or make) that say 'please don't speak to me, I'm on voice rest' which avoids having to explain your silence to everyone you come across, as that somewhat defeats the purpose of being on voice rest. If it becomes a regular part of your touring routine, those around you will get used to it and leave you alone for that period.

Resting your voice might also mean choosing to have an early night after the gig (generally always a good idea), which is a lesson musician Catherine Anne Davies learned from Simple Minds frontman Jim Kerr while on tour with the band. She explains:

> "One big thing that I took from [Jim] was the emphasis on not pleasing other people and not going to the after-show and chatting to your mates, your family, or whoever's there. They [should understand] that you're not being rude, that what you're doing is preserving your voice because you are respecting the fact that the audience the next day have paid a lot of money to come and see you and that you need to give them your best. It's very boring being a singer!"

Getting adequate voice rest can be a real problem for musicians who need to get a part-time job, which might involve bar work or teaching. Both those jobs require a lot of voice use that makes things worse and means you can't get proper 'days off'. If this applies to you, try and have silent time when you get home and don't speak to anyone, or carve out as much time as you can in the day where your voice can rest.

DIET

Depending on how physically active your set is, you may find it helpful to **think of yourself as a vocal athlete** from a nutritional point of view. You wouldn't see an athlete of any kind going on to the field without having properly set themselves up earlier in the day to make sure they were fuelled for the job they had to do. It's important that musicians adopt a similar attitude. If you're singing and dancing for two hours straight, skipping meals and having a

Snickers just before you go onstage may not give you the energy you need to give your best performance consistently throughout the gig. Equally, if you eat a large meal just before you perform, you may find that you become quite tired or sleepy, which isn't ideal either. It could be a good idea to have a well-balanced meal two to three hours before the show and a light snack before you go onstage. Again, the key is to experiment and find out what works best for you. Whatever you decide to do, **beware of the impact of late-night eating, and eating between sets**, which speech and language therapist Tori Burnay says can lead to increased risk of reflux symptoms.

When it comes to diet, don't believe everything you see on the internet. For vocalists, any sort of extreme diet won't necessarily make your voice any better and certainly won't protect you from vocal issues. The only person who can help with both of those things is a vocal coach. That said, some find that cutting out dairy helps if they have excess mucus, but this really is on a case-by-case basis, so there's no need to do that until it becomes an issue. Limiting alcohol intake, however, *is* worthwhile, as booze can be incredibly dehydrating for the voice and may encourage reflux issues, for those prone to them, if consumed late at night.

There are a few products on the market, like vocal teas and lozenges, that offer to help in this area. Some of them perhaps exploit the anxiety singers may feel about the fragility of their voices and some can be rather misleading about their effectiveness. If you find them helpful as part of your vocal health routine, by all means continue. But there's no solid evidence they will help vocal recovery or prevent problems, and they may even make matters worse if used as a replacement for proper medical assistance. Proceed with caution!

EXERCISE

Exercise is incredibly beneficial for singers, and cardio-vascular exercise such as running in particular can help to strengthen and increase lung capacity. Studies have also shown that if you run on a regular basis, a **gentle run on the day of a gig can help reduce anxiety for the show**[4], which could help prevent anxiety-related vocal issues too. This isn't to say that you should lace up your trainers and head out on a five-mile run after being a couch potato for months prior to a performance, as that's just going to make you exhausted. Think slow and steady – the NHS Couch to 5k programme offers a good plan to work your way up to longer distances in a safe way. Additionally, anything that involves stretching, like yoga or pilates, can reduce tension in the body, which has a positive impact on tension in the vocal tract too.

MUSICAL VOCAL HEALTH BASICS

We've looked at some of the physical vocal health basics that you need to sort out, and there are a few musical ones to consider, too.

- Warm ups and cool downs
- Repertoire
- Monitoring
- Workload

WARM UPS AND COOL DOWNS

The voice is made up of three main components: the breath, the larynx, and the resonators. We need to warm up all of these and get them ready for action, along with the physical body itself.

It's vital to warm up your voice before doing a performance — either on stage or in a vocal booth — and before rehearsing. Sometimes people get confused between vocal warm ups and technical exercises — the latter are there to help improve your pitching and tone or general vocal agility, but aren't appropriate to do just before you go onstage or you'll tire yourself out before you've even begun. So avoid vocal acrobatics in the green room! An ideal warm up is about ten to fifteen minutes max and is just enough to warm up the voice, but not to tire it out.

Although it may be tempting to hop onto YouTube and find a generic warm up, Dane Chalfin advises against this: "The warm up needs to be tailored to the athletic task that the singer is about to go through," he says. He returns to the sporting metaphor:

"A pole vaulter doesn't warm up the same way a marathon runner warms up as the sport is different. So a classical singer might be warming up differently to a pop singer, but a rock singer might also be warming up differently to the pop singer. You also have to be able to counter-balance all the athletic muscular gestures that you're using for your singing. You've got to cool down and stretch in the opposite direction afterwards to keep muscle balance so that you don't get stuck in an extreme position. This has to be created [in a] bespoke [manner] by somebody who really understands how the mechanism works."

You may want to clock off as soon as you leave the stage or recording session, but Tori Burnay says a cool down is especially important to remember. She explains:

"The cool down is the bit that we've got some really good evidence for[5] — it's really helpful in enabling somebody to bounce back again so they're in better shape 24 hours later. Vocal fold inflammation seems to resolve more quickly with people who are doing intermittent voice use for three or four minutes, every twenty minutes or so, when they've stopped doing that high intensity voice use. So we incorporate glides down the pitch. It might be a lip trill, a tongue trill, some Accent Method Airflow Exercises, voice fricatives down the range, stretch and release out. Just checking in, then back into modal pitch voice."

(If all that sounds like a foreign language then this might be where YouTube *does* come in handy.) "It's nothing onerous or complicated, but it's just allowing a bit of downtime," Burnay adds. Like Chalfin said, a vocal coach will be able to design a bespoke warm up and cool down that will be tailored to you and the work you're doing.

REPERTOIRE

When you're choosing repertoire for upcoming gigs, beware of 'challenging yourself' too much. As human beings, we all want to grow, develop, and improve at what we do, but in the world of singing, it's important to remember that we have different voice groups for a reason. In his voice clinic, Chalfin has to talk down many of his clients' ambitious egos if they forget where the real strength of a singer can lie. He explains:

"People always want their voice to do more, go higher, be louder. You have to work with your anatomy — size matters. If you've got a big juicy larynx, you are going to be happier at lower pitches. If you've got a tiny little sparrow's larynx, you're going to be happier at higher pitches. The high singers with the little larynxes seem to always want to be bigger, and the big beefy larynxes always seem to want to sing higher. Nobody ever seems terribly happy with what they have.

"You need to work with your anatomy because **your job is to be a vessel through which emotion and human experience can be communicated to an audience**. Your job is to hold up a mirror to your audience and say, 'Here's how I feel about life. How does that make you feel about it?' The audience won't come up to you at the end of the night and say, 'Great job, you've killed yourself up there singing really high. That was great. We love how high you sing.' They will tell you how moved they were. So you've got to put things in keys that allow you to be your most expressive and most flexible, in the most economical way, so that you can truly serve the purpose of facilitating communication with the audience. Always ask yourself the question: am I doing this for my audience or am I doing this for my ego?"

We have so much technological wizardry available to use now that if you really want to sing a certain song, why not just pitch shift the backing track to a range that works for you, or ask the band to play it in a different key? Most audience members won't notice, and it's far more important that you sing in a key you're comfortable in night after night than it is to try and reach that high note at the end (which could become a source of anxiety in itself and likely to cause yet more tension).

This also applies to songwriting. **It's worth being aware of what your most comfortable range is as a singer and where your voice sounds best**, and to make sure you stick to it in your songs. You may have had that experience where you write a good song but your voice doesn't sound as good as it does when you're singing covers, and often that's due to the fact that you're writing in a key that doesn't suit you. When picking your next track to sing, make sure that it is comfortably within your range. If you're challenging yourself, only do this in small increments alongside working with a vocal coach, so you can be sure that what you're singing is safe for your voice.

MONITORING

Have you ever had that experience where you can't quite hear yourself over the band in rehearsal, so you end up almost shouting to be heard, only to have a very sore throat afterwards? This happens a lot and it's often due to issues with monitoring or a lack of amplification. There have been discussions about whether it's helpful to have 'rehearsal' volume practice in popular music (particularly for drummers, who argue that they need to play at full volume in order to build up stamina in a realistic gig environment), but either way, as long you can hear yourself, that is the most important thing to prevent strain. Do what you need to do — bring monitors closer, turn them up, or, if you don't have access to monitors, turn up your vocal line and bring down the other instruments. **Don't shout to make yourself heard** or you'll be experiencing problems in no time.

Catherine Anne Davies credits remembering to sing quietly as one of the reasons why she hasn't had vocal issues, which is again a lesson she learned thanks to the wisdom of Jim Kerr. She says:

> "Jim told me that he maintains his vocal health by singing quite quietly because your microphone is up, so you know you don't need to yell and push yourself every night. You're producing that sound and the quality of that sound is not about the volume, it's about the quality of the tone."

WORKLOAD

Picture this: you've landed your dream support gig on an international tour for three months. You've never had a vocal workload quite like it before, but you've got the motivation and your songs are good, so it will be fine, right? Sadly, not necessarily. This 'step up' in terms of the expected workload is where vocal health issues can really start to be a problem for the first time in a singer's life. It's at this point where singers suddenly start to take vocal health seriously and often it's after problems have started happening. If you've been gigging once a week for the past few years, you may find that you can get away with the technique you've always used, or that your lack of attention to vocal health doesn't cause any problems. However, if you're suddenly expected to gig four or five days a week on top of lots of interviews, a gruelling travel schedule, and a lack of access to good food and rest, you may well find that you start experiencing issues.

Overload is what caused Jess Glynne to experience a vocal cord haemorrhage after performing nearly one hundred shows in a six-month period in 2019. She had to pull out of playing the Isle of Wight Festival (which she said wasn't, as widely reported, due to her partying with the Spice Girls the night before) and received strict orders from her doctor to rest in silence for ten days. She told fans at the time: "[The doctor] told me I have been completely overdoing everything. In the last six months, I've performed almost 100 shows, I've pushed through at times when I know I've been tired and overstretched and I got to breaking point, my voice literally got to breaking point."[6] In order to avoid this, try to increase the frequency of gigs slowly if you can. **If you're about to have a big step up in the number of gigs you're doing, go and have a session with a vocal coach to check you're doing everything properly**.

That goes for studio sessions, too. If you've had a few weeks off, it might be tempting to block book a studio for a week to rehearse, but singing for six hours continuously after having done next to nothing is a potential recipe for disaster. Studies have shown that the best way to rehearse is in small chunks of one hour or less, followed by a break,[7] but if you need to plough on through, you don't always need to be singing at full pelt. There's a process called 'marking' where you sing really lightly in rehearsal, and can often achieve just as much as you would have done if singing at concert level the whole time. Mental rehearsal[8] can also be a really effective tool if you don't want to tire out your voice — we'll cover more on that later in the Talent and Practice chapter.

PROBLEMS AND CAUSES

As we've seen above, **many of the problems singers face are a result of overuse and vocal overload** (which can lead to issues like laryngitis, nodules, and cysts) due to touring, recording and promotional demands, and inadequate amplification.[9] In theory, each of those factors can be adapted or changed to suit a singer more effectively. This can often mean reducing promotional activity and performance schedules — a short term solution that promotes long-term health. In practice, people in a singer's team, like managers, A&Rs, and tour managers, might cram a diary to breaking point without enough thought being given to overload. This is why a clear and direct dialogue about existing or impending vocal issues with any team members is required.

It can be hard for young artists to make executives understand the importance of avoiding overuse. For this reason, Burnay emphasises the value of a bringing in a professional. "It's very difficult, particularly for young artists with management who have a very poor understanding of voice and what people can actually cope with," she explains, "so I can't stress enough the importance of having a good and experienced vocal coach linked in — and linked in early." She continues:

> "Often, there needs to be an advocate for how to manage someone's schedule, who understands **it's not just about the performance schedule, it's all the other stuff around it, including travel time, lack of sleep, poor diets, and not enough time for rest and repair.** In an ideal world, it takes about 36 hours for collagen repair in the vocal fold tissue. When you've got back-to-back gigs and you're travelling through the night or flying, this is when things start to go a bit wrong. So having time to have enough rest in between and to also have a very, very good regime of technical singing style and a good voice care vocal health programme, that's the most important thing."[10]

Additionally, any sort of exhaustion, illness, or even a hangover will often have negative implications for the voice. It can be really hard to achieve vocal consistency night after night in the way a guitarist might be able to, especially if you're fighting a cold or didn't sleep properly the night before. Getting smashed every night of a tour might not affect some members of a band, but for the singer, a relatively early night might make the difference between finishing the tour or cancelling dates.

The medical problems singers might experience include occupational disorders (muscle tension dysphonia, vocal nodules, vocal cord haemorrhage, polyps, and general vocal deterioration), general health issues with vocal implications (respiratory diseases, gastric reflux, endocrine problems, medication usage), and lifestyle issues.[11]

Tori Burnay believes that **the main causes of these issues are muscle tension imbalances, along with oedema, which is vocal**

fold swelling. One such imbalance is muscle tension dysphonia, which is an imbalance in the muscles around the larynx[12] that's caused by excessive tension. Banishing that tension isn't always easy. After a two-year touring and promotional schedule for her debut album, La Roux singer Elly Jackson experienced exactly that predicament. She recalls:

> "I would do a sound check in the afternoon and sing perfectly, and then, come evening, no sound would come out. It was like this big ball of tension in my throat that had closed up and I had no control over it. I couldn't sing for about a year."[13]

Jackson was told that the tension was brought on by extreme performance anxiety, which shows that even with a great technique, vocal issues can still arise as a result of poor emotional and mental health. Burnay summarises it like this: "(Problems) may be linked to emotional shifts and **a lot of stress in someone's life may have an impact on what's going on in their body** with an emotional response, and increased tension in muscles."

PERIODS AND PREGNANCY

One issue not discussed widely enough is how menstrual periods affect voice use, and the prevalence of Premenstrual Voice Syndrome. Voice health specialist Jean Abitbol, who's Head of Clinic at the Faculty Medicine of Paris, explains: "The Premenstrual Voice Syndrome (PVS) is characterised by voice fatigue, decreased range, loss of power in the singing voice, and fewer harmonics, caused by the dryness of the vocal tract and the resonance chambers. There is also an increased tendency toward acid reflux."[14] Symptoms are said to start four to six days before the start of a period (in those who aren't taking the oral contraceptive pill), and continue for three days after the first day of their period. Abitbol says he sees this set of symptoms in a third of his patients who have periods, and that the voice is more easily injured during the premenstrual phase than at other times in the menstrual cycle.

"The singers with PVS complain of tiredness, loss of pianissimo (quiet dynamics), an alteration in certain harmonics in the higher registers, a deficit in the power of the voice, and a veiled voice," he adds.

Although information about this issue has only recently become widely known, there's evidence that it was recognised as far back as the nineteenth century. Back then, opera singers at La Scala in Milan were able to cancel their performances five days prior to and during their period, and still receive payment. For anyone working in the commercial pop world, you'll know how far-fetched and luxurious this idea sounds today. But it may be worth trying to avoid booking gigs at that time of the month if you're finding it hard to sing to your best ability. Additionally, contact a voice therapist, who will be able to give you more advice on treatment and how to manage the issue.

Pregnancy poses no real problem and vocalists should be able to sing well even when up to seven months pregnant — Beyoncé, Björk, Christina Aguilera and M.I.A. are all shining examples of this. The vocal folds are plump and well-lubricated, and the quality of the vibration can often be high, with some even saying that pregnancy appears to improve the voice.[15] The main issue pregnant women need to be aware of is gastric reflux — see the resources section for more details about that and how to avoid it.

HOW TO SPOT A VOICE ISSUE

Research into the specific vocal issues that pop and rock singers experience is still very limited, although it's been suggested that there is no significant difference between the prevalence of voice disorders in popular music or classical singers.[16] So, with a wealth of research into vocal disorders in classical music, we have a strong body of evidence that shows us how to prevent them.

VOCAL SOS

What do you do if you have a really sore throat and a gig that evening? The most important thing is not to panic. When we panic, we create tension in our bodies which is going to cause tension in the larynx and make matters worse. Hydration for the vocal folds is really important, and this can come by drinking water or inhaling steam. As mentioned earlier, vocal rest can help, too (which is essentially not speaking and resting your voice before the gig as much as possible). Teas and lozenges probably won't help and they certainly won't protect your voice. Seek professional help as soon as you can, and if it hurts to swallow, don't sing if at all possible.

The warning signs are:

- A lack of power or your voice cutting out
- Prolonged hoarseness
- Voice breaks over register changes
- A reduction in range
- Persistent throat clearing
- Heartburn or an acidic taste in the mouth

If you experience any of the above for longer than seven to ten days, contact a medical professional straight away. The vast majority of problems can be managed and prevented from becoming serious if they are caught early.

WHERE TO GO FOR HELP

The British Association for Performing Arts Medicine (BAPAM) offers a clinical vocal health pathway which makes sure you see the very best voice care specialists for your problem. If you have any of the above issues, contact them (see resources), and they will write a letter to your GP recommending that you attend a voice clinic that specialises in working with singers, has full diagnostic facilities, and offers a multi-disciplinary team who can work with you to sort your issue. Burnay says that in a specialist voice clinic, you should be seen by an ear, nose and throat (ENT) consultant specialising in laryngology, a laryngologist, and a speech and language therapist in the diagnosis room. "Being seen in a general ENT clinic where the equipment is not of the same standard as in a voice clinic is really not going to give you the best outcome," she adds. Burnay continues:

> "In the voice clinic appointment, a full case history will be taken and the laryngologist will carry out a laryngeal examination using an endoscope. A flexible scope will be passed through your nostril and moved back to look at your larynx and vocal cords. A full voice assessment should be carried out for speaking and singing. This will enable your team to provide you with a reliable diagnosis and to make a plan for treatment."

Even if the laryngologist detects issues such as nodules, these can often be managed with a vocal rehabilitation programme of exercises that will prevent the problems from developing into anything more serious. Surgery is a last-resort option, though, in most cases, it's unnecessary. Burnay explains: "We try to avoid surgery unless it's absolutely necessary, we look at every other approach." She continues:

> "Patients go through a minimum of four to six sessions of voice therapy, if not more, or they work with a vocal coach if they haven't already got one, in order to try to get the best biomechanical setup vocally. Therapy can be targeted at reducing any compensatory behaviours, which in turn reduce vocal fold swelling or tension patterns. This also enables us to get the best results from any surgery."

FINDING A GOOD VOCAL COACH

Knowing where to start when you're looking for a vocal coach can be incredibly difficult. There are thousands of vocal coaches online and without standardised professional accreditation, it can be a real minefield to find the right vocal coach or methodological approach for you. Burnay has some suggestions:

> "I advise people to contact the British Voice Association. They have a list of registered practitioners and those practitioners all over the UK certainly have an interest in ongoing learning. It's a good place to start."

When looking for a coach, make sure they are specialists for the genre you're working in. If, for example, you are in a heavy rock band and you scream a lot in your set, look for a coach who can help you with this specific problem – they do exist, and it is perfectly possible to 'scream' in a safe way! Equally, if at school you were trained as a classical singer but you now want to belt like Aretha Franklin or to try and mimic the power of Freddie Mercury, have a few lessons with a pop, rock, or musical theatre specialist who can help you to create that voice quality in a safe way.

Often vocal coaches will offer MOT-type sessions where you can go to check everything is okay and ask questions about specific issues you're facing. Sometimes, one of these every six months is enough, but if the coach identifies some key issues with your technique, it's a good idea to take the advice and, if necessary, have a course of sessions to sort the problems. It might take a few sessions with different coaches to find the right fit for both of you. Paloma Faith went through quite a few before finding the right one for her, but it was worth it when she did. "I didn't find a great singing teacher until my last album [in 2014] and this guy has changed my life." She continues: "He's given me so much in such a short space of time, it's been three years or something, and I do believe that my voice has got more powerful and stronger."[17] Chalfin advises:

"**Not every coach is going to be the right coach, no matter how good they are**. Don't be afraid to trust your intuition and audition a fair few versions of everybody on your team before you actually stick to your team. I know very quickly if a client is not going to be quite right with me, but I will always refer them on to the person I think they're going to be a great match with."

There can be a lot of conflicting advice within the world of vocal coaching, with different teachers being trained by different vocal 'schools'. Sometimes, there's secrecy surrounding what the vocal advice is within that school. This can even happen within just one genre. Chalfin offers some advice to help navigate these sometimes murky waters:

"Everyone should always remember that you don't have to necessarily follow the method you're subscribing to. There are two people you should have loyalty to as a singer: yourself and your audience. And you should do what's best for you. Sometimes that means you have to pick and choose bits and bobs from different methods or different teachers, or whatever, to find a model that's a map that works for you."

If you're in any doubt about what to look for in a vocal coach, get in touch with BAPAM or the BVA for guidance and support.

As a final word, there are many different problems that you might face as a singer but the majority of these are preventable. By looking after your vocal health on a regular basis, checking in with a vocal coach and immediately seeking help if you experience any problems, the chances of facing any career-limiting issues will be greatly reduced. Chalfin concludes:

"The gold standard advice is that, **if you notice a change in range, clarity, quality, physical feeling, or timbre, or any change lasting more than three weeks, or following the resolution of an illness** — because sometimes viruses have to run their course — then *that's* the time you go to your GP and ask for a referral to a specialist voice clinic."

To summarise, here are some of the key general vocal health pointers that the BVA recommend:

Do not:

- Misuse or abuse your voice
- **Smoke** — and if you can't give up, cut down
- **Talk above the noise** at social or sports events
- **Talk or even whisper if you are losing your voice**
- Answer by **shouting when you're upset** or anxious

Avoid:

- **Chemical irritants or dry, dusty conditions**
- **Eating a large meal before going to bed** at night
- **Excessive use of the telephone** (for talking – texting is fine)

Take care:

- If you have to **use the telephone** for your living
- About what you drink: **too much alcohol, coffee, tea, or cola will dry you up**

Try:

- **Not to clear your throat** unnecessarily
- To **warm up your voice** if you're going to use it for a long time
- To have a **humidifier** in your workplace

Make sure:

- You drink at least **six to eight glasses of water** each day
- That if your **voice sounds different for more than two weeks, you see your doctor**

Note:

- **Spicy foods and dairy products** may affect the voice
- **Hormonal changes** (such as the menopause, pregnancy, or menstruation) can affect voice quality
- The **voice is closely linked with emotion**, so tension or depression might show in your voice
- Get **medical advice** if you're worried

CHAPTER 9

MUSIC AND THE BODY

INSTRUMENTALISTS, PRODUCERS, DJS, and anyone else who uses some or all of their body while making music: this chapter is for you. Just as it's vital for a singer to look after their vocal health, those who play an instrument, or spend a lot of time at a computer, should prioritise taking care of their joints and body overall.

Frustratingly, looking after your musculoskeletal (MSK) health is one of those areas like your hearing, or buying a screen protector for your smartphone, where you only really understand its importance once disaster strikes — and often then it's too late. In the rock and roll world of the music business, making sure your posture is correct while holding your instrument or ensuring that you're lifting an amp in the right way may not be high on your list of priorities — particularly when some of music's most well-known performers have perfected iconic stances that would horrify your average physio. But over time, if you're not doing simple things to protect your joints, you might start experiencing pain when you're playing or develop referred problems in other areas of your body. Naturally, you want to try and avoid these issues at all costs because they could put an end to your performing career. In this chapter, we're going to provide you with the information you need to look after MSK health *before* it's too late, including common problems musicians experience, how to prevent them, and where to go if issues emerge.

If you're lucky enough to be young and fit (and perhaps feeling a little 'invincible'), we still urge you to read on. You may think that these problems won't ever affect you, but musicians at any age and state of health are at high risk of developing issues.[1] In one study of 226 popular musicians, **researchers found that 74% of participants experienced MSK problems**,[2] which is a considerable proportion of the musician population. So have a quick read and make sure that you've got the basics covered. Simple things like setting up your instrument correctly, making sure you don't suddenly increase your workload, and warming up your body before performance can make a massive difference.

COMMON PROBLEMS

What are the main MSK problems that you might be at risk of facing? Well, the first big one is pain, either from playing or from sustaining an injury of some kind. Studies have suggested **musicians experience high levels of self-reported MSK pain**,[3] along with performance-related musculoskeletal pain disorder (PRMD),[4] and issues arising from joint hypermobility.[5] There are some cases of instrumentalists developing career-damaging problems such as focal dystonia[6] (a neurological condition that can cause the muscles in your hands or elsewhere to spasm involuntarily). Then there are the regular issues that can affect anyone, such as repetitive strain injury, arthritis, accidental injury, or more general chronic pain (which can pose particular problems for musicians, for obvious reasons).

Lady Gaga had to cancel a European tour in 2017 due to a chronic condition called fibromyalgia, which causes her "severe physical pain" that impacts her ability to perform. Sia, on the other hand, suffers from a genetic connective tissue disorder that causes chronic pain called Ehlers-Danlos syndrome. Rolling Stones guitarist Keith Richards has a painful condition called osteoarthritis, which has resulted in swollen fingers due to a lifetime of playing. And Robbie Williams, who is known for his highly charged stagecraft, has the same condition in his back and has had to tone down his previously energetic performances as a result.[7]

As you can see from those examples, it's not just instrumentalists who are at risk in this area, but for instrumentalists specifically, studies indicate that problems with pain are particularly common in the neck, shoulders, and back,[8] which could be a result of poor posture or upper body strength. A study of 261 guitarists found that they were more likely to experience pain in their fretting hand, their back, and their neck.[9] There isn't a huge amount of research on this topic for other roles in commercial music, so we don't know to what extent DJs and producers are affected by physical issues. But anecdotally, songwriters and producers have reported that sitting for hours in front of a computer, clicking on a mouse, and staring at a screen can cause problems in their arms, hands, shoulders, and eyes — particularly for those who don't have an ergonomic desk setup that's specially designed to reduce the risk of MSK injuries and improve performance and productivity. That can create knock-on effects when they pick up an instrument to play and start experiencing pain (we'll come back to this topic shortly).

Rock and metal musicians are another section of the musician population who experience body pain, thanks to thrashing around on stage, throwing their heads up and down, or falling to their knees for particularly theatrical guitar solos. If that's you, have a think about how you're doing it, perhaps build some strength and a level of fitness to help your body sustain the movement, and if you start experiencing pain, see a professional as soon as you can.

For drum and bass musician Chris Polglase, aka The Jungle Drummer, pain in the hands was the most significant physical issue he faced while playing for artists such as London Elektricity, High Contrast, The Scratch Perverts, and Finley Quaye. In his super-fast jungle style, Polglase would hit the drums at around 187 beats per minute, which equates to approximately 11,000 hits per hour. As a result, he started feeling pain in his left hand, which was misdiagnosed as a break, and his thumbs. "I started getting pains in my left thumb and my right thumb and it got really, really bad," he explains. "When my hands were bad, I would be hitting a drum once and my hands would hurt." Polglase also experienced edema — unnatural inflammation in both of his wrists — and was told he had to wear thermoplastic splints in bed for the rest of his life. He adds: "I couldn't put my jacket on, I couldn't cut food, it hurt to turn the key when I tried to open a door. Everything was just a struggle, it was a really, really difficult time."[10]

Poor technique was the reason behind the pain Polglase experienced. "I realised that arthritis in my thumbs, osteoarthritis, I had got that from overuse," he says. "I used to kind of smash the drums, and drum as hard as I could, and as fast as I could, and I wasn't really being mindful and thinking about it. So that created really bad thumb pain."

Physiotherapist Dr Sarah Upjohn, who regularly works with musicians, says **poor technique or posture, along with heavy workload, are the most common causes of pain** in those she works with. She says that, according to scientific research, the risk factors for playing-related injuries are as follows:

- A sudden increase in playing time;
- Changing of repertoire to something with a different technical demand from the one you have been doing;

- Technique, the setup of the kit, the ergonomics, or your posture.

The two that Upjohn sees the most are "doing too much, so increasing playing time suddenly, or something to do with technique, posture, or set up of the kit."

Many popular musicians are self-taught, and you'll notice in interviews that many also wear this as a badge of honour, but behind the scenes, it can mean that some go into professional life having never consulted a teacher or physiotherapist about the way they play. Just like we advise singers to have a vocal coaching session to address any technical issues that might affect their ability to stay vocally healthy, the same applies to instrumentalists — get some lessons with someone who can assess your technique and make changes if you need to. Just like a good vocal coach, a good tutor in this area won't seek to change what makes you brilliant — they'll work with you to achieve what you want in a way that means you can keep doing it for a long time.

A bad technique can be overlooked for the odd gig, but when your workload suddenly picks up and you're performing every night of the week, that's when the problems will start to show and could cause damage in the long term. Upjohn continues:

> "All athletes and dancers tend to go on having lessons throughout their career. If you look at [tennis champion] Andy Murray, he still has a coach. Yet musicians tend to get to the end of conservatoire [or training, if they've had it], and may not have lessons after that point. And it's easy to slip into bad habits without knowing what you're doing."

Upjohn recommends **having consultation lessons every now and again, asking a friend with proper technique to observe yours and offer feedback, or recording yourself so you can see what you're doing**.

The other reason for taking care of your physical self as a musician is that when problems arise, they don't just impact your body. Experiencing pain and being limited by that is likely to have an impact on your mental health, too. This is something that Claire Cordeaux, who is Director of the British Association of Performing Arts Medicine (BAPAM), often sees in the work the organisation does with musicians. "The clinicians say that **pretty much everyone that comes in with an MSK issue has a mental health issue connected**," she explains. Upjohn expands on this:

> "Being a musician is a part of your identity, so if something is interfering with your ability to play at the level that you want to or you are usually able to, it can be enormously distressing. We see high levels of anxiety, we see depression, and it can be a very, very serious thing."

The good news is that **regular exercise can help**, which "is a superb stress buster as well", adds Upjohn. "So not only will being physically fit and exercising regularly make you less likely to get injured, if you are injured, it really helps you deal with the impact of that." (It's worth noting that BAPAM has many psychologists, counsellors, and therapists who offer talking therapies with performing artists who need it, to address the mental issues associated with injury or physical problems.)

Chris Polglase experienced mental health issues as a result of his physical pain and, just as Upjohn described, taking care of his body helped him to feel better overall. He got the right diagnosis, help from an osteopath, started doing yoga and meditation and was eventually able to return to drumming after being unable to play for over two years. His newfound healthy mindset is a stark contrast to his previous life in which, as someone who has struggled with addictive behaviour, he "would move from place to place trying to escape myself, and escape my mind." Some sage advice from a yoga studio owner helped him to revise his strategy. He explains: "She said to me, 'Look, it doesn't really work like that. If you exercised and put in work to your body, then you would start to think better because you feel better.' I know that might sound obvious but to me at that point, that was like a revelation." For Polglase, taking care of himself these days means trying to eat well, taking supplements, and doing things that are good for his health and his mind: "If I'm healthy, I can do what I love [drumming], and if I'm not healthy and go back to the musician that I used to be, I won't be able to do what I love."

POSTURE

As we touched upon earlier, musicians now spend a large amount of time at a computer. For many, days are filled more with admin and emails than with making music, and thanks to the wealth of digital production programmes available, a computer is where the creative parts sometimes happen, too. Ensuring you have good posture may not be high on your list of priorities but it's yet another way of avoiding pain in the long term. That means **checking that your desk and keyboard are at the right height for you and that you have a comfortable and supportive chair that is adjustable**, especially for producers and songwriters who might be sitting in the same position all day every day. The setup is going to change regularly for musicians on tour who are working from a laptop or tablet, and travelling from place to place, but some basics still apply so that you can make minor adjustments as you need. (And trust us, your body will thank you for it later.)

The following are pointers on how to reduce the risk of long-term injury at your desk:[11]

- Balanced head, not leaning forward
- Arms relaxed by your side
- Forearms parallel to the desk
- Sit back in your chair, ensuring good back support
- Screen approximately arm's length from you
- Top of screen about eye level
- Space behind knee
- Feet flat on the floor or on a footrest

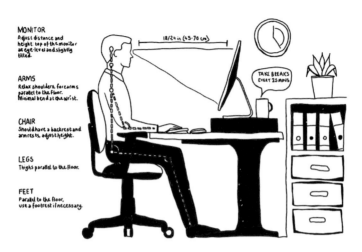

MONITOR
Adjust distance and height top of the monitor at eye-level and slightly tilted.

ARMS
Relax shoulders, forearms parallel to the floor. Minimal bend at the wrist.

CHAIR
Should have a backrest and armrests, adjust height.

LEGS
Thighs parallel to the floor.

FEET
Parallel to the floor, use a footrest if necessary.

18/24 in (45-70 cm)

TAKE BREAKS EVERY 25 MINS

From Ergonomics Health [12]

If you know you're going to be on the road often and will have a lot of screen time while travelling, it might be a good idea to buy a separate mouse, laptop stand, and keyboard. These extra items take up very little space (get a stand that folds flat) and can make sure that you have a safer setup, wherever you are. Even if you don't have a laptop stand, stacking a few books underneath a screen can help reduce neck pain by putting the monitor at eye level, and putting a cushion underneath you on a chair that is too low may be the difference between shoulder pain later or not. Having a perfect desk set up all the time is unrealistic but small changes can make a big difference, particularly for those prone to chronic physical health issues (hello, hypermobile community!).

While we're on the topic of posture, it's worth mentioning how you use your phone, too. We're probably all guilty of 'tech neck' or craning forward to type texts, which can cause real problems in the cervical spine over long periods. Here are a few guidelines:[13]

● Keep the phone at eye level — this will help keep the cervical spine in a more neutral position.

- Minimise the amount that the arms are floating in front of the body — this tends to engage the shoulder muscles which can engage the neck muscles.
- Find a place to rest your elbows.

It may be worth noting how high the phone needs to be for your neck to be in a neutral position, and therefore how far off it you are when it's down at the height of your lap. Again, this is just another thing to be aware of. And if you're really serious about avoiding pain, try to minimise time on your phone as much as possible. If you can't do that, find physical support whenever you can — such as elbows on a desk — or just type that message on your computer instead.

EYES

Lots of time spent staring at screens may also impact vision, and for musicians who use sheet music to play, good eyesight is pretty vital. It's not just about vision — poor eyesight can have a knock-on effect on the way musicians breathe, as optometrist Amy Ogden explains. "I have seen first-hand how musicians begin to struggle when they hit the presbyopic stage of their lives [when they begin to need spectacle corrections for reading]. It can have dramatic effects on their sound quality. Especially as they tilt their head to see the music — affecting the airways. This can lead to missed notes due to poor vision."[14] If you have started to notice any pain in your eyes when playing, or find that you're squinting to see clearly, book an eye test with your local optician or contact BAPAM or Allegro Optical (details in the resources section).

PREVENTION

As Sarah Upjohn mentioned earlier, it helps to think of your body as a musician in the same way that athletes and dancers consider their own physical performance, and to prioritise any preventative work you can do to support yourself. Protective tactics for musicians, according to Upjohn, include:

- **Increasing your levels of cardiovascular fitness**, which will mean getting fitter and increasing your strength. "There's research to show that strength training for musicians makes a massive difference, and they're talking about endurance training rather than bulking up training, and also increasing soft tissue flexibility," she explains. Those three things help prepare your body for physical work which, whether you're a drummer or a flautist, is so much of what being a musician really is. Upjohn continues by saying that your aim should be "getting fitter, getting stronger, getting more flexible, along with absolute attention to warming-up before playing and stretching after playing."

- **Warming up** might make you think of playing a few scales or sirening your voice, but Upjohn says musicians should also be doing a physical warm-up away from their instrument. She explains: "Warm up before tune-up — warm up before you get your instrument out of the case, in the same way that an athlete or a dancer would. The whole point of warming up is that you literally get warmer, you increase your heart rate, you increase the blood flow to the muscles that are using the oxygen that comes in the blood." A physical warm-up can be as simple as walking briskly to the practice space, or "trotting up and down a few flights of stairs," says Upjohn.

- She also recommends a **physical cool down** when you've finished playing, along with regular breaks. That means stretching the muscles that have been held in shortened positions when you're playing to get out of playing position. When it comes to breaks, Upjohn says a five-minute breather should be taken every 55 minutes, which can be used for stretching, rehydrating, and/or having a snack. Essentially, "all of the things that will keep your physical body well enough to play."

If you want to learn more about physical warm-ups, take a look at the resources section, where you'll find links to BAPAM's advice sheets on the topic.

SEEKING HELP

If you do develop some kind of pain from playing, the first thing you should do is take a break — carrying on and ignoring it is not going to result in improvement and may make it substantially worse. Upjohn explains: "The first thing is to follow the principle that soft tissue injuries simply need PEACE and LOVE.[15] Immediately after injury (one to three days) do no harm and let PEACE guide your approach:

Protection: avoid activities and movements that increase pain during the first few days after injury.
Elevate the injured limb higher than the heart as often as possible.
Avoid taking anti-inflammatory medications as they reduce healing. Avoid ice.
Compress: use elastic bandage or taping to reduce swelling.
Educate: your body knows best. Avoid unnecessary passive treatments and medical investigations and let nature play its role.

After the first few days, soft tissues need...

Load: let pain guide your gradual return to normal activities.
Optimism: condition your brain for optimal recovery by being confident and positive.
Vascularisation: choose pain free cardiovascular activities to increase blood flow to repairing tissues.
Exercise: restore mobility, strength, and proprioception by adopting an active approach to recovery.

If that doesn't work, the next step would be to source a free assessment with a clinician who has specialist knowledge at an organisation like BAPAM or ISM.

Claire Cordeaux encourages anyone with physical playing-related pain to seek help straight away. She says:

"People tend to wait for quite a long time before they come to talk to us about any health issue. So **if you have a health problem that's related to your occupation, stopping you playing for some reason or performing, seek help** because even if you don't have a clinical assessment, we can always point you in the right direction. **Do this as early as you can — don't sit on it — because that way you'll have a better outcome.**"

Activities that might help prevent an injury are those that keep you strong, improve your posture awareness, and increase overall movement. Upjohn suggests: "Any sort of yoga, Pilates, Alexander Technique, Feldenkrais, any of the movement disciplines would all be useful. In terms of therapy, as in medical therapy, osteopathy, physiotherapy, they're all absolutely appropriate depending on what's wrong with you."

It can be difficult to find regular classes for some of those movement disciplines that Upjohn talks about if you spend a lot of your life on the road. If that's the case for you, why not top up your regular practice with online classes? It's a good idea to start with in-person sessions so that a teacher can assess your posture and check that you have the correct alignment when holding poses, but after that, virtual sessions, either with your existing teacher or more generally on YouTube, can be beneficial. Adriene Mishler runs the incredibly successful Yoga with Adriene YouTube channel, where she (along with her dog Benji) regularly posts easy to follow yoga videos from her home to over eight million subscribers worldwide. For pilates, dance, or barre, celebrity trainer Tracy Anderson provides online classes, and there are many more besides, including gaia.com which offers tai chi, qigong, and general stretching. An important caveat: these options are there to keep you fit and strong and are not a substitute for consulting with the correct medical professional, who should be your first port of call if something goes wrong.

For Chris Polglase, being seen by the right professional took a while, but finding the correct diagnosis was what eventually enabled him to recover faster, along with sound support systems. **"You need to get a diagnosis, and the diagnosis determines how you recover from that**. You [also] need a lot of support and that's the thing that I think is really important." For Polglase, that support was not only for his physical state, but his emotional, financial, and mental states, too. "I'm very lucky that I've had support from Help Musicians, I have great friends, and I have family, and I've also had support for my mental health," he explains. "I've gone to places like Mind, the mental health charity, I have a decent GP, and still have moments when I need help. I think the most important thing I'd like to impress on people is that the start is getting help. Because that's the most important thing — to not feel like you're on your own or try and do everything on your own."

This is a message we're keen to endorse. **Whether looking at physical health issues such as those in this chapter, or any of the other mental, financial, or general health issues that you might be experiencing, you are not alone.** It's highly likely that someone has experienced something similar in the past, so there will be other people in the same boat as you, and there will also be resources, support, and help out there.

Keep in mind that so many of these problems can happen at the same time — a physical injury can lead to a reduction in gigs, which means less money coming in. That in itself can cause financial stress along with the mental challenges that injuries can bring. Don't feel embarrassed if, when you access support, you need help with several issues. Any of the organisations we've recommended will understand, and in many cases, they'll expect more than one problem to be presenting itself. The key is to make sure you get the right support as quickly as you can. Cordeaux concludes: **"Don't be surprised if you develop an issue because it is quite normal**. You have to try and be as healthy as you can to stop it from happening and you also have to go and get help from people who know what they're talking about if it does."

WAYS AHEAD

This chapter is about how you, as a musician, can look after your own health, but support is also needed from the wider music industry to endorse good practice in this area. If you're running a venue, for example, Cordeaux says: "You need to be thinking, 'Well, what is it that I can do that's encouraging people to think about their physical health?' You don't have to provide everything but you need to ensure you don't put any barriers in the way." That principle applies to everyone across the business – promoters, managers, festival owners, labels, and publishers. Cordeaux continues: "People should be getting the same messages all the way along so it's not a battle to be healthy, and you don't feel like you're running against the culture that you're trying to impress because you're trying to remain healthy."

The music industry can be an intimidating place to work, especially for newcomers, and until there's sector-wide education about this topic, it can be hard for musicians to speak up about their needs. Even seemingly small things like playing in freezing rehearsal rooms can cause tension in the body, which is what you're trying to avoid when playing an instrument (or indeed singing), and a lack of communication about access issues or stairs from venues for bands lugging heavy gear can negatively impact those who have pre-existing injuries or conditions.

There is some good work being done in the classical music sector, where a cultural shift towards prioritising physical health is starting to take place. The Royal Liverpool Philharmonic Orchestra, for example, provides membership to a gym for its orchestral players, while a massage therapist is available between rehearsals and concerts and goes on tour, too. Upjohn adds: "They're really good with their scheduling so that everyone gets a break over the summer. **It's important to build in rest and recovery time in training schedules because that's when bodies literally do recover**." A support package such as this one gives the orchestral players a strong message that management cares about the physical health and wellbeing of their players.

This kind of package is probably easier to provide for those on salaried roles in classical music (something that can be a rarity in pop) and a summer festival season offers little chance of a breather. Still, it outlines an interesting model of support that others in the industry could replicate, in various ways, to make positive changes. Relevant questions could include: how many consecutive shows is too many? Is there a limit to reasonable travel within a specific timeframe? Is there anything that could be done to better support the physical (and therefore overall) health of musicians while on tour, in the venue, and onstage? Are they being encouraged to rest and recuperate? And do they have support and help if an injury does arise?

CONCLUSION

MSK health is a pretty big topic and this chapter is just an introduction to a few of the main issues that may arise, along with some ways of preventing them. If you want to find out more, head to the resources section where we'll signpost you to further information about the specific issues we've mentioned and how you can get in touch with BAPAM to access that one-to-one physical health assessment.

We'll leave you with some final words of advice from Upjohn on how to look after your MSK health. "Increasing your level of physical fitness will help you, increasing your strength will help you, and getting more flexible will help you. If you're a sportsperson, you'd have a team of people looking after you. As a musician, you kind of have to carve those bits out for yourself, whenever you can."

What might *your* support framework look like, and what do you need to do in order to implement that?

Adapted from BAPAM's top tips for instrumental musicians[16]

Whatever your instrument, and whatever style of music you play, you should **take a holistic approach to practising and performing**. Here are a few tried and tested tips to remind you to think about YOU as well as your art.

- **Never try to play through pain** – stop beforehand.

- Always do a series of **physical warm-up exercises away from your instrument**, to prepare for each episode of playing. BAPAM's Don't Cramp Your Style factsheet covers warm-ups for musicians.

- Allow a **few minutes to adjust physically after playing. Do cool-down exercises to let your body unwind.**

- **Ensure your technique is as sound as possible**, allowing for individual physical proportions and level of experience. You should seek regular professional advice, whatever your level of playing; bad technique may become a habit and lead to further problems.

- **Ensure you are as comfortable as possible when playing** your instrument. Check your own posture when playing (a full-length mirror may be helpful – or even better, video yourself). Adaptations (e.g. chin rests, shoulder pads, supports, straps) are designed to help you so make sure that you take full advantage of what's available. Expert advice from a teacher may help.

- **Always check the position and height of things like a music stand, chair, piano stool** etc., to ensure that playing is as comfortable as possible and that you maintain good posture while playing. Changes made by others may not suit you and adjustments may be necessary.

- **Plan your practice sessions** to allow frequent breaks in playing. It's important to stop before any discomfort is reached – kitchen timers, mobile phones, or digital watches can be pre-set to remind you that a break from playing is advisable. Relax your muscles for at least a few minutes.

- Your physical build may make some repertoire more uncomfortable for you. Respect and accept this and design your repertoire and rehearsal schedules accordingly. **Try to play within your capabilities**.

- **Your general lifestyle can affect your playing.** Make sure you are eating and sleeping properly. Vision and hearing can affect your neck and upper limb posture; have them tested periodically.

- **A mixture of regular exercise** (e.g. a sport of your choice, such as swimming) **and relaxation will help you maximise your potential and reduce the risk of playing-related injury.** Performing is stressful and tension can lead to pain and stiffness. There are many forms of exercise and relaxation techniques. Find ones that you enjoy – they're more likely to help!

- Remember that **you are a musical athlete and that your performance depends on taking care of yourself**. Think twice before going rollerblading, painting the ceiling, or banging nails into walls in the days before a concert.

- **Get a life! There is a world outside music.** Find a hobby or interest totally unrelated to your music making and spend time on that as well.

CHAPTER 10

HEARING

HEARING IS A PRECIOUS commodity for musicians and, if you're lucky enough to have a pair of fully functioning ears, you'll find them coming in handy in pretty much every facet of working life — listening to the balance of a mix in the studio, staying in tune with the rest of the band on stage as a singer, fine-tuning an instrument before and during a gig, or hearing Annie Mac premiere your new single on Radio 1. **Having good hearing is an absolute necessity if you want to enjoy a long music career**. Yet, despite its importance, it's easy to take the ability to hear for granted and unknowingly abuse our long-suffering ears, which is very common for those who work in music and are regularly exposed to more extreme levels of sound.

For reasons we've outlined on the previous page, when hearing issues start to emerge, they can have a huge impact on the livelihood and wellbeing of someone who works in music, and as hearing loss tends to be permanent, it's something you want to avoid at all costs. For those who haven't protected their ears over the years, problems can often only become clear in their mid-30s, when the damage is already done. Protecting your hearing before that happens, therefore, is vital. The good news is that **hearing loss is entirely preventable and it's actually pretty simple to look after your ears**. In this chapter, we're going to take a look at the different types of hearing issues, find out why they happen, and how they affect musicians. We'll then look at ways to promote good hearing health and where to go if you think you might have problems and need some help.

THE ISSUES

To get an idea of how prevalent hearing problems can be in music, one study suggests that a huge **74% of rock and jazz musicians experience hearing issues**.[1] This figure isn't particularly surprising when you consider that noise exposure at rock concerts far exceeds daily advisable limits. In another study measuring the noise exposure and temporary threshold shift from a rock concert for 22 attendees, the peak levels of noise the audience was exposed to reached 139.5 dBA, which is just below the critical level of 140 dBA.[2] At that level, noise is thought to cause irreparable trauma to the ear. If you expose your ears to that level of sound night after night without protection, you can expect some damage as a result. Hearing issues aren't limited to rock musicians, either. A study measuring sound levels in the mixing booths of 29 French DJs, along with their responses to a questionnaire, found that three quarters of them experienced tinnitus and hearing loss,[3] which again is probably unsurprising for anyone who has spent long periods of time in a loud club.

Alongside **hearing loss**, clinical audiologist Gladys Akinseye says the most common hearing-related complaints she sees amongst musicians include:

- **Tinnitus**. This is the perception of sound, often described as a distant ringing noise, in the ear or the head that's not coming from an external source.
- A condition called **hyperacusis** — increased sensitivity to everyday sound — is also common among Akinseye's patients. "Sometimes I see musicians who are sensitive to their own voices, which can be devastating for them," she explains.
- **Diplacusis** is another common issue — that's the perception of a single pitch that comes through as *different* pitches in each ear. Akinseye believes that regular exposure to excessively loud noise is the cause: "The hair cells in the inner ear get damaged, sometimes it can be temporary and they recover, and sometimes it can be permanent."

Thankfully, due to a lot of education about this topic, attitudes are changing in live venues to protect the musicians and crew working in them — but it wasn't always so. In the '80s, drummer Nigel Elliott was playing stadium shows around the world with artists, including gold-selling post-punk hitmaker Toyah Willcox, where he was exposed to the prolonged loud volumes that Akinseye is talking about. "I remember on [a] Toyah [tour], I had two massive column speakers, right on either side of me, and it kind of squashed your head sometimes," he says. "But as the tour went on, it got louder. So yeah, it can get excruciatingly loud, but it was just the style of things in the day."[4]

Elliott developed tinnitus and hearing loss as a result, which took a while to emerge. By the time they did, it was too late to treat and his only option was a hearing aid. "The ringing in the ears started to last a little bit longer after some of these gigs, and I started to get slightly concerned as to what was actually happening to my hearing and the frequencies. My right ear was definitely affected more than my left ear because I think, in my playing style, I tend to face towards the left. I would say the bell of the ride cymbal was a big culprit." Black Eyed Peas founder will.i.am also suffers from tinnitus, which affects him in that "there's always a beep there every day, all day." He says: "I don't know exactly how long I've had this, but it's gradually getting worse."[5]

It's not just speakers and instruments that are to blame — headphones aren't totally safe either. Singer Pete Townshend of The Who attributes his hearing loss to earphone use in the studio, as opposed to playing too loud onstage.[6] Dean Garstecki, an audiologist at Northwestern University, agrees with Townshend about the issues headphones can cause and says he is now seeing the kind of hearing loss in young people that you'd normally expect in ageing adults. "Unfortunately, the earbuds preferred by music listeners are even more likely to cause hearing loss than the muff-type earphones that were associated with the older devices," he explains. These earbuds can boost sound levels by six to nine decibels (four to eight times louder), which, over a long period of time, can make a real difference to the levels of noise you can comfortably tolerate." Although six decibels doesn't sound like much, if you increase sound by three or more decibels, it doubles the sound energy, making the potential for hearing issues much greater. Boost levels by six decibels and it doubles it again, and so on.

Thankfully, there are now laws in place to protect gigging musicians from hearing issues. The Control of Noise at Work Regulations 2005 (which came into effect for the music and entertainment sector in April 2008) sets out the minimum standards required by law to prevent hearing injury in the workplace. Occupational physician Finola Ryan explains:

> "Sound exposure can be a hazard to hearing so there are legal limits on workplace exposure. Three factors determine exposure: the **intensity** of sound (how 'loud' it is), how **close** a person is to the source of that sound, and the **duration** of time they are exposed.

"Noise exposure is calculated over an eight-hour working day, so you'll see the figure 85 dB quite frequently. Both the intensity and duration of exposure contribute to this figure of 85 dB. A musician's working day may be longer or shorter than eight hours, so the exposure value should be calculated over the correct number of hours. Always consider non-musical sound exposure: public transport, kitchen appliances, canteens, and so on, all contribute to your daily sound exposure."

Ryan adds that, "the Noise Regulations require employers and venue operators to do a risk assessment. That means they must identify who might be harmed and how, and take all reasonable steps to prevent or reduce the risk of harm. **Prevention includes reducing sound exposure at source, taking adequate breaks from moderate to loud sound exposure, allowing sufficient space between performers, continuous monitoring of sound levels in the environment, and hearing protection.** The Noise Regulations also cover freelancers and part-time workers."

In 2018, a landmark case was won against the Royal Opera House by viola player Christopher Goldscheider, who claimed that exposure to sound of over 130 dBA during one rehearsal led him to develop 'acoustic shock', attributed to brass instruments being placed behind him in the orchestra pit. That caused symptoms of tinnitus, hyperacusis, and hearing loss, and he was forced to give up his music career as a result.[7] It's the first time a musician has won a court case against an employer for exceeding noise levels and causing hearing issues, and will no doubt have implications for all those responsible for maintaining safe levels of sound in the future.

Hearing problems such as tinnitus won't just affect your ears — they can also impact mental health and create issues such as anxiety and prevent your ability to sleep. Constant ringing in your ears can even be life-destroying, as was the case for drummer Craig Gill, who had a lot of success in the '90s in Manchester band Inspiral Carpets. In 2016, he died by suicide, with his wife subsequently blaming his tinnitus, which she said had become "so unbearable he felt there was no cure".[8] This is an extreme example, but it illustrates why it is so vital to protect your hearing as best you can.

This is an important point we really want to reiterate: **you will not know something is wrong until it's too late to do anything about it, which is why prevention is vital.**

PREVENTION

There are some pretty simple ways to protect your hearing:

- **Reduce and monitor your overall noise exposure (the most effective option)**;
- **Wear earplugs around loud noise**;
- **Have regular hearing tests**;
- **Recognise warning signs.**

Firstly, try to reduce the overall amount of sound you're exposed to, although we appreciate that, for musicians, this isn't always easy. One simple option is to **take regular breaks**. Akinseye recommends to step out of the studio or rehearsal space 15 minutes of every hour and allow your ears to rest. This can apply to heavy headphone use, too. Some train lines, particularly the tube in London, can regularly break that recommended 85 dB limit, so you may find wearing hearing protection helps in those situations, too. Overall, be aware that you'll need to give your ears time to recover after being exposed to prolonged loud noise.

Help Musicians works in partnership with **Musicians Hearing Services** to provide access to specialist hearing assessments and bespoke hearing protection. For more information, and to apply for the scheme, visit **hearformusicians.org.uk**

Then, make sure you wear earplugs when you're exposed to sounds over 85 dB, and, ideally, custom-moulded ones rather than the small foam earplugs given out for free at gigs (but these are definitely better than nothing). Custom-moulded earplugs used to be prohibitively expensive but Help Musicians and the Musicians' Hearing Service have teamed up to offer a hearing test, with personalised earplug creation for a fraction of the usual price. The Incorporated Society of Musicians also offer discounted ear protection from a range of suppliers.

It can be hard to get used to wearing earplugs initially, which is something Nigel Elliott struggled with. "The first set [I played] with the new hearing protection was really odd. It just felt wrong," he says. "So I took them out after the first couple of numbers because it was just this weird chatter between my ears and my brain and everything." Akinseye agrees that, given the choice, most musicians would prefer to use their natural hearing. But patience is key here — stick with the earplugs and eventually your brain will adjust to the new way of hearing. She explains:

> "What I usually recommend is that if you **put the earplugs in maybe half an hour before you even step into the festival,** or before you step onto the tour bus, or onto the tube, your brain has that time to acclimatise to the sound. So it's not that sudden shock of attenuation [a reduction in the strength of the hearing signal]. A lot of people, if they're not used to it, the first inclination is to take the ear plugs out, or, if they don't have the ear plugs, they'll stick cotton wool in their ears or tissue but that's not an effective way of protecting your hearing. We can't measure how much of the sound is being attenuated so we can't guarantee that your hearing is being protected."

If you opt for custom-moulded earplugs, make sure they are fitted correctly to get the best possible results. BAPAM's Hearing Conservation Guidance explains: 'Errors can occur during manufacture to affect the fit so although comfortable, some samples will not fit properly and this leakage will result in a significant reduction of the real world protective value.'[9] We've linked that guidance in the resources section if you want to read it in more detail, along with the BBC's Music, Noise and Hearing Guide.

So how do you know when you've hit that 85 dB level? In the past, you may have had to hire an expensive piece of kit to find out, but now there are free apps on your phone that can give a pretty good estimation of levels — these include Decibel X, Decibels, or Decibel Meter. There's a graph below that tells you how much time you can spend in an environment per day at the levels that you're experiencing. It's just a guideline, but it helps to know what is advisable and when you should be using ear protection.

Audiologist Frank Wartinger advises the musicians he works with to think about monitoring as a way of protecting their hearing, particularly for DJs, and is a real advocate for in-ear monitors. Although they're commonly used by musicians in bands, for DJs, they allow more control over volume levels. As he explains in a vlog on YouTube titled 'about my hearing',[11] Laidback Luke endorses that approach. He told fans his in-ears "function as my hearing protection, in the club as well, and in these I apply the same rule where I don't go over living room volume." We'd like to point out that not all in-ear monitors attenuate and protect your hearing, so check with

SOUND LEVELS AND SAFE EXPOSURE TIME [10]

Continuous Sound Level	Safe Exposure Time
85dB	8 hours
88dB	4 hours
91dB	2 hours
94dB	1 hour
97dB	30 minutes
100dB	15 minutes
103dB	7.5 minutes
106dB	Less than 4 minutes
109dB	Less than 2 minutes
112dB	About 1 minute
115dB	30 seconds

an audiologist to see if yours do. In the video, Luke also advocates regular hearing tests and describes the process that takes place during them. It's worth a watch.

Wartinger believes that, **for DJs, an awareness of sound levels can help them to understand how to protect the hearing of the audiences who have come to listen to the set, who are also at risk**. "Oftentimes, you can have control over the house volume so try to make some adjustments there," he explains. "Sometimes it doesn't mean quieter, sometimes it means having a more dynamic set, having loud moments and quiet moments, and also maybe pushing the bass more than pushing the 2-4 khz range, where you're causing the most damage. Little tweaks can make what you're doing safer."[12]

WHAT TO DO AND WHERE TO GO

As we've heard, hearing problems are common for musicians, so it's good to know the warning signs and what to do if you get them. Some of these warning signs can include:[13]

- **Ringing, buzzing, or whooshing in the ears.**
- **Sounds seeming muffled or garbled.**
- **Difficulty understanding speech, especially in the presence of background noise.**
- **One ear hears better on the phone.**
- **You ask people to repeat themselves.**
- **You're frequently told that you play, sing, or speak too loudly.**
- **Pitches seem different in one ear than in the other.**
- **You've become hypersensitive to sound and feel discomfort or pain when others don't.**

If you start to notice any of the above, have your hearing checked as soon as possible by an audiologist who regularly works with musicians. You can do it through the MU hearing scheme we've mentioned, or get in touch with BAPAM or the British or American Tinnitus Associations (see links in the resources section). From there, the audiologist will assess whether you have an issue, and if you do, they will discuss options and strategies to manage it. For some, it may be using earplugs more regularly or, for those with tinnitus, it could be identifying triggers other than sound that cause problems. Matthew Barnes, who performs as the artist Forest Swords, says his tinnitus triggers are "drinking, or if I haven't slept, or if I'm stressed — which is quite often on tour — then it really gets worse."[14]

Wartinger explains that, like Barnes experiences, **tinnitus triggers can include excesses of caffeine and alcohol, stress, and also sleep deprivation**. "So if you go out for a nice dinner and there's a band playing and you come home and your ears are buzzing, you don't have to say, 'Oh no, I've damaged my ears because that band was in the background playing quietly!' It might have been those seven glasses of wine that you had [that are] making your ears buzz tonight. Recognising that usually reduces the stress level that people have."

If the audiologist does diagnose an issue, such as tinnitus, what then? Wartinger's advice is: "Don't cancel anything. Don't cancel your [tour] dates, because that's going to be emotionally draining and rough on you in a psychological way, and that's not going to help you deal with the trauma [of tinnitus]. So definitely don't stop. Give yourself a break and reduce the overall stressors in your life. Allow yourself to just take a nap, go for a couple of days where you don't have to do anything except read a book. Usually, what you're going to find is that you're not thinking about the tinnitus as much."

Although some musicians have been advised to quit music after being diagnosed with hearing problems, Wartinger understands that it's just not that simple and believes there are always ways to make it work. He says:

> "Although your hearing is precious, and you don't want to lose it, still, music is going to win out. **There are so many**

musicians out there who have hearing impairment, and they find ways of doing what they love."

For Nigel Elliott, that meant being fitted with a hearing aid, which totally transformed his hearing and ability to play. For Barnes, it was a long-term acceptance of his tinnitus. "The older I get and the more I get used to it, the less it bothers me," he says. "But I'm also aware that I can't let it bother me because I'll never get rid of it. It's just something that I have to accept."

If you are diagnosed with an issue, don't despair as there are probably ways to deal with it that will allow you to continue playing, and there are also simple prevention tools. Akinseye concludes:

> "We only get one pair of ears, so treat them like they are precious. **Noise induced hearing loss is 100% preventable, but it's also 100% permanent**. So, if we can do something about it to try and prevent it from occurring in the first place, why not?"

HEARING TIPS INSPIRED BY FRANK WARTINGER [15]

Rehearsal management

- Think about the **length and venue of rehearsals** from an acoustic perspective.
- Plan the length of rehearsals with hearing in mind. **Take regular breaks** or reduce time spent on louder sections.
- Think about **alternative rehearsal formats**, such as unplugged sessions that reduce the need for amplification.
- Try to **reduce 'noodling' in between songs** to give your ears a break (guitarists, we're talking to you!).

Hearing protection

- Consider using **custom-moulded earplugs**. Although better than nothing, simple foam versions won't do the job as well.

- Try **rehearsing and listening to music with earplugs in** so that your brain is able to adapt to music at lower volumes.
- **Use earplugs in other day-to-day situations**, for example, on a loud tube train or whilst attending a concert or operating loud tools. This will help save your hearing for what really matters — music.

Effective monitoring

- Try to **reduce your exposure to sound levels** by reducing monitors in practice and then in performance.
- If possible, **turn down amplifiers**.
- Work with your sound engineer to **reduce excess noise** and lower overall sound levels onstage.
- **Consider using in-ear monitors** instead of traditional wedge monitors to control exposure to sound (although we appreciate these may be prohibitively expensive for some musicians).

CHAPTER 11

MENTAL HEALTH

WORKING IN THE MUSIC INDUSTRY can be extremely fun and fulfilling, but it also brings about incredibly challenging situations and environments that aren't necessarily conducive to good mental health. As we've discussed, the rigmarole of touring, for instance, can wreak havoc on the body and mind, making you more susceptible to mental health issues like depression and anxiety over time. That lifestyle also brings about a high likelihood of using substances as a way of coping with the challenges. There's the potential for extreme levels of performance anxiety that can come with playing live, stress as a result of the financial insecurity of freelance life and travel, long and anti-social working hours, and competitiveness within the industry. It's not hard to see how this particular career choice is often far from helpful when trying to maintain a balanced state of mind.

The perception of mental health is currently going through a seismic change across the world at large. We are, finally, accepting not only that our mental health can be just as important as our physical health, but that the two are closely linked. It's a hugely welcome development that's resulting in researchers and doctors making all sorts of incredibly interesting realisations. One relates to the relationship between our minds and our guts[1] — the impact that rising levels of stress might have on our digestive systems[2], and how gut bacteria can influence inflammation, which can contribute to depression and fatigue.[3] Then there's the role that exercise and maintaining a healthy diet play in maintaining wellbeing,[4] and how physical health problems significantly increase the risk of mental health issues,[5] and vice versa. Mental health is an incredibly complex phenomenon and there is still a lot yet to learn, particularly around its management and treatment. However, what we do know is that mental health challenges can be as commonplace as physical ailments, and that no-one is weird or abnormal for experiencing them.

In the music world, this shift in perception has resulted in a host of well-known artists making honest public statements about their own struggles. Justin Bieber has spoken about a period of depression following his rise to fame,[6] Lady Gaga has experienced panic attacks, acute trauma responses, and "debilitating mental spirals",[7] and Kendrick Lamar has experienced depression and suicidal thoughts.[8] Adele has talked about having postnatal depression following the birth of her son[9,] and Ariana Grande has opened up about depression and anxiety that has resulted in panic attacks.[10] Halsey has bipolar disorder,[11] and Stormzy's battle with depressive experiences[12] is clear in his lyrics. To back up these individual accounts, research suggests that **musicians and performers have higher reported rates of mental health challenges and substance misuse than the general population.**[13]

BARRIERS TO HEALTH AND WELLBEING IN MUSIC [14]

- Bad eating habits, drugs/alcohol use, lack of exercise, getting ill, and travelling while on tour.
- Antisocial/long hours considered 'the nature of the work'.
- Self-management and the pressure that brings.
- Competition from peers and in the business.
- Dealing with trolling and bullying online.
- Industry culture centred around drinking alcohol at gigs and rehearsals.
- Mental demands, including the pressure to create songs to deadlines and write 'hits'.
- Emergence of an 'artist character' as an alter ego and potential loss of true identity as a result.
- Lack of support from friends and perceived lack of support from services.

Psychotherapist Tamsin Embleton, who works with musicians at all career levels, says a motivation to express oneself through music, alongside pressures that come with turning it into a career (detailed in the list above), can result in a perfect storm. She explains:

"[Musicians] often use creativity to express their innermost thoughts and feelings, and to figure out their perspective on their life experiences. Sometimes, it also helps them to process and cope with pain. However, careers in the music industry involve many other factors that add pressure, stress, competition, and uncertainty. For those with pre-existing psychological issues, this highly stressful environment can exacerbate underlying issues and create new difficulties."

Psychotherapist, musician and Babyshambles member Adam Ficek says problems can arise from managing a desire to pursue music for passion with the pressure to turn it into a commercial career. He explains:

"From my experience as a professional touring musician and a psychotherapist, the real challenge comes when we evolve our relationship to music. We are all inherently drawn to music as a way to create and regulate ourselves emotionally. This changes from a personal to an intersubjective experience when we move to performing. The real tension comes when we apply this in a commoditised framework and it becomes the job we always dreamt of. It's a difficult transition and I subsequently lost touch with the original essence of meaning that music had once provided. It took a while to balance and rekindle the original passion and find myself again."

DEFINING MENTAL HEALTH

Before we go any further, we want to clarify some definitions for this chapter. Firstly, the distinction between mental health, and mental health problems or mental illness, is a separation which can sometimes be overlooked. To quote the World Health Organization:

"Mental health is a state of wellbeing in which an individual realises his or her own abilities, can cope with the normal stresses of life, can work productively, and is able to make a contribution to his or her own community. Multiple social, psychological, and biological factors determine the level of mental health of a person at any point of time. For example, violence and persistent socio-economic pressures are recognised risks to mental health. Poor mental health is also associated with rapid social change, stressful work conditions, gender discrimination, social exclusion, unhealthy lifestyle, physical ill-health, and human rights violations."[15]

This definition suggests that mental health is a spectrum that includes the ability to cope with the normal stresses of life. It's worth noting that these 'normal stresses' can sometimes make life exceptionally hard. However, if you're going through a tough patch due to a breakup or life transition, it may not mean that you are experiencing a mental health problem, such as depression, just that your mental health is temporarily suffering. Equally, natural levels of anxiety around exams, performances, and stressful life experiences are also to be expected and can help us mobilise the resources that we need to get through difficult periods.

Mental health problems, however, are slightly different (you'll find a list of the most commons ones alongside their definitions on the next page). Mental health charity Mind offers some clarification: "**Mental health problems affect around one in four people in any given year**. They range from common problems such as depression and anxiety to rarer problems such as schizophrenia and bipolar disorder. They can happen to all kinds of people from all walks of life. And it's likely that, when you find a combination of self-care, treatment, and support that works for you, you will get better."[16]

If you're struggling with your mental health, the first step is to have a chat with a mental health professional, like your GP or a therapist, who will be able to identify which of these experiences you are going through. The quicker you seek support, the better, so if you are in any doubt, don't hesitate to have a chat with someone who can help. To reiterate what we said at the beginning of this health section: we're not mental health professionals and cannot offer treatment or advice for anything that requires medical help. However, we do have some self-care tips from Mind as well as examples of what artists like Ella Eyre, George Ezra, Ellie Goulding, Lady Leshurr, and MNEK do to look after their general mental health day-to-day. Read on for that, and to learn more about the common mental health problems that research suggests may be associated with a career in music.

Common mental health problems

Approximately one in four people in the UK will experience a mental health problem each year[17], and one in six people in England report experiencing a common mental health problem in any given week.[18] The most common ones (in order of prevalence) are as follows (definitions taken from Mind). Mixed anxiety and depression is said to be the most common, impacting just under 8% of people.

Generalised anxiety disorder (GAD) means having regular or uncontrollable worries about many different things in your everyday life. Because there are lots of possible symptoms of anxiety, this can be quite a broad diagnosis, meaning that the problems you experience with GAD might be quite different from another person's experiences.

Post-traumatic stress disorder (PTSD) is a type of anxiety disorder which you may develop after being involved in, or witnessing, traumatic events. The condition was first recognised in war veterans and has been known by a variety of names, such as 'shell shock'. But it's not only diagnosed in soldiers – a wide range of traumatic experiences can cause PTSD.

Depression is a low mood that lasts for a long time, and affects your everyday life. In its mildest form, depression can mean just being in low spirits. It doesn't stop you leading your normal life but makes everything harder to do and seem less worthwhile. At its most severe, depression can be life-threatening because it can make you feel suicidal.

A **phobia** is a type of anxiety disorder. It is an extreme form of fear or anxiety triggered by a particular situation (such as going outside) or object (such as spiders), even when there is no danger. Someone with a phobia may even feel this extreme anxiety just by thinking or talking about the particular situation or object.

Obsessive-compulsive disorder (OCD) has two main parts: obsessions and compulsions. Obsessions are unwelcome thoughts, images, urges, worries, or doubts that repeatedly appear in your mind. They can make you feel very anxious (although some people describe it as 'mental discomfort' rather than anxiety). Compulsions are repetitive activities that you do to reduce the anxiety caused by the obsession. It could be something like repeatedly checking a door is locked, repeating a specific phrase in your head, or checking how your body feels.

There are many conditions beyond this, like bipolar disorder, disassociation, and schizophrenia. For further reading, head to **mind.org.uk**

THE BIG PICTURE

We've heard about some of the mental health problems musicians face, like anxiety, depression, and substance misuse, but what else may arise? Tamsin Embleton says she sees a broad range of issues in her work, which include "relationship challenges, both inside and outside of the industry, insecurity, identity issues, suicidality, loss, and bereavement." She continues: "Some clients I've worked with are still picking up the pieces of having been dropped by a record label 10 or 15 years ago and losing their management, label, career, community, future plans, and sense of self overnight." Embleton also sees patients with histories of "deprivation, neglect, trauma or abuse, which can result in post-traumatic stress disorder (PTSD), diagnoses such as personality disorders or schizoaffective disorder, or maladaptive coping strategies like addiction and eating disorders". Then there are mental health problems that are a direct result of work, like "stress and burnout, anxiety that's been exacerbated by work schedules, job uncertainty, career transitions, band breakups, the pressure to gain and maintain success, negative press, online trolling, bullying and stalking."

Adam Ficek says that it's important to take a holistic view of the journey to becoming a musician in the industry. He explains: "**There is an innate struggle with being a creative musician in terms of the constant artistic pursuit, technical development, and the learning involved. We then add the extra tension of the working environment and, of course, the underlying 'life wounds' of the person. It makes for a potentially dangerous cocktail.**" He also adds the pressure involved in trying to be authentic while working in "an inauthentic commercial music industry."

Embleton points out the paradox expected of musicians — that they are expected to be vulnerable on stage, in songwriting sessions, and interviews, but then somehow also have a huge amount of resilience to weather the music industry's pressures, disappointments and challenging lifestyle. She explains:

> "The industry asks artists to be vulnerable but also resilient, and it's a big ask. We're not really teaching artists how to cope. **It's a competitive and unpredictable industry**. You have to weather all of these really unpredictable ups and downs, long hours, exposing your art for others to critique. There's a lot of pressure to gain and maintain success, pressure to self-promote and network, and a lifestyle that of course has a lot of access to drink and drugs."

Studies looking at the mental health experiences of musicians suggest depression,[19] anxiety,[20] music performance anxiety (MPA)[21], and high levels of stress.[22] In a randomised study of 246 popular musicians in the UK, published in 1987, researchers found that the main predictors of challenges to mental wellbeing for musicians included:

- **Performance-related anxiety**;
- **Poor physical working conditions** (like working at night and performing in substandard circumstances);
- **Work overload** related to travelling and the impact of the job on social and family life.[23]

Although that study is now over 30 years old and much has changed since within the music industry, the nature of performance and touring life has remained relatively consistent (as we delved into in the first chapter of this health section).

A 1989 study looking at sources of stress in popular musicians found:

- Complaints about **public ignorance around the stresses of the job**;
- Experiences of **low self-esteem**;
- Problems with **work overload or underload**
- **Career development worries** (which includes associated financial issues);
- Problems with **relationships** at work.[24]

A more recent study of 18 young musicians in 2011 backed up the findings of financial stress, with participants expressing concern over their lack of job and financial security.[25] The research included in Sally Gross and George Musgrave's 2020 book, *Can Music Make You Sick?*, agreed with some of the stressors above, and added the lack of esteem musicians are held in by the general population.

The prevalence of mental health and substance use issues within the popular music community has a worrying impact on the mortality of its musicians. In recent years, Lil Peep was misusing drugs and experiencing several mental health issues, which led to his incredibly premature death from an accidental drug overdose at just 21-years-old.[26] Avicii died by suicide after having taken steps to reduce his workload following ten years of charging full steam ahead in the music business, but struggling to find "meaning, life, happiness" as a statement from his family revealed.[27] Mac Miller died from an accidental overdose aged 26,[28] and both Prodigy singer Keith Flint and Linkin Park frontman Chester Bennington died by suicide aged 49[29] and 41[30], respectively. Amy Winehouse died following years battling with alcohol, drug misuse, and an eating disorder,[31] and Scott Hutchison of Frightened Rabbit died by suicide after experiencing anxiety, depression, and alcohol misuse.[32] All of these examples are heartbreaking for the people close to those who died, as well as the fans who loved their music.

Sadly, there are a wealth of stories beyond these. In a 2016 study of the death records of more than 13,000 musicians, researchers found that popular musicians had life expectancies that were up to 25 years shorter than those who didn't work in music, and that suicide rates were two to seven times higher.[33] There were also higher rates of suicide and liver-related diseases for those working in country, metal, and rock music.

American sociologist Steven Stack believes we should look at the occupational and financial stressors on musicians to find answers for the high suicide rate.[34] He says specific factors that contribute to a musician's suicide risk include perceived unfairness in rewards and workloads, toxic relationships, work insecurity, the inability to prioritise work that one enjoys, social isolation, and overall career dissatisfaction. In the 2016 study, half of those who died from substance use or risk-taking had experienced childhood adversity, and researchers point to this, as well as factors inherent in the working culture of the popular music industry, as the reason behind the stats. It's important to note that this study was a retrospective one, looking at records of those who died between 1950 and 2014, and there's since been a lot of work to raise awareness and support of health issues within the industry. Over the coming decades, we hope this will result in a marked change in these statistics.

THE 'TORTURED ARTIST'

It could be easy to dismiss these stats as being part of the 'tortured artist' cliché, point to famous examples of what might once have been termed 'eccentric' creative talent, and assume mental health issues are just part and parcel of life as an artist, and an intrinsic part of creating good work. But, the truth is, **research into this area draws no concrete conclusion.** While there have been studies that suggest a higher prevalence of mental health issues in creative people, others have found the total opposite.

For example — a study published in 2012 of more than a million people in Sweden found that aside from authors, who had a higher prevalence of experiencing bipolar disorder and schizophrenia, people in creative professions were no more likely to have a psychiatric disorder than those in the control group.[35] A study in India that was published in 2007 rubbishes the idea of the tortured artist entirely.[36] From a sample of 40 musicians, 40 writers, and 40 random non-creative people, the prevalence of mental illness was similar between groups and was not found to be statistically significant. In fact, **most creative respondents said that they were only able to produce work of good quality when they were free from stress.**

Writer, producer, and musician Catherine Anne Davies, who performs as The Anchoress, has seen both sides of the coin and concludes that from her own experience, pain or poor mental health is not a prerequisite for producing good work. She says:

> "I've just finished making my second album, which unfortunately is hugely influenced by a lot of terrible things that have happened. Equally, I made my first record in quite a stable, very reasonably contented frame of mind.

So I see both ends of the spectrum and I don't think that one produces better art than the other. But it was more difficult to make the second record because nobody really wants to write or record when they're in a lot of pain. I think any person would acknowledge that to be healthy and on a generally even keel, and to be able to put the work in every day to your craft, is a better frame of mind to be in to achieve what it is that you want to in a sustained fashion."

Grammy-winner Imogen Heap has also grappled with the tortured artist cliché for the best part of her career. She says:

"I wish I'd known before starting my career that you don't have to be sad and depressed, or invite bad stuff into your life to be able to write a good song. There's this belief that 'tortured artist' equals 'creativity in the brain' but I think whatever sad thing has happened just gives you the license to have the confidence to be creative. If you believe you are creative and believe you have it in you, you can do it anytime."

Storme Whitby-Grubb, who has worked as an artist manager and tour manager, also rubbishes the tortured artist trope. She says that seeking help for her mania and depression *improved* her ability to be creative. "I'd like to say to all musicians (and non-musicians) who fear medication and seeking help will diminish your creativity, for me, suddenly the noise stopped. I could think clearly. I could hear properly. I suddenly became a better writer, my ideas were more vivid, my thoughts stronger," she writes.[37]

"My creativity has only grown from quietening out the constant drill of mental illness. That's just my experience, but I know a lot of people are afraid that it'll change you for the worst. In my case, I moved to Los Angeles, have a great life, make cool shit, and write stories. That's all I need. I couldn't have any of that before."

MANAGING MENTAL HEALTH

As we have already clarified, unless there's an underlying mental or physical illness that requires treatment, generally being mentally healthy is within reach and there are steps we can all take to try and maintain a positive state of mind. While working in music, the key to creating mental resilience, according to Tamsin Embleton, is self-education. "It's about really getting to know yourself, your sore points and your limits, and **learning how to put in boundaries and feeling comfortable with saying no**", she says.[38] That can be difficult if you're feeling insecure about your job, want to say yes to everything, or feel like you need to be always available. But as cellist and singer Ayanna Witter-Johnson points out: "I think that passion and perseverance and drive can cause you to neglect your health until it gets to a chronic point where you're not able to [work] anymore."[39]

Mental health self-care doesn't have to be overwhelming and it will probably look different for each person. For you, perhaps it means taking good care of your physical health, going to regular therapy, eating nice and healthy food that's matching your energy needs, keeping active, remaining in contact with family and friends, watching the grass grow, or staring at the sea for a bit. Maybe it's listening to extraordinarily loud music and playing video games. Perhaps you just need some time off. In *Lost Connections*, author Johann Hari puts forward a strong case for what we need, as humans, to be happy and healthy.

> "You need to have a **community**. You need to have **meaningful values**, not the junk values you've been pumped full of all your life, telling you happiness comes through money and buying objects. You need to have **meaningful work**. You need the **natural world**. You need to feel you are **respected**. You need a **secure future**. You need connections to all these things. You need to **release any shame** you might feel for being mistreated."[40]

Here are a few examples of what mental healthcare might mean in the music world. Ayanna Witter-Johnson feels the benefits of easing herself into the day, which starts with going for a run first thing or doing a yoga session. She says: "I usually start the day with some form of physical activity to wake me up and get the energy going and blood moving. I then have something to eat, enjoy the process of mindfully eating, and ease myself into whatever the to-do list throws up for the day. So just a bit of me-time. I usually journal a little bit in the morning and have some affirmations of what I want for the day, like inner peace, gratitude, something like that."

Singer, songwriter, and two-time BRIT winner Ellie Goulding uses exercise to combat feelings of anxiety that she says she experiences as a result of insecurity. "I know I chose this job but nothing could have prepared me for the ups and downs that come with it. I know for sure that a lot of my anxiety has come from what they call 'imposter syndrome' not believing in myself enough and thinking that I don't deserve happiness, which results in wanting to sabotage my own success," she says.[41] "I keep my head straight by training every day (running and boxing mainly) and although it is so hard sometimes to be motivated, the feeling of blood pumping through my veins and a human body performing the way it so impressively does reminds me how cool it is to be alive."

For Adam Ficek, managing his way through the sometimes opposing forces of authenticity and commercial success was about learning to be less precious with his art. He explains: "As an artist, I feel that we need to remember that it is a continuum between commoditised entertainment and art. Wherever we are on the 'authenticity' continuum, once it is released, it will impact people in their own unique way so we can learn to be less precious. I was once struggling with navigating this and remember [The Who legend] Roger Daltrey telling me, 'It's just show business'. Once I adopted this mantra, it all became easier. I was just as authentic, but realised that once in the hands of others, it becomes something else. Tension relieved!"

Mental health self-care might also mean making some big changes in your career. Singer and songwriter Lauren Aquilina found herself spiralling into a period of depression after a string of professional disappointments and to get her health back on track; she parted ways with her record label, her then boyfriend, and her manager. She explains: "There were a lot of big changes that happened at once, which was difficult at the time, but I told myself that it was probably going to have to get worse before it got better. As a result of those changes, I was able to put in place the new surroundings in my life, which are still present now and are working much better for me in general. One of those was that I decided to stop being an artist for a while, and just not put pressure on myself, which I really needed to do." Aquilina found a new manager, who gave her the confidence she needed to start writing songs for other artists, and spent a year and a half doing that, before feeling ready to put herself front and centre as a solo artist again.

For Everything Everything frontman Jonathan Higgs, adopting a healthier approach to touring, and creating boundaries between his work and home life is what he and the rest of his band members have learned to do. "**We've all tried to get healthier and to drink less**," he says. "We tend not to drink before shows now, we used to get quite drunk before and we've found that when we don't drink at all, we actually play a lot better and have a better time. We try to exercise more and eat properly and to think about things beyond the band and where our lives might go other than, 'Let's just keep doing this insane thing until we can't', because we are getting older and that time might not be that far away."

BRIT Award-winner George Ezra, who has experienced anxiety and OCD, uses **meditation** as part of his self-care routine. He explains: "I've learnt this meditation where I've got a mantra, which is a sound that isn't a word I know so I can't relate it to anything. For 20 minutes, I close my eyes and repeat it in my mind. The way I see it is that any intrusive thoughts or worrying that I do is either worrying about something that might happen or something that has happened, and neither of those things are happening while

I'm having the thoughts. The way I relate to this mantra is that it's just reminding me to come back to where I am."[42] As fellow BRIT-winner Ella Eyre points out, meditation, as well as yoga, don't always have the best connotation, and might be considered a bit "hippy-dippy", but they are both fairly easy ways to do something good for both your body and mind. She says:

> "Quite often, I find it hard to think straight and to get simple tasks done because my head is clouded with lots of things, but meditation is really good for resetting that. Whenever I feel myself not being able to complete a task for no reason other than just pure fear or stress, **taking 10 minutes out of my day to do some breathing and relax my body**, and just keep reminding myself that everything is all right, really helps."

Eyre says that meditation and yoga help facilitate self-development, which results in her being able to feel more positive and accepting about where she's at in life. "I feel like the happier I am in myself, and the more self-development that I do, the more accepting I am of my surroundings and who I am, and the more positive my output is," she explains. "My dad dying a couple of years ago was a real hit for me because I felt like my Jamaican heritage had escaped me, so the last couple of years have been about finding balance and reconnecting with that. In doing that, I've been a lot happier and things are a lot easier because I've worked on myself. I think I've learnt the importance of taking time out from work and not having to work your butt off to the point where you can't compute or do anything."

Rapper, singer, and songwriter Lady Leshurr also values self-development and education, which she practises by spending time on her own. She says:

> "To build on yourself, grow, and learn about yourself a bit more, you have to **take time for yourself**. I know a lot of people who just fill the gaps with friends, family, or people

that they want to surround themselves with, but they are not mentally there. I've had so much stress and I'm not really a vocal person, so I don't talk about stuff, but by being on my own, I've been able to face up to my demons and try and tick things off the list one by one. That has really helped my anxiety."

Leshurr also uses **prayer** to get through tough times, as she explains: "Prayer is a really huge part of progress, strength, and guidance. I lost my sister recently so that really affected my mental health and it took me a while to get back into the space where I'm able to make music again. I think praying, or just talking to someone who has passed in your life and keeping them alive, really helps you to build and get stronger."

Part of artist, songwriter, and producer MNEK's mental health self-care is making a conscious effort to **separate his work and home life**, and foster his relationships with friends and family so that he always has an objective ear to call upon. He explains: "When I'm doing my artist thing, I definitely get a bit anxious, get quite obsessive, and I sometimes then have imposter syndrome. When it comes to my mental health, the best preservation I have is being able to separate work with my life situation. I know I have people I can talk to for that amongst my friends and people I love, even if I don't always have people to talk to within my job."

Two-time Mercury Prize nominee Laura Mvula, on the other hand, has worked on stepping up her "bullshit barometer". She says:

> "I try and speak my mind in the moment without the fear of, 'What if they think I'm a diva? What if that person now has a particular opinion of me?' I can't control the population's opinion of me, I have to get on with it and be cool in myself. So if I do feel like rescheduling that fifth interview because I'm really tired, then I'll say that rather than do it and not do it very well and feel exhausted."

Stephen Buckley from Mind says his definition of self-care is similar for both mental and physical health. "Mental health *is* health, so some of the self-care tips that we might recommend for people who are struggling with anxiety or depression are very similar to the kind of things that you might expect if someone has been told they perhaps need to look after their physical health a bit better," he explains.[43] Buckley's self-care tips are:

- Do what you can to **make sure your diet is good**;
- Keep an eye on things like **alcohol, drugs, caffeine, and sugar**;
- **Sleep** is really, really important to good mental health;
- Wherever possible, if you can find 10 or 15 minutes each day, **take some time out to do what's important to you** — whether that's sitting quietly, doing a little bit of meditation, or staying in touch with people back home.

Catherine Loveday, Professor of Social Sciences at the University of Westminster, offers her five tips for looking after your mental health in the music industry:[44]

- Number one is to make sure that you **maintain a good solid base of friends and family** away from the music business who are still going to be there whether the band breaks up or whatever happens.
- My second piece of advice is for people to **take regular breaks in their schedule**. So if they have got a lot of live work, make sure they have good chunks of time where they can live a normal routine and do their usual health-promoting behaviours to try and compensate for what happens when you're on tour.
- A third and related tip is about where you sleep. I think **sleep is really important** and being away from home is not good for sleep. It's about weighing up: 'Am I better going home and getting in my own bed?' [A tour bus

is] not great, certainly on a long-term basis, because disrupted sleep is not good for us.

- Another piece of advice is for people **to have alternative methods of relaxation.** One of the problems of being a professional musician is that the thing that's your relaxation and your hobby and your love, is also your job. I think it's really important for people to find something else they can do so that you can have a break from music sometimes.
- My final tip is **to use music in a positive way.** Go back to the music that you love, the music that inspired you to become a musician, the music that fills you with positive warm memories, and use those to remind you why you love music and why you're performing.

MENTAL HEALTH TREATMENT

As the Mind description outlined towards the beginning of this chapter, approaches for managing mental health problems will be determined on an individual basis, but may include **self-care, support, and treatment.** This treatment could be talking therapies, such as psychotherapy or cognitive behavioural therapy (CBT), and you may be offered medication. This will be a personal choice and is a conversation for you and your GP or therapist, so we're not going to go into too much detail here.

However, if you're interested in talking therapies and you're not sure where to start, have a look at the box on the next page. Be aware that these tips apply to private therapy and may not be relevant for the NHS approach assigned to you by your GP. If you access treatment through the NHS, it could be that you are offered six sessions of CBT with a therapist you are unable to change. If this is the case and you are unhappy with the situation or individual therapist, go back to your GP and have a chat about other options. The most crucial aspect of your approach to mental health problems is that if you're struggling, speak to a mental health professional as soon as you can.

Therapy can be an essential element of mental healthcare, which helps untangle negative thought patterns and addresses past trauma. So how do you find and choose a therapist?

- **The therapist and client dynamic is important to get right**. You'll benefit from being with someone you feel comfortable to share your innermost workings with, which is why choosing the right one is a bit like dating: you might have to keep going until you find the right match. There are many different approaches out there, some of which will work for you, others of which won't. Have an initial phone call and/or face-to-face session to see what the dynamic and approach are like, and if they don't work for you, move on.

- Having the right qualifications is important and it might be helpful to find **someone with music industry experience** who understands the world you're operating in, and who **specialises in whatever issues you're dealing with**. Ask for recommendations within your circle, and check out those who are working under the Music Industry Therapists and Coaches collective at musicindustrytherapists.com, or Adam Ficek at musicandmind.co.uk.

- Before your first session, **think about what you want from the therapist and what it is you're struggling with**. Therapists aren't mind readers who can work out your issues for you, they are great listeners who hold space and ask the right questions to help guide you towards answers you need that are within yourself. It may be that the initial issue you go in with leads to the exploration of something else in your life, and being clear about what you want to change will expedite that process.

- **It's not going to be an overnight fix**. If you've been struggling with mental health issues for years and have some unresolved trauma that's buried deep, it's going to take a while to work through that. Be patient, give yourself time to heal, and trust that it will be worth it in the end.

When seeking help from those around you, you might be surprised at the reaction. Laura Mvula has experienced depression, anxiety, and panic attacks throughout her career, and there have been times when she's been bed-bound for long periods. At first, her management weren't aware. "I was terrified that if people found out, it was going to be over for me," she recalls. "I was ashamed and embarrassed, I didn't want people to know that I'm not this invincible being that makes music. I thought it would make it difficult for them to like me or something. I didn't say anything to my team for a long time." However, when she did eventually tell them, it was all hands on deck. "Everybody was super resourceful, gracious and gentle and understanding. What it did do was humanise me again. I think it's easy for people that are working closely with me to see me as some kind of thing because I am a project, I'm a brand, but the danger with that mindset is that you neglect the human being. Luckily, in my case, sharing had the opposite effect."

As Mvula says, having the courage to talk about mental health issues is where those working in the music industry can start to foster a healthier working environment:

> "We live in a culture of 'keep calm and carry on', but when mental health issues get to the stage where they are debilitating and you are trying to deal with it in secret, for

me, it becomes deathly. The minute that I spoke out about it, it lost its power as this taboo thing in my own head. I didn't see myself as some weird other species that is set apart in a negative way from everybody else. When I've spoken publicly about it in interviews, what's surprised me is the response. People say, 'Hey, I struggle with this' or 'I know a person who struggles with this'. Once it's out, there is freedom in that and strength in solidarity."

Being open about struggling isn't going to come naturally for everyone and we know that men, in particular, shy away from talking (this is said to be one of the reasons why men are three times as likely to die by suicide as women[45]). According to south London-raised MC Loyle Carner, "loads of things stop guys talking. People are caught up in certain ideas of masculinity. In the parts of London where I grew up, there weren't many male role models doing something positive. So as a teenager, you might have a lot of responsibility; you might be the man of the house, looking after your family. And when you have to be strong for everyone else, it's seen as a weakness to be upset."[46] In an essay for the book *It's Not OK To Feel Blue (And Other Lies)*, singer and songwriter James Blake says he thinks the reason behind this reticence to share is "systemic toxic masculinity ('boys don't cry', basically) and an ostensibly homophobic fear of sensitivity being beer-bonged into us by our friends, family and the media from as early as we can remember ('Chug, chug, chug!'), to the slow realisation as we get older that the world is actually stacked towards our success." He concludes: "We end up thinking that our individual psychological decline is shameful."[47]

As a result of this, BRIT-winner Dave says you might be the one who has to take the lead in a circle of friends: "**If you are open yourself, it will encourage others to be open**."[48] He continues: "Ranting works for me. If you're speaking to your friends correctly, then every conversation should feel like therapy." Carner advises finding places to chat that will help create a relaxed environment. "Talk whenever you feel comfortable," he says. "You don't want to feel like you're under scrutiny. Go to the pub, go to their house, talk while you're watching the football. Get a coffee. Go where there's something else to do if you get embarrassed." As well as talking to friends and family, Carner sees a therapist whenever he has time. "It's essential, especially in a high-octane, stressy, angry, fake, bullshit world like the music industry," he says. "You've got to have at least one person you can chat to who doesn't have an ulterior motive."[49]

It's also vital to know that **whatever pain you have is valid**, regardless of what might be perceived as privilege in other areas of your life. This can be especially pertinent while pursuing a career in a highly coveted industry like music, where many might assume you're 'living the dream' and don't have anything to complain about. But, as we've discussed elsewhere in this book, all that glitters is not gold, and everyone experiences challenges and struggles, regardless of how it looks from the outside. Of course, it's not just the musicians who struggle. Crew, management, agents, and label staff are all susceptible to mental health problems. That's why it's vital to notice the signs of when things might be going wrong in those around you, be it bandmates or management.

Stephen Buckley says things to look out for include "marked changes in behaviour, particularly if someone becomes very withdrawn when normally they're quite chatty and friendly." He continues: "Equally, if someone is generally a fairly quiet person and their behaviour becomes more outgoing, that might be a sign that something's not quite right for that individual. I think it's always worthwhile keeping an eye on how someone eats, how they drink, and how they sleep. Again, if someone is noticing changes in those kinds of behaviours, that might be a sign that someone is finding their mental health difficult."

What do you do if you see this kind of behaviour in the people around you? Buckley's advice is first to have a chat. "It doesn't need to be a heavy mental health question, you can just ask how someone's doing. 'How are things going for you at the minute?' And I think once you have the open question, it's important that you listen to the answer respectfully and without judgment. **That individual might not want to talk about what they're experiencing, and you can't pull them down that road if they don't want to go there**. Equally, they might want to disclose something quite difficult to you. So if you do ask that kind of open question, sit back and listen to the answer and respond appropriately."

How you then support someone close to you with mental health issues is up to you, depending on how involved you want to become. As Buckley explains: "I think it's really important to think about the role you want to play with someone else for their mental health. A key question someone might want to ask themselves is: 'Do I want to be a carer for this person?' Because in some relationships, that might be entirely appropriate and the right thing to do. In other relationships, it might not be. It's important for someone supporting someone else to think through a few things. That might be stuff like recognising there are practical things you can do for someone. You perhaps, for example, could say, 'I can come to an appointment with you if you like,' or, 'I can help you with some specific tasks that you're struggling to do at this point in time. I can be there for you as a friend and I can listen to you.' But there are things that you might not be able to do or might not want to do. You might not want to take on someone's emotional distress. You can't fix someone's problems for them, you can help them and support them, but you need to recognise that they are grown up, they can make their own decisions as well. It comes back to being self-aware. If you become aware that supporting someone has been difficult for you, take some time out."

Alongside learning how to look after yourself, as Mvula, Carner, Dave, and Blake discussed above, it's vital to know how to ask for help. If you're struggling to know what to do or where to go, speak to a trusted friend, family member, team member, or health service. There's loads of support out there and all it takes is one conversation to start moving in a more positive direction.

Mind, Help Musicians and Music Support have free confidential helplines that we've listed in the resources section, and the Incorporated Society of Musicians also has a helpline and a free counselling service for members. BAPAM offer access to approved psychotherapists with financial assistance if you need it. The first conversation might not always be the most fruitful, so keep trying different avenues until you find a supportive ear.

Mind recently did some research on the users of their helpline and found that, for many people, it was the first time they had spoken to anyone about their mental health concerns and it took them around six months to make that initial contact. As Buckley explains, that's "an incredible amount of time to wait before asking for help, to hold and sit with the fact that you think your mental health is deteriorating or not in a good place." He continues: "Mental health is like other health problems or other problems more generally. The longer you leave it, generally speaking, the harder it is to figure out what's happening and how to fix it." So get into the habit of addressing problems straight away in order to find the most effective treatment, and get better as quickly as possible.

To reiterate points we've made in this chapter:

- There is a wealth of research to suggest that **musicians are at a higher risk of developing mental health issues** due to the pressures of the job.

- However, unless you're experiencing mental illness that requires treatment, **there are some steps you can take to foster good mental health** in your daily life.

- That starts with **education and learning what it is that you need to be happy and healthy**. What does that look like for you?

- You then need to **implement self-care into your daily routine and career**, which might mean making changes, big or small, and articulating those needs to people around you.

- If you do need mental health treatment, **get professional help as soon as possible** so you can find the support and tools you need to foster good health. If you don't find the right treatment the first time, keep looking until you discover a route that works.

- When it comes to helping others with their mental health, offer them a chance to talk while **avoiding judgement and being respectful**. Think carefully about how you can best support that person whilst still prioritising your own mental health.

CHAPTER 12

SUBSTANCE USE AND ADDICTION

MUSIC, DRUGS, AND ALCOHOL have an extensive shared history. This goes as far back as at least the 1800s, where 'medicine shows' would see musicians providing the entertainment around sales pitches for 'miracle cure' drugs.[1] More recently, there have been the supposed party legends of the rock and roll era, the proliferation of psychedelic drugs in the 20th Century, ecstasy booms around both acid house and EDM in the '90s, and the significance of everything from cough syrup to Xanax in the SoundCloud rap scene. It's not hard to find references to booze and drugs within the lyrics of today's biggest pop tunes; in the past, famous musicians might, at some point, have feared being 'outed' for drug use, but in 2020, more than ever, it's front and centre.

Because of the lack of structure that comes with life as a musician, and workplace norms you'd hardly associate with a 'proper' job, alcohol and all kinds of drugs can be very easily accessible and are totally socially acceptable. Some sort of consumption might follow a good or a bad gig, notably in an attempt to maintain the adrenaline high most performers experience when they're on stage. Drugs and alcohol are excused in the studio as tools to 'heighten creativity', there's little reason for business lunches to be dry, and late nights and late mornings enable a multitude of excess. Throw in the pressures of the job — maintaining a certain level of perceived success; performing live, in interviews and in the studio — and it's easy to see how you might develop reliance on some sort of substance to get through the day.

There's been quite a bit of research looking at substance use in the music industry that outlines what we already know: popular musicians have widespread use of substances overall.[2] Alongside musicians, business executives are known for risk-taking and substance misuse, too.[3] Part of this is down to the working environment. In a study of 24 band members, variety acts, and DJs in Glasgow, researchers found a workplace that had continual opportunities for free alcohol consumption.[4] Drinking 'on the job' was normal, expected, and sometimes encouraged by peers, the public, and employers. This reflects an environment that endorses and supports substance use behaviours, and may create a culture of drinking that enables pop musicians to drink more frequently and develop problems more readily than both classical musicians and the general population.

The result of that research is confirmed by Everything Everything frontman Jonathan Higgs, who says drinking and drug taking to excess is accepted as part of life in the music industry, especially while on tour. He explains:

"It's quite a strange lifestyle being in the music industry. Being in a touring band, you are quite disconnected from normal society in lots of ways and you don't have a nine to five. You are essentially going out every night, so the norms about excess get very quickly forgotten. You forget after a few years what's normal. **Addictions can start really easily, and the weird thing about the job is that bad behaviour, drinking to excess, and taking drugs is almost encouraged, it's part of the role you are supposed to fulfil**. If you haven't got your head screwed on right then you get lost in it all. That happens all the time unless you know what the hell is going on."

In another study, responses from 249 male musicians — 113 working in classical music and 136 in heavy metal — suggested differences in drinking behaviours between the two genres. Those working in heavy metal consumed more alcohol than the classical musicians, and 85.3% reported regular use, compared to 76.1% of those working in the classical genre.[5] Heavy metal musicians also drank alcohol more frequently (76.8%) than the general population (64.9%). Results from both genres suggest a pattern of regular substance use activity in musicians overall.

Beyond the workplace, what else makes popular musicians likely to engage in substance use? Although there is no conclusive link between creativity and mental illness, there has been a link made between creativity and sensation seeking in jazz musicians,[6] and all forms of substance use have been positively associated with sensation seeking in popular musicians more generally.[7] On top of this, lifestyle, prescription, and illicit drugs have been described as ways of managing:

- **Music performance anxiety;**[8]
- **Dealing with stress;**[9]
- **Enhancing creativity;**[10]
- **Coping physically or emotionally with the pressures of a musical career.**[11]

Imogen Heap, who entered the music industry aged 17, found herself immersed in a culture where drinking alcohol every day was considered the norm. As well as drinking because of unlimited availability, she accepts that she also used alcohol as a crutch to give her confidence in intimidating situations. She says:

> "In the beginning, I had three or four different producers [helping to make my record], so I was on my own a lot with a group of older people. They had been in the business and knew all the tools and [how to use] the mixing desks that I didn't yet fully know as well, so I felt insecure and intimidated. Dealing with that involved a lot of drinking. It was like, 'If I have a glass of wine, I'll lighten up and won't feel so intimated.'"

In short, there are several reasons why musicians might start experimenting with drugs and alcohol, and then progress on to using them as a coping mechanism, particularly when things start going wrong.

DEFINING ADDICTION

Don't think we're making any moral judgements here: substance use isn't necessarily bad in and of itself. But we've also seen that problems can arise when use crosses the line into misuse, and then addiction. There's a sliding scale of use that will impact everyone differently, but a clear red flag to look out for is **continued use despite negative consequences**. That could mean behaviour that continues despite clear impact on someone's relationships, health, work, or bank balance.

While this chapter focuses on drug and alcohol use, addictive behaviour doesn't only happen with those substances. Addiction generally is defined by the NHS as not having control over doing, taking or using something to the point where it could be harmful to you[12] and is said to impact one-third of the population. It can include compulsive engagement with a variety of things including gambling, work, internet, porn, sex, solvents, shopping, and food, all of which are worthy of treatment. Various addictions may coexist in one person at any time, and transferring addictions from one to another is also common (but doesn't ultimately solve the problem, which is the addictive behaviour).

Addiction is not experienced by everyone who fancies trying out some sort of substance, or whatever their vice may be. Some people can have a night of heavy drinking and call it a day for the rest of the week, or might only take drugs a few times a year. For others, those who have what Shireen Janti, an addiction counselling specialist at Grammy-supported music and health charity MusicCares, refers to as "an allergy of the body," the drive to continue consuming can feel impossible to ignore.

There can be myriad explanations for this. When it comes to substance use, the most common reasons for the addictive behaviour Janti sees in the musicians she works with involve misusing drugs or alcohol to try and mask feelings of depression, anxiety, stress, and exhaustion, and to manage the pressure to be 'good enough'. Psychotherapist and Babyshambles member Adam Ficek frames addiction within an 'affect regulation' framework and views it as "our attempt to regulate ourselves emotionally through external stimuli — which is even more impactful in an industry of tension", he says. Therapist Adrianna Irvine additionally points to loneliness, the emotional turbulence of being away from home, highs and lows, and identity issues — as well as if musicians 'make it' and if they don't. She adds: "Substances get layered on top of an inability to feel good about oneself; to feel talented, to feel clever, needed and wanted. Addiction isn't really about the substances. It's an illness of feelings and appetites and for our inability to control, enhance, annihilate, or tweak certain feelings, so we will feed, or starve, an appetite."[13]

The NHS says there are lots of reasons why addictions begin:[14]

- In the case of drugs, alcohol, and nicotine, **these substances affect the way you feel, both physically and mentally**. These feelings can be enjoyable and create a powerful urge to use the substances again.
- **Gambling may result in a similar mental "high"** after a win, followed by a strong urge to try again and recreate that feeling. This can develop into a habit that becomes very hard to stop.
- Being addicted to something means that **not having it causes withdrawal symptoms or a "come down"**. Because this can be unpleasant, it's easier to carry on having or doing what you crave, and so the cycle continues. Often, an addiction gets out of control because you need more and more to satisfy a craving and achieve the "high".
- Some **studies suggest addiction is genetic, but environmental factors,** such as being around other people with addictions, **are also thought to increase the risk.**
- An addiction can be a way of **blocking out difficult issues**. Unemployment and poverty can trigger addiction, along with stress and emotional or professional pressure.

According to the World Drug Report 2019, 35m people were estimated to be experiencing drug use disorders in 2016, or 0.7% of the world's population aged 15–64.[15] In the UK, drug and alcohol dependence is said to impact 3.3% of the adult population, and research suggests that both types of substance dependence are twice as likely in men than among women.[16] However, MusiCares suggest those stats are higher within the music profession due to the "occupational related hazards of being a musician, like playing in clubs and bars, and stresses of touring and availability".

In Russell Brand's book *Recovery*,[17] he points to unresolved pain as the reason behind substance misuse, noting the comments of a counsellor at a treatment centre where he got clean. In response to Brand's suggestion that drugs allowed him to just about manage to navigate the complexities of life, she replied: "How clever of you to find drugs. Well done, you found a way to keep yourself alive."[18] It was a sympathetic response to an ultimately ineffective and unhealthy coping strategy: keeping yourself alive with drugs or alcohol isn't a plan that's likely to pan out well in the long term, particularly if you won't seek help to sort out what's going on underneath. The tragic early deaths of much-loved talents like Amy Winehouse, Whitney Houston, Lil Peep, and Mac Miller may all have been alcohol and drug-related, but it's also fair to suggest that each of those artists were using substances as their way of coping with deeper issues. Resolution of those issues may, therefore, have prevented such extreme substance use. As Brand later puts it: "**The reason you must tackle your addiction, no matter how moderate it may seem or whether it be socially sanctioned is it will, in the end, fail you.**"[19]

An important addition to this: you don't need to be conscious of an underlying issue for consumption to become a problem. Addiction isn't picky, and it can strike even if you consider yourself to be in tip-top mental health with no concerns in the world.

WHAT DOES ADDICTION LOOK LIKE?

Addiction is described as a progressive illness that gets worse over time, so doesn't immediately manifest as something extreme. In early use, it can be as simple as not being able to stop once you've started — so not being able to have one or two drinks and leave it at that, or always wanting the party to continue, despite the consequences, even if you can often go days or months without using in between. In a music industry context, according to Shireen Janti, an early warning sign of substance misuse in particular is unreliability — so not showing up for work, or showing up but not being fully present. "All of a sudden they have excuses, why they are late or can't even be there, or they do show up but you know that something is off," she explains. Anger, belligerence, overly-emotional or isolating behaviour can also be tell-tale signs. Which is precisely what Jonathan Higgs recalls going through while excessively drinking during the making of the band's third record. He says:

"I was going through a very odd time at home and while we were writing and recording, I was just moody, angry, pissed off with everybody the whole time. I remember trying to record something at some point and I just didn't get out of bed. The guys came in like: 'What the hell are you doing? We've got to do this.' And I was like: 'Fuck that!' Our manager came a bit later to visit us and I just wouldn't talk to him. It wasn't long after that one of the guys in the band said something like, 'I don't really want to do this because it's shit if it's going to be like this,' and I thought, 'What am I doing? What is this even about?' It's just bollocks really, it's me thinking there is some great tragedy when there isn't, it's just me drinking all the time and being a very immature little person. In the intervening years, the guys have said that making the third record was really hard and I was kind of like, 'Was it? Oh, I don't remember that...' Clearly it was for them and not as much for me because I was the one that was being hard!'"

Discussing his own issues with drugs, The 1975's Matty Healy recounted in a 2018 interview that crunch time came after George and the rest of his band attempted an intervention over dinner one evening. His initial response to the intervention was not positive: "Listen, everyone has to get on board because I'm the fucking main deal. If you want songs, we're just going to have to get on with it." He said that the next morning he woke up and realised he was in a real pickle. "I realised that [what I'd said] was absolute fucking bullshit. So I went downstairs and told George I should go to rehab."[20]

It's worth pondering how different Healy's or Higgs' experience might have been as a solo artist, without a close support network at least attempting to sort things out. While it's possible to spot evidence that there's something up with others, recognising a substance use issue within yourself, especially without the benefit of hindsight that Higgs has now, isn't so clear cut. Janti, who has been in recovery for alcohol and drug misuse for 30 years, explains:

According to MusiCares, the following could be warning signs of drug and alcohol addiction in musicians:

- Missing gigs, showing up late
- Being late to the studio, not knowing parts
- Fighting with bandmates
- Hiring and firing of management
- Band breakups
- Using drugs and alcohol to get through gigs
- Major financial problems resulting from drug or alcohol use
- Loss of motivation to play
- Not 'feeling' the music anymore

"In my experience, because addiction is so cunning and powerful, you minimise it. **It's an addiction of denial, you keep minimising and making excuses and justifying. Even though you can see your life falling apart, you make excuses for it**. A lot of people will *blame*. Instead of owning and being responsible, it's like, 'Oh, my wife this or my husband that, or my kids or my manager or band members this.' It's always somebody else's fault why they need to take the edge off. 'Well it helps me, I need to do this, or I'm happy,' whatever. It's very hard for most people who are in the grips of alcoholism or addiction to just right away admit that they have it. Most people around you are going to see the problem before you."

For Andy Franks, who spent most of his time as a functioning alcoholic while working as tour manager for Coldplay, Robbie Williams, and Depeche Mode, it took getting sacked for him to seek help, at which point he was drinking morning, noon and night. "Alcoholics are very clever about concealing what they do, they hide it either through embarrassment or necessity," he says. "I used to get up when I was at home in the night and start drinking spirits, which I never used to drink, to get a hit really. I don't know if my body craved it, physically or mentally, but there was always an excuse that I would be able to use to justify that I needed it. There was always a reason to do it and never look past that what I was doing was crazy."

Franks makes a good point about acknowledging changes in behaviour. Drinking spirits when you never did before, or drinking at home by yourself where previously you've only drunk socially, or finding that drugs have moved from a social distraction to a solitary endeavour, are all signs that you may be more reliant on substances than you'd like to admit. It's useful to keep tabs on these changes in behaviour when they're still a habit, rather than a lifestyle.

Addiction can be especially hard to identify when everyone around you is doing the same thing. This can be particularly pertinent in the music industry, where drinking and using are so entrenched in the culture of the business. Recovering addict Yasmine Ben-Afia, who supports other addicts through the 12 Step programme and worked on the business side of music for eight years, says that when addressing problems in your own life, it's important to avoid comparison. "You have to look at your own individual circumstances," she explains. "Everyone around you might be using similarly to you, but that doesn't mean your own using isn't problematic or that their using isn't either. Ultimately, **it is down to us to define what our personal limits are** and if we feel our behaviour has become problematic, that cannot be measured against the behaviour of others."

Unless you're struggling with addiction, it is possible to just say no if you feel that engaging with drugs and alcohol isn't what you want to do (and of course that's vital to do if you are in recovery from addiction). Ben-Afia continues: "It might seem like everyone is drinking or using and it's 'uncool' not to partake, but as the rate of youth sobriety rises[21] and wellness culture pervades society, now more than ever, health is considered a priority and we all have a right and responsibility to look after ours, regardless of what those around us are doing."

DEALING WITH IT

If you *are* able to recognise that you might have a substance use or general addiction problem, the first thing to do is get help. You'll find lots of suggestions of where to go in the resources section at the end of this book. We understand it might feel hard to approach a professional with this sort of concern, although if your reticence is because you consider your situation a 'shameful secret', that might already be all you need to know about whether help is needed. In any case, approaching clients in a non-judgemental way is pretty much day one training for any therapist or counsellor.

Speaking of treatment, Adam Ficek says: "It needs to be attacked with a two-pronged approach because the addiction isn't really the problem, it's the underlying factors which drive people to create clunky ways of getting their needs met, as it were." As Russell Brand outlines in his book, his impulse to engage in addictive behaviour was triggered by "a matrix of disturbances" which were, in reality, everyday emotions that he wasn't equipped to handle without the help of 'something else'. "The stimulus-response relationship between me, myself and the world was like this: 'I'm lonely – have sex', 'I'm sad – get drunk', 'I'm bored – eat a cake'."[22]

Since working a 12 Step programme and admitting he had issues that required addressing, he was able to address the root causes of those unconscious responses. Brand writes: "Once I had 'admitted I had a problem', drinking and drugs and the impulse to use them were under observation. When I 'came to believe' there was another way to live, this gave me pause, a moment to consider. When I 'made the decision to turn over my will', that meant that when the impulse to use came I conceded that my mental processes were no longer to be trusted. I had to ask for help." Which is where a therapist, sober coach, and community-based support, like 12 Step programmes (which are used by the anonymous groups we'll point to in resources), come in handy — to untangle impulsive behaviour by providing people with new mental processes and a balanced listening ear that can be trusted.

There's also no one size fits all solution — Brand is an advocate of the Minnesota model of treatment aka 12 Steps, but Self-Management and Recovery Training (SMART) is a popular alternative for people who need a more self-directed approach. The key is to do some research and find the one that works for you. Don't suffer in silence and expect to be able to work your way through what can be some very messy and complicated thoughts alone, because there is lots of support out there (as we detail in the resources section).

ADDRESSING ISSUES IN OTHERS

Acknowledging a potential substance misuse issue in somebody else — like a band member of anyone within an artist's team — requires some introspection first. Shireen Janti describes addiction as a 'family disease' that relies on co-dependency around an addict to continue. Co-dependency is described by Mental Health America as an emotional and behavioural condition that can result in people forming one-sided, emotionally destructive and/or abusive relationships.[23] Those who have the condition try to take care of a person who is experiencing difficulty, like those struggling with addiction, but the caretaking can become compulsive and defeating. The organisation continues: "Co-dependents often take on a martyr's role and become "benefactors" to an individual in need and typically sacrifice their own needs to take care of another person."

This is a problem because when co-dependents place other people's health, welfare, and safety before their own, they can lose contact with their own needs, desires, and sense of self. You might remember us talking about boundaries in the Fans and Boundaries chapter when we referenced research by Brené Brown, and this is what's needed here, too. To reiterate: it's only by creating a healthy distance between yourself and others that you'll be able to have enough energy to be the most energetic, kind, and compassionate version of yourself in all areas of your life.

"So anybody who is close to that person, they need to do their own work too, to be true to themselves, and not always be focusing on the person who is in trouble," Janti says. "Because a lot of times when they get better and stronger, they are able to help the other person. **People feel guilty that if they start taking care of themselves, they are abandoning the other person, but if you don't take care of yourself, you go down with them.**"

Co-dependency can turn into an addiction in and of itself, which is what mental health and wellbeing consultant Sam Parker has been in recovery from for 20 years. She explains:

> "It's a weird addiction to have as it doesn't have the outward signs that other addictions have. No messy or life-threatening drug or alcohol induced dramas, no gambling debts, risky sexual activity, nothing in fact that seems terribly 'wrong'. It's subtle and the only reason I came to know I had it was because of my experience of my best friend's spiral into drug addiction in the mid '90s in our twenties working in the music industry."

At the peak of her friend's health issues, Parker says she'd been helping her for four years, despite friends and family telling her she should let go. She says that becoming so consumed with another person's problems meant she lost all sense of self. Parker continues:

> "I found that I couldn't walk away and felt that it was my duty to save her, as 'that's what you do when you love someone' and if I didn't, she would die and it would be my fault because I couldn't hack it. I was very confused about where she ended and I began. I would often feel her feelings so keenly that they felt like my own. I had no idea about self-care, as my 'self' was lost deep inside me, cut off from my consciousness. I was convinced that I was okay and that my only problem was her addiction. If she stopped being an addict, then I would be fine!"

With a lot of introspection and support from the co-dependency recovery programme, Parker has gained more awareness about how to manage relationships. "It was never about what my best friend was or wasn't doing, I was so detached from my core self and my feelings, that sometimes the only way to feel was to do so vicariously through someone else's drama, with the added bonus that if the pain was outside of myself, then I had a chance of fixing it," she continues. "Only when I failed at fixing her and was left with my own feelings of despair, failure, and exhaustion that would not go away, did I realise there was something wrong with me and get the help I needed to heal."

In her previous work as an artist manager, Parker found that some of her co-dependency traits made her very good at aspects of her job, and in her own words, "terrible at others!" She has come across many artists and managers who are co-dependent and now leads workshops to help others and shine a light on this particular addiction. To find out more about co-dependency, head to the resources section.

Alongside maintaining healthy boundaries, when it comes to having a conversation with someone you're worried about, sensitivity and understanding are key. Janti continues: "I've found that **attacking or immediately assuming that you know what is going on usually sets people up to be defensive and not responsive**."

Instead, asking someone if they are okay and offering them the opportunity to open up might kickstart a conversation and course of action. If that isn't received well, Janti recommends offering reassurance that you're there for them and setting some boundaries if behaviour escalates. She adds: "The limit at first may be; you need to control yourself, you can't come to band rehearsal or play loaded." If the person keeps crossing those limits, then perhaps the next step is to ask them to seek the help they need, before the working situation becomes unmanageable. Having an open culture of dialogue and the promise of support within a team is something anyone can do to try and ensure situations don't reach rock bottom before being addressed.

In an industry of deadlines and schedules, and with lots of money hinging on those being met, it can also be helpful to try and play the long game. Janti adds:

> "A lot of managers, labels, or tour people who are supporting the band will be scared to say anything because if they did, they would either get fired or not get paid, so they are scared to have a voice and just continue to watch the artist or the person slowly start spiralling out. But over and over again, I have seen people that are so scared to get help or tell someone they need help because of the monetary thing, and what happens is they either end up just not showing up anyway, or even dying or ODing, so that is not really the answer. **It's about not being quiet and supporting people to let them know that you are there and you care and that their life matters first**. If somebody is willing to get help and they really need it, I always say, 'What's a month out of your entire life, give or take, whatever that would look like?' A period of time which changes your life so you can always show up and never have to disappoint your people or your fans, period."

None of this is to suggest that getting someone else to realise they need help is easy, as the motivation ultimately has to come from the person who's suffering and at a time when they are ready. This is why it's important to take a step back if needs be. That's something Adam Ficek has experienced, as he explains:

> "I've been in situations with some very high-profile people I've worked with and management have tried to push [for help] and the artist hasn't [been willing]. Other times, management have pushed and the artist has gone to rehab and they come out and are back on it and it's more dangerous. When I work in addiction now, [threats from]

family members, spouses, or children ultimately really lack the potency that people need to get through those struggles. But you can create a dialogue and offer support or some of the systems that are in place, whether that be fellowships or charities."

To conclude this chapter:

- Substance misuse and addiction aren't experienced by everyone who engages with drugs, alcohol, and other vices, but **it's worth keeping an eye on consumption if you feel you can't go without or can't stop once you've started**, especially if doing so has negative consequences.

- This is especially true in the music industry, where drugs and alcohol are often accepted as part and parcel of life as a musician and addictive behaviour can be difficult to identify due to widespread and accepted use. **Only you know what's problematic for you and what your personal limits are**.

- If those around you are concerned about your behaviour but you think there's nothing wrong, it's worth remembering that Janti said **denial and blame are often associated with addiction** and that most people around you will see the problem before you do.

- If you are able to recognise that there's an issue within yourself, **seek help as soon as possible**. You'll find lots of ideas of where to go in the resources section at the end of this book.

- Before approaching others who you suspect might have an issue with addiction, it's vital to make sure you're in a **strong place with your own health and sense of self first**, and that you understand that the motivation to get help must ultimately come from the person themselves.

CHAPTER 13

DISORDERED EATING AND BODY IMAGE

THESE DAYS, WE'RE BOMBARDED left, right, and centre with messages relating to the physical benefits of getting the 'right' kind of nutrition. So much so, it's easy to forget just how vital a healthy and balanced approach to food is for our mental health, too. **You need to be adequately nourished to function at your best on both an emotional and intellectual level** — it might surprise you to know that 20% of your body's energy output is used by your brain[1] — and malnourishment is associated with difficulty concentrating, disrupted sleep[2], and general poor mental health, including anxiety and depression.[3] The good news is that your body is a highly intelligent machine that knows what it needs to keep up with your energy demands, and it sends a variety of signals to your brain to indicate hunger. When we're born, we have an innate knowledge of how to recognise those cues and what to do about them. We know what we want to eat and when, and don't have any issue with making that clear to whoever's looking after us.

But at some point along the journey from child to adult, there are a few things that can mess up that intuition. 'Diet culture' is one such impediment — as intuitive eating dietician Christy Harrison explains in her *Anti-Diet* book, many types of diet have proliferated in mainstream culture since the mid-1830s.[4] The first example to be recorded was by Presbyterian minister, speaker, and LOL avoider Sylvester Graham, who decided that eating austere, bland, and non-stimulating foods was key to both health and moral virtue. Since then, a seemingly endless number of movements have attempted to convince the masses that various ruled and rigid ways of eating are the 'right' way and, as well as having nutritional value, foods have gained a moral value too: some are 'good' while others are 'bad'. (To be clear, we're not talking about medically recommended diets as a result of allergies and health conditions like Celiac Disease, which are absolutely the right way to go for some people. There's also nothing wrong with dietary preferences relating to culture, religion, or ethnicity.)

Today, Instagram is awash with modern-day versions of Graham, preaching 'clean', restrictive, and oftentimes expensive ways of eating, accompanied by filtered photos of meals, bodies, faces, and crockery sets that are designed (and focus-grouped) to be 'aspirational'. Through social media and the media at large, we all hear and see constant messages that suggest we should mould ourselves into and follow what is a very limited representation of the variety of healthy bodies and diets that exist in the world at large. It's also strange that some influencers are attempting to dictate (whether consciously or not) what's right and healthy for a body that they don't inhabit. Only your body knows what it needs and what size it wants to be, and BMI scales and cultural pressures don't have any influence on that.

Think about this: how often do you see an 'average' looking person in the media? In the entertainment industries, we usually see tall, skinny models, tiny and toned pop stars, ripped men, and curvaceous bodies hailed as part of the body positivity movement (whether they identify as such or not). With a few exceptions, there isn't much representation out there for a bog-standard (and inherently beautiful) healthy body — which is strange, because that's in total contrast to the reality that surrounds us on every high street, at every gig, and in every office, school, and supermarket. And we *know* it's strange, but if we're not careful, we forget. Which has the greater influence on our perception — the extremes we see in the media, or the average we see in everyday life?

For **musicians who may be in the public eye, the pressure to meet unreasonable standards is especially intense**. We hear countless examples of musicians who have been told to lose weight by their teams. Brand campaigns, modelling deals, red carpets, and photoshoots all add pressure for artists to look a certain way, dictated by fashion directors, stylists, artists, and advertising, and looking that certain way may simply not be someone's natural or healthy state.

Discourse in the media regarding the bodies of famous people piles on further pressure. The conversation and opinions surrounding Adele's weight loss were deafening, and Billie Eilish began her 2020 world tour with a commentary on the scrutiny she experiences regarding her body. "While I feel your stares, your disapproval or your sighs of relief, if I lived by them, I'd never be able to move," she said. "Would you like me to be smaller? Weaker? Softer? Taller? Would you like me to be quiet? Do my shoulders provoke you? Does my chest? Am I my stomach? My hips?" As *Guardian Music* Deputy Editor Laura Snapes writes, whether living in a media-approved 'ideal' body or one that sways further towards the average, female stars in particular often can't win.

"Being anointed a liberating force in the body-image stakes is its own kind of prison, one that preserves physicality as the ultimate measure of a female star's worth — and the standard by which they can be undermined," she says.[5]

It's not just female artists who face the expectations of what a 'perfect' body should look like, or fall into the trappings of diet culture. One Direction member turned solo artist Liam Payne, for instance, doesn't beat around the bush when he discussed his regime before shooting a mostly-derobed Hugo Boss ad campaign: "I had to eat five meals a day and drink 1,200-calorie protein shakes almost every hour — to pile on loads of weight. Then you have to train hard every day. I call it fish month because white fish was the only thing I was allowed to eat for four weeks."[6] He didn't have much fun. "I wouldn't rule out doing another campaign," he added, "but I wouldn't want to repeat that diet." Aaron Flores — a dietitian in California who specialises in intuitive eating and eating disorder recovery — says the way men engage with diet culture is often through what he calls the "life hack". He continues: "It's all about how can we optimise our performance, how can we hack eating to be this much more efficient at work, this much more successful."[7]

EATING DISORDERS

This obsession with weight and bodies, and the idea of an 'ideal', can result in dieting, disordered eating, and excessive exercise, which can lead to mental health issues, malnutrition, and the inability to function at your best. It can also lead to eating and body image related disorders. Diet culture and societal pressures are just two factors that can lead to the development and exacerbation of food related mental health problems, which may not be tied to a desire to be 'thin' and can also be influenced by food insecurity,[8] trauma, low self-confidence, family history,[9] and act as a coping mechanism to deal with the tougher facets of life.

These are the most common types of eating disorders:[10]

- **Anorexia nervosa**: characterised by trying to keep weight as low as possible by not eating enough food or exercising too much, or both.
- **Bulimia**: people who have bulimia go through periods where they eat a lot of food in a very short amount of time (this drive to eat can be because the body is starving) and then make themselves sick, use laxatives, or do excessive exercise, or a combination of these, to try to stop themselves gaining weight.
- **Binge-eating disorder**: this involves regularly eating large portions of food at once until you feel uncomfortably full, and then feeling upset or guilty, which can be followed by a period of starvation (which may cause or further the drive to binge — it's the body's survival mechanism).
- **Orthorexia**: an obsession with proper or 'healthful' eating. People with orthorexia become so fixated on so-called 'healthy eating' that they damage their own well-being.

Demi Lovato developed bulimia at the age of nine, which she says was a result of eating disorders, substance misuse, and mental health issues in her family, as well as being bullied at school.[11] Kesha, on the other hand, has said that she was "slowly starving herself" as she became more famous and avoided food for fear of becoming "fat".[12] She says: "I remember being like, 'If I'm fat, I can't be a singer because pop stars can't eat food—they can't be fat.'" She continues: "**The music industry has set unrealistic expectations for what a body is supposed to look like**, and I started becoming overly critical of my own body because of that."[13] Elton John suffered from bulimia for six years after becoming "paranoid" about his weight during his younger years,[14] while former One Direction member Zayn Malik started going days without eating while dealing with the pressure of being in the band. "I think it was about control," he writes. "I didn't feel like I had control over anything else in my life, but food was something I could control, so I did."[15]

Taylor Swift has spoken about starving herself and engaging in obsessive behaviour, including over-exercising and keeping lists of everything she ate. She says that was a result of media attention on her body and perceived praise from stylists for being a small size. She says:

> "I remember how, when I was 18, that was the first time I was on the cover of a magazine, and the headline was like 'Pregnant at 18?'. And it was because I had worn something that made my lower stomach look not flat. So I just registered that as a punishment. And then I'd walk into a photoshoot and be in the dressing room, and somebody who worked at a magazine would say, 'Oh, wow, this is so amazing that you can fit into the sample sizes. Usually, we have to make alterations to the dresses, but we can take them right off the runway and put them on you!' And I looked at that as a pat on the head. You register that enough times, and you just start to accommodate everything towards praise and punishment, including your own body."[16]

BODY DYSMORPHIC DISORDER

While body image concerns are commonly associated with eating disorders, and the symptoms for **body dysmorphic disorder** (BDD) are similar, they aren't the same thing. According to mental health charity Mind, someone experiencing an eating disorder is generally mainly concerned about their weight and shape, while someone experiencing BDD, which is an anxiety disorder, is likely to have other concerns around body image — for example, they may also be worried about a particular facial feature.[17]

Mind says that you might be given a diagnosis of BDD if you:

- **Experience obsessive worries** about one or more perceived flaws in your physical appearance, and the flaw cannot be seen by others or appears very slight.

- **Develop compulsive behaviours and routines**, such as excessive use of mirrors or picking your skin, to deal with the worries you have about the way you look.

If you have BDD, these obsessions and behaviours cause emotional distress and have a significant impact on your ability to carry on with your day-to-day life.

Risk factors that might mean you're more likely to experience BDD include abuse or bullying, low self-esteem, fear of being alone or isolated, perfectionism or competing with others, genetics, depression, anxiety, or obsessive-compulsive disorder. Psychotherapist and body image specialist Liz Ritchie (who we heard from in the Social Media chapter) says the main cause of body image issues she sees in the patients she works with at St Andrew's Healthcare is low self-esteem and self-worth, which can progress to self-harming, eating disorders, and social anxiety. She adds: "A lot of the young people, men, and women that we see have history of trauma, emotional, sexual and physical abuse. We've also got [patients who are on the] autistic spectrum disorder, which is an awful lot of our men and some women, who have been undiagnosed for many years. We usually find that with patients who have had trauma in their lives and a history of abuse as children, they never had any sense of validation, nurturing, or even how to look after themselves."

Garbage frontwoman Shirley Manson has spoken about experiencing BDD, and describes her experience like so:

"I always turned up five hours late because I'd be fussing about my hair and make-up. I would change into a million different outfits, and make them change the lighting a million times, I would spend two hours crying in the toilet – and whatever the result, I always thought I looked disgusting. I would look in the mirror every morning and be upset. I would get dressed and look in the mirror again, and be upset. It could be anything; I could be too fat, too thin, too flat chested. My hands were not long enough, my neck was too long. My tummy stuck out, my bum was too big... It was driving me crazy and I was wasting energy – precious energy – that I should have been putting into my music or my family or friends."[18]

Manson says BDD is something she'll "always battle with" and defines it as not seeing yourself "physically as you actually are." She continues: "I always feel embarrassed talking about it because I feel a lot of people will roll their eyes and say: 'Oh look, there she is, harping on about the way she looks. Well, she can't feel that bad as she has her photograph in the paper.' But I feel I should tell the truth about how women feel and how we do things that are contradictory. That's just human nature. Yes, I do have my picture taken, and I look glamorous and I have my hair and make-up done for me, but don't mistake that for being in love with the way I look. I look at those photos sometimes and, well ... it doesn't make me feel good."[19]

PREVALENCE IN MUSIC

While we don't have research to suggest how prevalent BDD is in the music world, **there is evidence to suggest that musicians and performers may be particularly susceptible to disordered ways of eating**. In a 2017 study of 301 musicians aged over 18, 32% of participants said they had experienced an eating disorder in their lifetime (42% of females and 18% of males).[20] In addition, 19% of participants showed pathological values in the Eating Disorder Examination Questionnaire Global Score (a tool to measure the range and severity of eating disorder features), suggesting that they were experiencing an eating disorder at the time of the survey. It's difficult to provide a sound comparison of how prevalent eating disorders are in the music community when compared to the general population due to issues with data gathering; however, research suggests that between 1.9% and

5.1% of the British population suffers from an eating disorder.[21] This suggests quite strongly that the issue may be disproportionately prevalent in musicians.

According to the 2017 study, reasons for this are:

- Increased **perfectionism, depression, anxiety, and stress** due to the demands of their job.
- **Various developmental and biopsychosocial factors** which are present in many musicians' lifestyle and training, including an unpredictable work schedule. Performing and low income are major factors that result in a mental (loneliness, anxiety, depression, personality disorders, substance misuse) and practical (irregular meals when travelling) predicament that can draw people into a vicious circle of restrictive and disordered eating.
- As we alluded to earlier, other possible risk factors for eating disorders in musicians include **the cultural idealisation of thinness and attractiveness, pressure from parents and teachers, competitiveness, and peer pressure.**
- Also, **puberty can be a particularly at-risk stage** — it constitutes a significant transition (and a weak point) in the control of musicians' eating habits, as it's usually a time when they attempt to launch their careers while experiencing heightened body awareness and increased eating concerns.

It's important to note that despite eating disorders being commonly associated with young people, women, and low weight, there is research that challenges those perceptions. According to eating disorder charity Beat, studies suggest around a quarter of people with eating disorders are male, 80–85% of people with eating disorders are not underweight, and in 2015, 15% of the calls made to their helpline were about someone aged 40 or over.[22] As Beat says, stereotypes about who gets eating disorders might make them even harder to spot among older people, men and boys, and ethnic and cultural minority groups. This means that the real number of sufferers overall could be much higher than we think, particularly among groups like these.

SYMPTOMS AND SIGNS

So why does all of this matter? Well, in addition to having a severely negative impact on your overall health, quality of life, energy levels, and ability to spend stress-free time with others (especially since food is such an intrinsic part of social activity), experiencing an eating disorder in particular can have a direct impact on your career. As the study we referenced above points out, symptoms for musicians can include:

- **Voice dysfunction** due to vomiting or gastroesophageal reflux disease as part of bulimia;
- **Increased injuries** due to muscle atrophy and osteoporosis from malnutrition, with females at particular risk of the latter;
- Then there's koilonychia (aka '**spoon nails**' — a condition resulting in abnormally thin and misshapen nails, which isn't great for some instrumentalists);
- **Fatigue and impaired brain function**.

Although eating disorders often have many physical symptoms, at the end of the day, the diseases themselves are very mind-based. Someone with an eating disorder can often be totally consumed by destructive thought patterns that seem very real and true, creating a tricky mindset to get out of. But it's not impossible, and with the right support, lots of people make a full recovery. If you suspect that you, or someone you know, might be dealing with an eating disorder, the most important thing to do is reach out for help. Your GP or an eating disorder charity like Beat, which offers a helpline, is a good place to start. If you feel unsure about your relationship with food and body image, it might be worth having a look through the list of emotional and behavioural symptoms detailed at the end of this chapter.

Psychotherapist Emmy Brunner, who is CEO of The Recover Clinic, says:

> "If you recognise that how you feel has led you to make negative choices with regard to your food, then that is an indicator that something isn't quite right. When we don't have issues with food, we just eat intuitively and enjoy our relationship with it. **As soon as food becomes something that creates anxiety and starts impacting our social choices, that's when you know there is something to work on.**"

Examples of choices to be wary of include missing social events due to fear of what you might be expected to eat at them, and often making food choices for reasons other than what's available, your hunger levels, and what you want to eat (that could include calorie numbers, compensating for what you've eaten at an earlier time, and how you feel about your weight and body image). As Brunner explains, it doesn't have to reach crisis point before you get help — and the sooner you start getting out of a challenging mindset, which can become very entrenched over time, the better. "I think what a lot of people don't realise is that **it doesn't have to escalate to a full-blown eating disorder, or you don't have to be in a complete place of physical crisis to get help**," she says. "People can have low-level anxiety or a negative relationship with food, and that is very worthy of attention and support."

As we alluded to earlier, one of the **key signs of an eating disorder is an internal dialogue that might be giving you 'rules' about eating and exercising**, and you may feel bad or guilty for not following them. It's not a positive or kind voice and can be characterised as negative and mean. What does yours sound like? "We want our overriding internal dialogue to be one of compassion and kindness," says Brunner. "If we find that voice is predominantly critical and unpleasant, that is something we need to become really mindful of." Rather than getting into battles with that critical voice and trying to negotiate with it, Brunner suggests "we need to step back and go, 'Wow my critical voice is really strong today.'" She continues: "I think what a lot of people do is get drawn into trying to placate the critical voice and soothe it, and actually the nature of that beast is that it can't be soothed. It's much better to take a step back and focus on nurturing a more compassionate alternative."

When it comes to body image, Brunner says: "If you find that your mental time is preoccupied with how you look and you are putting a lot of pressure on yourself to conform to a certain body or physical type, and if it's making you unhappy, it's a problem." Instead of trying to obtain an 'ideal' that might not be your natural body type and being overly critical of what is, Liz Ritchie encourages working towards a place of self-acceptance. She says:

> "**Look at what your strengths and weaknesses are because we've all got them. Perfection is unrealistic and it's extremely damaging to be striving for because it's unobtainable**. Self-acceptance and self-compassion is a huge thing. Anything that we don't like about ourselves, anything that we hyper-focus on, instead of thinking: 'That is something I would like to change,' we can reframe it to: 'Well, this is me, this is part of my identity that I want to accept and learn to love and to eliminate that sense of self-loathing as much as possible.' If you don't, you're going to be continually dissatisfied, and longer-term, that is something that will absolutely limit the potential for personal growth."

Some people might be able to *start* the journey of practising a kinder internal dialogue and self-acceptance alone, but we really can't stress enough the importance of getting professional help. As Brunner says, eating disorders don't have to be fully developed for sufferers to require treatment. There is a bit of a grey area between dieting, disordered eating, and clinically diagnosed eating disorders and only you, or those who love you, will be able to judge whether your health and happiness are negatively impacted.

If you think you might be in that grey area and perhaps are being influenced by pressure to conform to a certain 'standard' or bow to the (completely unreasonable) demands of those that you are working with, we get it. You might even be reading this and thinking, 'Well, this advice is all well and good for someone whose image isn't part of their job, but for me it is so I have to maintain a certain look.' To be clear, there's nothing wrong with taking pride in your appearance and working to stay fit and healthy, but there is something wrong when it becomes an obsession that adversely impacts other areas of your life.

If that chimes with you, all we'll say is that **it's worth spending some time questioning the culture that's dictated food and body-related rules and ideals, and whether your own personal values and needs truly align with those.** Who do you respect and why? What it is that you love about your friends and family? Those answers are probably not going to centre on how someone looks, what they eat, or what they weigh. So why are you (and those you may be working with) holding yourself up to different standards? With all the influences we have, it could actually be considered an act of personal activism to reject any pressure and stand up as your complete, happy, and healthy self. If anyone doesn't vibe with that, it's their problem, not yours, and they don't deserve a place in your life. When it comes to influences, here's a tip: if your perception of beauty is limited to one particular 'ideal', you can use your social media feeds to challenge that by following accounts that feature a diverse variety of bodies and faces.

According to the NHS, the list at the end of this chapter can be signs that someone might be experiencing an eating disorder. It isn't intended as a checklist — someone struggling generally won't display all of these signs and symptoms at once, and the warning signs vary across eating disorders and don't always fit into neat categories. Rather, the list is intended as a general overview of the types of behaviours that may indicate a problem. You'll also find a list of the symptoms commonly associated with body dysmorphic disorder, taken from Mind. We'll say this again: if you recognise any of the following within yourself or someone you know, please seek out some support as soon as you can. You'll find more details of that in the resources section at the end of this book.

Finally, when it comes to trying to help other people, Brunner says that the message may not always be well-received, but it's worth mentioning something because it could help the person who is unwell recognise that there's an issue. She explains:

> "I think what so many people do is, when they have concerns about a loved one, they don't say anything because people react badly and get defensive, and they are worried about upsetting people. But **these illnesses thrive on shame, they keep people isolated, and they keep secrets**, and so when we are acting like there is not a problem, it makes it very difficult for the person suffering to be able to identify it themselves. If they intuitively feel that there is something wrong, but everybody else around them is acting like they are fine, it's actually not very helpful. It can be an uncomfortable conversation saying to somebody, 'I love you, but I'm quite concerned about you, is everything okay?' but I think it's so much more preferable than ignoring the problem."

Symptoms of eating disorders include:[23]

- Spending a lot of time **worrying about your weight and body shape**
- **Avoiding socialising** when you think food will be involved
- **Eating very little food**
- **Deliberately making yourself** sick or taking laxatives after you eat
- **Exercising too much**
- Having very **strict habits or routines** around food
- **Changes in your mood**

You may also notice physical signs, including:

- Feeling **cold, tired, or dizzy**
- **Problems with your digestion**
- Your **weight being very high or very low** for someone of your age and height
- **Not getting your period** for women and girls

Common signs and symptoms of body dysmorphic disorder[24]

People with BDD see themselves differently to how others see them. Although everyone's experience of BDD is unique, there are some common signs. If you have BDD, you experience intrusive, negative thoughts about one specific area of your body, or several areas of your body, which you think are:

- **Out of proportion**
- **Too big or too small**
- **Disfigured**
- **Lacking symmetry**

These thoughts cause you significant anxiety and you will often spend several hours a day thinking about the area or areas of concern. BDD can affect any area of the body, but common areas of anxiety include your skin, hair, nose, chin, lips, or genitals.

BDD and eating disorders share similar symptoms, such as: having poor body image, worrying excessively about your physical appearance, developing compulsive behaviours to try to deal with these worries. Some people with BDD experience an eating disorder, but not all people with eating disorders have BDD. A mental health professional, such as a psychiatrist, can assess your symptoms to help you find out whether you are experiencing BDD, an eating disorder, or both.

SOUND ADVICE

PART 3:
IMPROVING SKILLS

In this third section, you're going to learn about the skills needed to further your career, whilst remaining passionate and motivated about what you do, and how to improve your musical, performance, and creative abilities. Unlike in the classical world, practice and strategy aren't always associated with careers in pop, which can result in musicians feeling like they lack the skills and confidence to reach their full potential. The following five chapters aim to equip you with the information and strategies you need to get there. We'll offer tips and tricks for effective practice, improving performance by alleviating unhelpful anxiety, and other sound advice to help you deliver your best show. We'll end with a chapter on creativity – how to harness it, where inspiration comes from, and navigating blocks.

CHAPTER 14

SETTING GOALS

BEFORE YOU READ THIS final improving skills section, it's important to get clear on what you want from your career, and how you're going to achieve that. After all, you could be the most seasoned performer, well-practised musician, or creative genius, but without a clear plan on how to make the most of those skills, you won't fulfil your potential. So assuming you want to use your talent to achieve your dreams, we're going to first talk you through how to set goals and work towards them in an effective and considered manner.

Whatever level you're at in your career, it's worth considering the simple question: **what do you want from a career in music, and why?** For instance, is your goal to secure a childhood dream of a million-pound record deal? Or do you want to develop a deep and meaningful connection with your audience, releasing music on your own terms? Or both? Or something else altogether? Let's go one step further — what is *your* definition of success, and what does it look like to you?

Alongside the distraction of simply working to survive, all the noise from influences like social media, TV, magazines, newspapers, and the expectation of others, means it can be really hard to hear that voice inside that tells you what your heart truly desires. As we discussed in the Social Media chapter, it's easy to get sidetracked by what other people are doing, what we're being told we *should* aspire to be or do by adverts and articles, or measures of success that a manager or label might be trying to achieve (the latter is particularly pertinent — other people on your team might have their own agendas and those won't necessarily correlate with your own).

Case in point: Imogen Heap has released four albums, written a soundtrack for the acclaimed *Harry Potter and The Cursed Child* stage production, created her own musical gloves (as you do), written for Taylor Swift, been sampled by Jason Derulo, and delved into the complex world of blockchain with her Mycelia project. Despite all of this, without a Top 10 chart hit under her own name, she's unlikely to be deemed 'successful' in music by the average person who doesn't recognise her on the street. Does she care? No. She says:

> "My idea of success has always been *not* other people's version of success. If I get in a taxi and the taxi man says, 'What are you? Are you some kind of singer?' because of the way I look or they might half recognise me, or maybe I was talking on the phone and they were listening. I tell them I do sing, make records, do musical gloves, and all these things. But when they talk about music, they say, 'Oh well, maybe one day you'll make it.' Their idea of success is being on the radio, something they recognise, a famous person who must have made it.

"But **you don't have to be famous to have made it. For me, success is being able to be free to be who you are.** I think we can get set on these ideas about what success is, whether it's money or fame, but it's just an imagination of the thing, it's not real. Day-to-day, having the time or money to go and get a coffee in your favourite coffee shop, read a book, or go on a little trip to the mountains with your daughter — that is success. Having the time to experience the world, learn and collaborate, and not have to worry too much about when the next paycheque is coming."

As well as practising a mindful approach to any messages or perceptions you're bombarded with when figuring out what you want in life, it's also important that you have a clear idea of why you're doing what you do, and that you maintain that throughout your career. That sense of certainty can act like an inner compass that keeps you focused, despite all the other noise. There's no point in making vast amounts of money or achieving a number one album if you realise that, when you get there, it wasn't what you wanted in the first place, or that you were chasing a dream for the wrong reasons.

Equally, you might dream of selling out the O2 Arena in London, and be totally clear on why you want it, but without a clear plan (along with a lot of good luck and hard work), it will always remain just that — a dream. Gaining clarity and focus about what you want in life has been shown to help with motivation[1][2] and drive, and aligning goals with your passion, while knowing how you want to contribute to this world, can be a great way to make your mark, truly enjoy life, and fulfil your potential as a human being.

In this chapter, we take a deep dive into finding out what you really want to achieve and giving you the skills to structure your own journey towards it — a sort of roadmap to where you want to be. Pursuing life as a musician is tough, it's often a non-linear career, and takes deliberate intention, hard work, and the fulfilment of specific goals to achieve personal and professional success.

There's a lot of luck involved, too — unfortunately, being supremely talented doesn't always guarantee global stardom.

Or, as Ed Sheeran puts it, success is often a combination of talent and opportunity. "**I think luck is when preparation meets opportunity**," he says. "So if you work hard enough to better yourself and make yourself good and the opportunity comes, you're good enough to be elevated to the next level. For me, I just loved what I did and worked really hard at it because I loved what I did. Then an opportunity would come up and I was good enough to take it by the horns and let it take me wherever."[3]

PASSION

The majority of musicians put up with long hours, rubbish pay, and ludicrous travel schedules because they really love what they do and are passionate about taking their music to audiences around the world. However, motivations change over time, which is totally normal and will affect everyone at some point. So, to start, it might be worth checking in and asking yourself:

- **Do you still feel passionate about what you're doing?**

If you're a professional musician, chances are you know what passion and energy feel like. Those early on in their careers probably feel it a lot — when playing for the first time with people you respect, being totally in the moment while performing a gig that's going well, or getting lost in a sense of timelessness when creating new music. If you're not sure, check the amount of energy you feel about your career on a regular basis. When we love what we do and are aligned with our goals, motivation comes easily and we have a sense of excitement and energy about the future and our work. Not everyone is lucky enough to experience this every day, and even the most driven musicians may feel a lull in motivation from time to time. However, if you have committed to a goal that feels meaningful to you, you should be able to ride the highs and lows of motivation over time, and stay committed to your action.

If the answer to the question above is a resounding yes, that's brilliant news: go forth and conquer your chosen area of the music landscape. If the answer is no, take a moment to recall the activities or locations where you last felt that energy and excitement.

- **What were you doing?**
- **Who were you with?**
- **What were you working on?**

If you're struggling with motivation right now, some things in your life may need to change so that you can rediscover the zest and zeal that you once felt about your career. Sometimes looking to the past can be helpful.

- **Are you able to pinpoint a moment in the past when things *did* feel right**? If so, you may be able to identify particular elements of that situation that it's possible to engineer once again.
- **Are you able to emulate the decisions you made to find yourself in that position**? If you were last truly happy when you were working with a particular collaborator, for example, you could try to work with them again. Or, look at how you came to work with them in the first place, and use a similar method to find a new collaborator who ignites your creativity in a similar way.

Another approach is to ask yourself why you're doing what you're doing. As previously mentioned, motivations may change over time and you may need to understand why you've changed direction. There may come a time in the future when you would like to start a family, for example, or make a similarly big life change, and at that point your goals may need adjusting. In that situation, the motivation may be to be more financially stable than you are now, and prioritise work that pays better, or to reduce stress and workload. Even if the joy isn't as strong in the daily work, the sense of meaning arising from providing for a family, or maintaining a higher level of day-to-day happiness, may create a different sense of satisfaction that's no less fulfilling over time. Understanding why you're doing what you're doing can also be a key factor in creating meaningful goals and aiding motivation. Additionally, you may need to look ahead and pre-empt the fact that you'll probably want slightly different things in ten years' time, and that will be okay.

It's also worth noting whether your goals are achievements based on society's standards of success or things that you know, deep down, will make your heart sing. In other words, are they 'intrinsic' (i.e. they'll give you a sense of internal meaning and fulfilment), or 'extrinsic' (focused on external factors such as a flash car, piles of cash, and a robot vacuum cleaner for every floor of your mansion)? Aligning yourself with some intrinsic goals that relate to internal meaning and relationships with others, instead of chasing a paycheque for monetary reasons alone, can provide greater fulfilment, more happiness, and improve mental health.[4] Equally, for some, making money and finding personal fulfilment may not necessarily be mutually exclusive.

WHAT DO YOU WANT?

To start getting clear about where you want to go in your career, it can be helpful to set some goals. You might find a 'future self' visualisation exercise useful. This is where you imagine yourself at a point in the future and notice what you're doing, where you're living, and who you're with. To try it, we'd recommend working with a coach or finding a video online that can walk you through the process. Visualising what she wanted to achieve and combining it with targeted goals is something that Nina Nesbitt did before creating her second album, *The Sun Will Come Up, the Seasons Will Change*. She explains:

> "Something I found really helpful was goal setting. I'd never really tried visualisation or proper goal setting before, but thought I'd give it a go before my most recent album and the results were everything I hoped for. It made it a lot easier and less daunting to work towards short term goals, which, achieved one at a time, would help me eventually reach my long term goal."

We'll take a look at visualisation and mindset in more detail in the Stage Strategies chapter. In the meantime, to start the process Nesbitt went through, try the following:

- **Write down a list of goals** — they don't just need to be career-focused (and would be better if they weren't). The idea is that your list represents a rich, full life, not just a single track path to stardom. Things on this list could be anything from 'play a solo gig at [insert dream venue here]' or 'shoot a video with a budget higher than £80', to 'travel to Machu Picchu' or 'build and maintain a thriving 30-gallon aquarium'. It could involve getting married, owning a home, running a marathon, and much more besides. Jot down goals that are important to *you*.
- Write down **as many as you can think of** and at least 30, if possible.
- Try not to be too 'realistic' at this stage — **throw caution to the wind and let your imagination take over**.
- If you're struggling to think of anything, maybe it's time to bring out the big guns: ask yourself **what would you do if you were told you had six months to live**? Where would you go, who would you see, what would you want to leave behind as your contribution to this world? It might seem like a morbid task, but giving yourself a short time limit will help bring focus on what's important, and you may find that the answers surprise you.

As well as creating specific goals for items we want or achievements in our career, another approach is to take a broader values-based view to create an overarching intention in your life. This then drives all the smaller goals and makes you know why you're working towards them. Understanding why you do what you do, finding meaning in your work, and feeling as though you contribute to society in a broader sense can even improve your wellbeing levels.[5] For example, you may want to set the intention of connecting with audiences around the world and spreading a message that is important to you. If you're struggling for ideas, try answering these questions:

- **What kind of person would I like to be in the world?** (i.e. kind, generous, authentic.)
- **What meaning do I want to create in my life?**
- **What do I want to contribute to the world and why?**
- **If I could sum up the reason why I do what I do, it would be…**

Have a think about whether those goals feel any different to the ones you set previously. Now…

- Take the goals from the first exercise. Check that they are coherent with the values you've identified above. Next to each one, **write down when you would like to have achieved it by.** You can write three months, six months, one year, three years, five years — whatever works for you.
- Take one goal that's particularly important to you and that you want to work on first and write down the answers to the following questions:

  - **What do you want?** (This is your 'end' goal)
  - **When do you want to have achieved it?** (Set a completion date)
  - **How will you know when you're there?** (What will it look like, where will you be, how will you feel?)

BREAKING THE GOAL DOWN

Let's say, for instance, that you want to become a world-class musician. Firstly, we need to tighten this up a bit, as becoming a world-class musician is quite a broad remit and it's hard to be specific about knowing when you've achieved it.

When setting goals, to maximise the chances of them being realised, they need to meet the following specifications (known in areas like the coaching world as SMART goals):

- Specific
- Measurable

- **Achievable**
- **Realistic**
- **Time-bound**

It's also vital that they are stated as positive intentions (rather than saying, for example: 'I don't want to be a rubbish musician anymore'). You'll notice that the original statement of becoming a world-class musician is positive but it isn't specific (what does world-class mean?), measurable (there's no international register of world-class musicians), or time-bound. It's a great overall intention for a career, but there needs to be a more specific goal associated with it. Perhaps a more targeted intention could be to have an album in the Top 10 sales charts within three years. However, if you can't sing and you've never written a song or picked up an instrument, there are a lot of steps you need to take before that goal can become a reality.

So let's take a few steps back and start with a goal of, for instance, recording and releasing an EP, which is totally realistic for an artist, while also being specific, measurable, achievable, and time-bound (more on this shortly). It will also be a goal that, once completed, will take you closer to your next big goal — for instance, recording an album, en route to having a Top 10 album. We'll use this example as a way of showing you how to break the goal down into simple, manageable steps.

First of all, you need to be clear that it's an EP, not a whole album or a single. There are a lot of tasks involved with that one goal so write down some of them now. These are your 'process goals' – all the actions that will lead you to your 'end goal'. You might need to find some source of funding, so research industry schemes that support artists (you'll find lots of information about this in the Money Management chapter). Alternatively, if you've already got GarageBand and a SoundCloud, maybe funding isn't your first concern. But you'll definitely need to write the songs and perhaps collaborate with producers, musicians, and other writers, so put that down. You may need to buy some studio equipment, or upskill yourself with an online course in a digital audio workstation (DAW) such as Logic. Think about all the tasks that need to happen to get from where you are currently, to where you have an EP released. Can you do the artwork? If not, who do you need to contact? Do you have any plans for marketing? The priority is listing the steps you need to take to get you to the 'end goal'.

Once you have all of those tasks written out, you need to get clear on timing. As the saying goes, 'a goal without a deadline is just a dream'. So when do you want to release the EP? Without a release date, you can't create a campaign, and it would be easy to keep putting it off until five years have passed and it still isn't out in the world. Once you've decided on a realistic date, put it in your calendar. Let's say, for example, that the EP will be released in one year. Now, break down your other tasks and put them into time slots. For example:

One year	EP released
Six months	Songs written and recorded EP sent to be mastered Release campaign created
Three months	Funding secured Songs written Research engineers to master EP
One month	Funding application submitted One song written and recorded Completed Logic skills course online
One week	Create budget for funding applications Decide on what funding schemes to apply to Approach co-writers to work with
Today	Write a list of costs associated with release Research funding schemes Order new microphone

This grid shows how you can break down a goal that can be overwhelming or vague into simple steps, and, most importantly, tasks you can start on now. Don't worry about booking out huge chunks of time, just commit to 10–15 minutes a day of doing small activities that will take you in the direction you want to go. Getting started is the hardest part. If you think you'll just be doing something for 10 minutes, it's easy to get going, and once you've started, chances are you'll carry on for a lot longer, particularly if you're enjoying your work!

If you're finding it hard to sit down and get going, it can be helpful to set a timer on your phone and commit to concentrating until the alarm goes off, at which point you can decide to take a break or continue. Many creative people swear by the Pomodoro Technique — a time management framework that promotes short bursts of activity, punctuated by regular breaks. If you're interested, there are plenty of free timers and apps online.

> *"Create a big dream. Keep it simple, easily understood, and measured. Attract the right people who work together. Measure results consistently. You can create, run or improve anything with this formula."*
>
> Harvard Business School, 2009

CREATING ACCOUNTABILITY

The next step is to create a sense of accountability.

- **Write out your plan**, in a similar way to the table on the prior page, outlining the goals that need to be met along the way.
- Now, **put those into your diary**. If you use a calendar on your phone, set reminders for each step of the way, and review your progress at the end of each week.

- Ideally, **have your goals somewhere that you can see daily** to remind yourself of where you're going.
- You may find that you want to **repeat the process above for different areas in your life**, too. For example, if you want to run a marathon, you can break that down into simple weekly tasks, and you may have financial, relationship, or health goals, and others besides.
- **Find someone who will hold you accountable**. This might be a mentor, friend, or family member. Share your goal with someone you respect and make sure they help you follow it through.
- You may also find it easier to achieve your goals if you **surround yourself with people who have a shared vision,** or at least a strong appreciation of yours. If there isn't anyone in your inner circle who is aligned with what you want to achieve, find ways of connecting with others who do, or join networking groups or attend workshops to find your tribe.

Things will happen along the timeline that may throw you off-course. This is completely normal and you'll need to review and update your plan as you go along. Try not to get disheartened — sometimes goals take a lot longer to achieve than you initially hoped, even if you plan meticulously. Often this can be due to circumstances beyond your control and that's okay. Just stay focused on why you wanted them in the first place, commit back to taking regular action, and you should be able to stay on course. Connecting daily with your goals and planning can help to keep you on track, and there are all manner of planners and diaries that help you to prioritise daily tasks, while reminding you of your bigger intentions.

In the peak performance world, morning routines have been shown as a tool that can be used to help start your day with the best possible mindset.[6] If you find that you regularly hit snooze and end up rushing out of the door with a piece of toast hanging out of your mouth, already feeling stressed, chances are you'll arrive wherever you're going unfocused and unprepared (and you probably won't enjoy the process). If this sounds like you, think about whether there are any changes you could make that would improve your mental state, energy levels, or focus. In an ideal world, how would you really like to start your day? Maybe set your alarm 30 minutes earlier (and go to sleep 30 minutes earlier) and give yourself time to do something you enjoy, such as meditating, yoga, or going for a short walk or run. Choose how you want your day to unfold, rather than leaving it all to chance.

ALTERNATIVES

People often work very differently from one another and routines or approaches to work that are freeing for one person can feel highly restrictive to others. So if this all sounds a little too 'daily schedule of a mindful CEO' or you're struggling for ideas, we've got a few final suggestions. Vision boarding, otherwise known as mood boarding, can be a useful non-verbal way of identifying what you want in your life and can work well alongside goal setting.

- To do it, find a stack of magazines (or go on Pinterest) and look for images that inspire you. It could be as simple as a shot of a beach, someone standing onstage in front of a huge audience, or a feeling or mood that you identify with and want to recreate.
- Go through and rip out (or screen shot) anything that appeals to you, paste it onto a large piece of card or create a virtual board on your computer of all the things you want, places you want to visit, feelings you want to create, or milestones you want to reach (marriage, children, owning a home etc.).
- It can help to put this somewhere prominent so that you see it frequently and remind yourself of what you want and where you're going. Just make sure that you use it as a tool to gain clarity about what you want and take regular action towards achieving those things.

A final suggestion when setting these goals is to **think about what you would like your life to look like**. You may think you want to be a global superstar, but do you want the kind of schedule that comes with that? How would you feel about getting up at 5am to do promo or spending every night in a different hotel room, rarely seeing family or friends for months on end?

Similarly, do you want to own a home in an expensive city and commit to working hard to build up the level of finances that would facilitate that, or would you prefer a quieter and relatively cheaper life that affords you more freedom? As Imogen Heap puts it: "You can still have success in life with very little, it's just that you pay for where you choose to live. If what is valuable to you is living in London and having a fancy house and that is your version of success, then you're going to have to work very hard for that. Are you willing to give that time up that you might have put into becoming a painter or living in a hut somewhere that wouldn't cost you any money?" The alternative to an expensive lifestyle doesn't necessarily have to be the polar opposite, like a hut in the woods with no plumbing (although if the Bon Iver lifestyle is your jam, don't let us deter you) — but thinking outside the box often leads to surprising (and exciting) ideas.

Getting clear on how you want to spend your days may change your goals, and you might find that what you actually wish for is to have time and space to pursue the music you want to make, or that spending quality time with loved ones is high on the list. It's entirely possible to have a long, successful, and balanced career in music without becoming a household name and while still being able to hit other important milestones. As life progresses, you may find you seek different meaning and purpose, and for musicians, this can be an important aspect of their career. Once upon a time, singer and songwriter Amanda Palmer was blinded by the bright lights of superstardom, but she's since realised that the desire to be loved by all was really just about being seen and feeling connected. And that's something that can be achieved in many different ways. Palmer explains:

"When I was 12 and looking up with wide eyes at Cyndi Lauper, Madonna, Prince, and Michael Jackson, I was like okay, if I want to be an artist, I need to be huge, everybody needs to love me. But actually, the older I got, the more I realised that was, first of all, a losing game because look at a lot of people who became superstars and gauge their level of happiness. Also, I realised **the thing that was driving that desire to be loved by everyone was [the need] to just be seen and [to feel] connected**. That was it. For so many artists, that's just the fundamental building block — to be seen and connected, and provide connection for others so that they may see themselves and see the world differently."[7]

BARRIERS

As we've highlighted, you will face external barriers along the way to achieving your goals, but sometimes the worst ones will be those you impose on yourself. Procrastination and perfectionism are genuine blocks in the road and you need to be aware of those behaviours in yourself if these are things you struggle with. As we mentioned in the section about breaking goals down, one way of solving procrastination is to commit to five minutes of action. Chances are, once you get going, you'll continue.

For perfectionism (which we discuss further in the Performance Anxiety chapter), remember that mistakes are where the lessons are — you only really start to find out how to do something by taking action and doing it, and learning along the way. That may be easier said that done, so if you're finding perfectionism is sabotaging your work, it may be worth seeking professional help.

Sometimes, we feel as though we need to wait for the perfect time to start a project or write a song. Here's a tip that will save you a lot of time: it will never feel like the perfect time, but there are times when it might feel good enough. Those are the times when you just need to get going. If you wait for inspiration or for everything to be perfect before you begin, you may be waiting for a very long time and miss valuable opportunities and chances that won't be repeated. Get started and refine along the way.

PARADISE SYNDROME

Here's a curveball: some people find that when they've achieved life goals that they never thought were possible, they feel a sense of anti-climax or emptiness and that there are no mountains left to climb. There's even a term for this — *paradise syndrome*. Although not officially recognised by psychologists, it's used to describe a sense of dissatisfaction despite achieving all of one's dreams.[8] We assume a goal will make us happy, when often we were just chasing a feeling in our minds, and achieving great things will most likely lead to wanting to achieve more great things. Dave Stewart of the Eurythmics reportedly experienced paradise syndrome[9] — once he had achieved fame and fortune, he found that it didn't lead to everlasting happiness.

Ed Sheeran has ticked off pretty much all the major milestones in music: his *Divide Tour* set the record for the highest grossing tour of all time in 2019, which included four nights at Wembley Stadium, he has the most streamed song in the UK (at the time of writing) with "Shape of You", and became the first artist in UK history to have three different albums in the Top 10 albums chart for 12 months in 2018.[10] However, when ticking off his major goals, Sheeran says he didn't really "feel anything." He explains:

> "You get to Wembley Stadium, you finish it and you're like, 'Well, what do I do now?' You'd think it would be like, 'Ah ha, this is it, I've made it!' But it's such a weird feeling. I think especially in this industry, no one is ever really satisfied."[11]

This is why it is so important that you **set goals aligned with your values and understand why you want them in the first place**. If we achieve those goals, we not only create what we want in the world, but become who we want to be in the process. Long after the excitement has faded from performing in front of 10,000 people (or whatever your goal might have been), what remains is the feeling of being proud of the person you are, and true to who you want to be. Along with achieving values-based goals, you also listened to what you wanted, took regular action, and manifested something into reality which once only existed in your mind. That ability to shape the world you live in brings about a lasting sense of self-confidence, knowing you're able to create what you want to see in the world on your terms.

Another vital point about pursuing goals is to **enjoy the process of working towards them**. There is no point in going after your dreams, only to be exhausted and burnt out when you get there, realising that you sacrificed the last five years of your life and hated every minute. So often, we don't take stock of where we are and what we have achieved so far in our careers and life — focusing only on what we've yet to do. It really is a privilege to be able to work in an area that you enjoy, and it can help your mental state and level of contentment to be mindful about what you're grateful for in your life and what you have accomplished so far. As Sheeran says, the journey is also the most valuable part: "You don't learn anything from your achievements, you learn everything from your failures. I learnt more playing in a room to one person in Exeter when no-one came to my gig in 2009 than I did playing Wembley Stadium for four nights. The journey is the fun part."[12]

Keep a record of your big wins and the things you've already achieved that you may never previously have thought possible, and celebrate and reward yourself whenever you hit milestones.

Finally, look back at the goals you've set, and ask yourself:

- **How will I feel when I've achieved them?**
- **Do I want to feel confident, loved, strong, calm, abundant, or creative?**
- **How could I create the feelings I've listed right now?**

For example, if you want to feel strong and powerful standing up on the Pyramid Stage at Glastonbury in front of 50k people, what could you do to make yourself feel strong and empowered daily, whether you get the gig or not? Equally, how can you create a sense of calm and peace in your life, without having to decamp to the Himalayas and join a Buddhist monastery? In the end, we are only going after goals because of how we think they'll make us feel and most of those feelings are available to us right now, in different formats. If a goal is to live in LA, surrounded by creatives and walking on the beach every day, could you move to Brighton and recreate that feeling there? The sooner you try it out, the quicker you'll realise whether it is as important as you thought it was (and it could save you packing up your life to travel across the Atlantic).

Finally, a note on happiness. You may think that this is a key driver behind some of the goals you've set — 'when I have £100k in the bank, I'll be happy.' But it's worth doing a bit of myth-busting. An extensive study on the correlation between high income and emotional wellbeing suggested that once we have our basic needs met, happiness levels increase only up to an annual salary of $75,000 (which is approximately £60,000 with current exchange rates).[13] After that point, **any increase in income doesn't make a significant difference to our emotional wellbeing**, even if we *believe* we're more satisfied with life. This doesn't take into account the variability in rent prices and the astronomical cost of living in a city like London, for example, which regularly eats up vast chunks of anyone's pay packet. But you get the idea — infinite amounts of money do not lead to infinite levels of happiness; earning twice as much won't make you twice as happy.

Also, whilst being supremely focused and going after what you want are important, remember not to sacrifice the simpler things in life in the process, such as good relationships with the people around you, which will be vital in keeping you happy[14] and healthy[15] along the way to success.

If you find yourself suffering a comedown after achieving a big win, it might help to channel your creativity and energy into something different for a while. For example, after his *Divide Tour*, Sheeran took up painting for a month to find happiness outside of music. He says: "The last day of tour, we played in my hometown to 40,000 people and all my friends and family came down. It ended and the day afterwards it was like, 'I know that's never going to happen again.' [So] I took up painting for a month because I [thought] I should probably find something else to give me happiness than music, because music is a weird thing when you feel like you've achieved everything you can achieve. I bought 30 canvases and painted a canvas a day for 30 days. It was really fun."[16] After that, Sheeran found it helpful to create a nine to five working structure in his life and get up for a run every morning in order to avoid feeling lost and without direction.

Remember, too, that despite your best efforts, **life will throw some unexpected curveballs and sometimes you just won't end up going down the path you imagined**. You could suddenly get chronically ill or injured, take up a full-time caring role for a loved one, or fall on difficult financial times. During these periods, all your efforts might have to go towards paying rent and keeping food on the table, and might mean that you consider a career change or hiatus from music. Even if you don't experience an individual threat to your career, a larger situation beyond your control might prevent you from achieving the goals you know you're capable of, at least in the short term. When the coronavirus crisis hit in 2020, many musicians had significant albums ready to be released, with sold-out shows booked around the world, only for all plans to be cancelled and their work not given the platform or marketing campaign it deserved. This was heartbreaking and financially challenging for those who saw months of work wasted or opportunities not being fully maximised, as many sat at home waiting for life to return to some approximation of normality.

Regardless of whether it is a global pandemic or a personal issue, life events will throw you off track, and that's okay. Musicians' lives can be chaotic and non-linear at the best of times, and life will give you both opportunities and setbacks you could never envisage. Keep that in mind when thinking about what you want to create. Have an idea of where you'd like to go, and then hold your goals lightly, knowing that whether or not you achieve the exact thing you're after, this process in itself will have been useful in pointing you in the general direction of where you're going and who you want to be. Sometimes that is good enough.

Here are a few takeaways from this chapter:

- While pursuing a career in music, it's important to **work out what your goals, passions, and values are** to ensure you're always working towards your own personal definition of success.

- The first step to doing that is **asking yourself whether you feel passionate about what you're doing** and identify if your goals and motivations have changed over time.

- You can work out what you truly want by using a **visualisation exercise** or **vision boarding**, **defining your values** and **aligning your goals** with them, or thinking about what you'd **like your daily life to look like**.

- The next step is to work out **a plan for achieving those goals**, making sure they are specific, measurable, achievable, realistic, and time-bound.

- Ultimately, **enjoy the journey** and be aware that there might be a feeling of anti-climax when you've achieved something. Keep a record of your big wins, and **try not to sacrifice your health or relationships in the pursuit of big goals**.

CHAPTER 15

TALENT AND PRACTICE

IF YOU'VE COME HERE straight from the previous chapter, you may have set some goals and it's likely that, as a musician, there may be some 'skills acquisition' goals in there, which is basically a way of saying you want to learn or improve something. For example, you might be a singer who wants to 'belt' songs more effectively or an instrumentalist who wants to be able to play a specific solo with ease. You may want to learn a new instrument or get better overall at the one you already play; perhaps you want to learn how to use Ableton. We all know that to do any of that, you need to practise. Simple, right? In some ways, yes, but perhaps not how you might expect. For instance, you may already know that excellence and improvement require time and patience, but you may not know about specific strategies that have been shown to speed up and simplify that process.

Over the last twenty years, there has been a surge in research about the science of practice, which has helped uncover some suggestions that are surprisingly simple but offer big results. Want to reduce the time spent practising and improve faster? Read on. The techniques we'll delve into have been shown to focus your brain on what you want to achieve, improve the speed at which you make the change, and protect your mind and body in the process. Most of us aren't taught these strategies when we learn an instrument, and forge ahead with our own approaches that then stay fixed for many years. But learning how to practise effectively is a great tool you can equip yourself with if you want to continue to improve as a musician throughout your life (and who doesn't?).

THE MYTH OF TALENT

To be good at something requires skill and practise — that's a given. But before we get deeper into strategies, it's worth pausing briefly on the concept of talent and the role of practice alongside it. Think about it for a moment. Have you ever thought that someone was more talented than you, and that they possessed some kind of innate musical greatness that you're unable to access? For years, people have discussed the concept of talent as an innate, fixed thing, believing people were either born with a predisposition to achieving great things or they weren't. However, recent research is moving in a different direction, more focused on a concept of talent with *practice* at its core.

Anders Ericsson, researcher and author of *Peak: Secrets from the New Science of Expertise,* believes there is no natural predisposition to talent. He's spent his career studying how people become brilliant at what they do, with surprising results. By now, most people have heard of the claim made famous by Malcolm Gladwell in his bestselling book, *Outliers,* that the world's best performers (in any domain) need 10,000 hours of practice to master a skill. Well, the original research for Gladwell's book was actually conducted by Ericsson and two other colleagues, and it's bad news for the inspirational meme industry: the findings weren't quite as black and white as *Outliers* made out.

The amount of time needed to become an expert depended on the nature of the task, with some musicians needing 20,000 hours of practice before they could win a piano competition. Practice was absolutely essential, but what truly made people great, whether it was in music, sport, business, or literature, was the ability to conduct the *right* sort of practice in order to improve. It wasn't enough to just sit there going through the motions — Ericsson found that those who followed a specific process during their practice sessions were able to get where they wanted to go faster and more successfully than the others.[1] In short, he believes we all have the capacity for great talent, not just a chosen few.

In his *Differentiated Model of Giftedness and Talent*, psychology researcher Françoys Gagné takes a slightly different approach. He sees the concepts of giftedness and talent as being distinct from each other and suggests we separate them out when approaching this topic. A gifted individual, Gagné believes, is someone in the top 10% of the population for their age, who has a *natural potential* to achieve an above-average level of ability in one or more areas of skill. Similarly to Ericsson's theory, Gagné sees talent as demonstrating superior performance or skill as a result of systematic training in a specific field. At the most basic level, the suggestion here is that **giftedness is something we receive without having to do anything, while talent is something we earn.**

But is talent enough? Angela Duckworth of the University of Pennsylvania believes not. In her study of 2,235 adults, in which she investigated the individual differences that predict success, data suggested that the achievement of challenging goals needed sustained and focused application of talent *over time*.[2] This tallies with Gagné's requirement for systematic training. Duckworth saw this focused application as requiring perseverance as well as passion for particular goals, which she calls *grit* (if you want to read more about Duckworth's work, check out her book *Grit: The Power of Passion and Perseverance*). So Duckworth is implying that even effective practice is not enough, and that there needs to be a high level of motivation to keep you going long-term. This all makes sense and underlines the importance of setting goals you feel passionate about. Achieving them will take time, but passion can fuel your motivation to stay focused all the way to completion.

Considering these approaches, **whether or not you're 'gifted' with an innate musical ability, you can still become 'talented' through focused practice**, which is great news for anyone who has doubted their potential. Of course, there will always be exceptions to this rule, with genetic factors making some musicians pre-disposed to playing certain instruments with more ease than others. If you want to try playing Rachmaninov on the piano, for example, you'll need to be blessed with large hands to span the notes of the chords. However, no matter what your genetic make-up, if you combine talent acquired through focused practice with working towards goals you feel passionate about achieving, your chances of success will improve.

PRACTICE – THE TRADITIONAL WAY

Imagine for a moment that you want to learn how to play the guitar. You start by buying one in your local music shop and sign up for a few lessons with a teacher. Initially, your improvement is rapid as you learn a selection of easy chords and incorporate them into songs. Motivation levels are probably high at this point. You may then start to play with a band, and your skill improves the more you play, as you continue to learn more chords and solos. Eventually, though, you reach a plateau and don't feel like you're improving any more. At this point, it's often assumed that the greater your experience, the better the player you are, and that continuing at this level of playing will naturally improve your ability as a performer, as long as you carry on doing it.

Sometimes that works, but it's not always the case, and any progression might be slow and unfocused. As humans, we tend to train ourselves for the job we need to do, then once we perform that job, the training stops and we stay at the same level for years. But because we also have an innate drive towards mastery, this can be a really unsatisfying place to stay, and over time our motivation may be affected as we yearn for more challenge and improvement. Classical musicians understand this concept — you're unlikely to find a platform soloist who doesn't continue to find ways to improve in their career through focused practice and regular coaching. Yet, many working in the commercial music world find that when they sign a record deal or release some music, they stop learning and improving as the demands of the job take over. Initial artistic goals are often temporarily shelved as new priorities involve learning about the 'business' side of music and adapting performances to the requirements of the industry and audiences.

Maybe you feel, though, that you've reached your personal limit and there isn't any point continuing with individual practice. That's an understandable way of thinking, but is it possible to reach a natural 'peak' in terms of what we can achieve? Or to put it more simply, is there a limit to what practice can improve? Ericsson believes not, as he explains in his book:

> "**In pretty much any area of human endeavour, people have a tremendous capacity to improve their performance, as long as they train in the right way.** If you practise something for a few hundred hours, you will almost certainly see great improvement — but you have only scratched the surface. You can keep going and going, getting better and better and better. How much you improve is up to you."[3]

Remember, though, that it's the quality of practice which matters here and any negative habits or approaches will be reinforced long-term, resulting in 'practice makes permanent' rather than the old adage 'practice makes perfect'. If you want to achieve the kind of improvement mentioned above, Ericsson says that this is done through deliberate practice: "Imagine you want to climb a mountain. You could just start walking and hope for the best. Or, you could find a guide who has been to the peak before and knows the best way to get there."[4] This will be the quickest, most efficient way to climb the mountain, and is the easiest way to describe deliberate practice. You know how good you want to be. How do you get there?

PRACTICE – THE EFFECTIVE WAY

As we've established, noodling around on the guitar with no particular plan is not a way of improving quickly. Instead, you need to manage your practice sessions effectively, being very clear about what you are trying to achieve and why, then reflecting on how you did in the practice session and how you can improve next time. There are five important elements involved in high-quality practice, as identified in *Musical Excellence* by Professor of Performance Science at the Royal College of Music, Aaron Williamon, who offers strategies and techniques to enhance performance through effective practising.[5] We're going to break those elements down and simplify them over the next couple of pages. They are:

- Concentration
- Setting and meeting goals
- Constant self-evaluation
- Flexible use of strategies
- Seeing the big picture

The purpose of using this approach to practice is to improve ability by accentuating your strengths and reducing weaknesses, which will achieve results quicker. So how do you do it?

- Plan and prepare
- Execute
- Reflect and evaluate

Firstly, be clear about what your over-arching goal is — for the purposes of this chapter, we've used learning the guitar. Then, for each practice session, set some micro-goals for what you're trying to achieve and stick with them. For example, it may be that when you first start, your strumming pattern sounds off, and this is something you've identified as an issue (being able to self-evaluate and know what you need to work on is a crucial part of this process, as we can see in the list on the previous page). So now you can identify that a practice session goal might be 'to improve my strumming pattern'.

PLAN AND PREPARE

It might be tempting to launch in and start strumming furiously, but a little planning and preparation will help first. In the practice literature, this initial stage is really key — using strategies and mental tasks to find out how best to solve the problem. So, could you look on YouTube first for a lesson on strumming patterns? Could you video how you're playing to see if there is something off in your posture or hand position? Taking some time to think and plan the session will help save a lot of time and effort. Now you've decided on a plan of action, write it down, along with the original practice goal you decided on. This can be in a journal or notebook, or there are specific apps (like Sessions: Music Practice Log and Modacity) dedicated to helping you with this process of effective practice.

EXECUTE

It's now time to do the practice. Check first of all that you have the right location. Is it quiet, with minimal distraction? If you're in a communal section of your house or practice room and know you'll be interrupted every five minutes, it might be worth finding somewhere else that is more private. Do you feel comfortable and is it warm enough? (Playing an instrument with freezing fingers that won't move freely isn't going to help you achieve the best results.)

Once you have a good location sorted, research suggests that, during practice sessions, it's a good idea to balance physical playing with mental rehearsal strategies. The latter part of this sounds like a potentially enticing idea on its own — could you lie in bed all day, practising by just thinking about it? Unfortunately, not quite. But used in a structured and intentional way, mental rehearsal has been shown to be *almost* as effective as the real thing.[6] It can be used to help learn and memorise songs, to overcome technical difficulties, improve focus, enhance confidence onstage, and achieve peak experiences.[7] Performance Psychologist Dr Ellis Pecen explains how mental rehearsal can be achieved through imagery:

> "Imagery is about practising your imaging ability in a targeted way so it will help you to practise and perform better. It is not about 'relaxing' or 'fantasising' about what you want. You ideally want to train your imagery skills so you can come as close as you can get to the experience of the actual event. It can make people feel better prepared, as if they have already been there before, and it can help to hone imagery skills so you can use them for learning and focusing. PETTLEP is an example of a more comprehensive imagery model that encourages performers to think about various aspects of imagery practice. The acronym stands for **physical, environment, timing, task, learning** and **perspective**. What you ultimately want to achieve with imagery is to image as many facets of the performance as possible, and practise this skill regularly as you would with normal practice."

If you'd like to have a try, we've included an exercise below. It's based on the PETTLEP model Pecen described, which is one of the best ways to improve your visualisation skills for mental rehearsal.

First of all, there is no need to relax when using PETTLEP for performance. You will not be relaxed in the real event and you need to be as accurate as possible.

- Ask yourself, how will I feel **physically**? What will the emotions and symptoms be? What does the task feel like to execute physically?
- What will the **environment** be like? Will the room be large? Old? Warm? What will it smell like? Be as specific as you can.
- What will the **timing** be? Not just time of day, but also the timing of the task you are about to start. For instance, many performers find that doing a mental 'count-in' helps them to execute a skill well because we have natural rhythm to all things in life. Music, sports, speech — what is the rhythm I want to set? Something like a paced one-two-three-GO! could be incorporated into an imagery routine.
- What are the **task**-relevant considerations you need to think about? Are there parts where you need to focus on something technical? And where should you pull your focus back to 'letting it flow'? What does the task demand you to think about, and where are the parts where you will let go of thinking?
- **Learning**. Imagery will need to be refined continuously as the performer improves and outgrows strategies. You can also use imagery to learn new material, to do mental rehearsal, or to improve your overall skill development.
- The final point concerns **perspective**. Generally, imaging from a first person perspective has been considered superior, but you can experiment with shifting perspective when your preparation and cognitive load allow. For example, during passages where you do not need to focus on technicality, you could imagine the audience watching you thinking, 'Wow. This is amazing!'

Let's imagine that you've done some mental rehearsal and now want to play. Firstly, make sure you warm up your body physically for playing in whatever way you usually do (and if you don't have a warm-up, head to the resources section to find out from BAPAM how to create one). Now, as you practise, be mindful of that goal you set at the beginning and stay focused on achieving it. You want to make sure that you're concentrating fully throughout the practice session, without your mind wandering off to what you're going to have for lunch. The best way to do this is:

- To **practise in short chunks**, ideally of no more than 30 minutes. Any longer and it's almost impossible to keep laser-focused concentration, which is the vital element to improving fast.
- It's easy to get absorbed in what you're doing, so **set a timer** on your phone and once it's done, get up, have a walk around and a drink, and return to playing after 10 minutes. If you find this hard to stick to and want a longer session, you can extend it to one hour.
- **Try not to exceed that** as anything longer increases your susceptibility to musculoskeletal problems, especially if you don't have good posture when you play.

REFLECT AND EVALUATE

Once you've finished the physical practice session, it's a good idea to do some self-evaluation. One of the best tools to help with that is either recording audio or video of yourself while you practise. If you have a smartphone, these tools are available to you anywhere, so make the most of them. Set up a passage that you might be finding difficult and video yourself while playing it. Again, focus on what you're trying to achieve — if there's a tricky passage you want to improve, just record that and get clear on what's going wrong and how you can improve it next time.

To finish:

- Take out your journal or practice app, and **record whether you were successful at achieving your goal** in this practice session. To use the example of our original practice task, did your strumming improve? You may find that having videoed yourself, it became obvious what the problem was, and you adjusted your hand position accordingly.

- Note down in the journal that yes, it did improve, as well as what you did to enable that, including if a particular video or online lesson helped. It's so easy to forget what we've learned and jotting it down can make sure it's there as a reference in future if we need to brush up on a particular skill. It can also serve as a confidence and motivation boost — whilst improving, **it's easy to forget how far you've come and looking back over a journal or notebook to review progress will help jog your memory**.

Another option is to compare the videos you've made with experts in your field doing something similar, otherwise known as 'observation learning.' For example, with guitarists, how are their hands moving? Are their movements smaller or more relaxed than yours? What is their posture like? This can be a quick and effective way of improving technique and learning.

CONCLUSION

As we've discussed, practice, and in particular, the right *kind* of practice, is essential to mastery in music. If you want to improve quickly and effectively, you need to:

- Adopt **a systematic approach to your practice** sessions.
- Choose the **right environment in which to practise** (one with as few distractions as possible) and combine it with a warm-up to prepare your body and mind.
- **Practise in short bursts and take regular breaks** to protect your joints and use your brain more efficiently.
- Use a journal, notebook, or app to **monitor your progress**, and reflect on what you achieve and how you can do it better next time.

We worked on setting up a big picture goal in the previous chapter, and this chapter has described how you can set yourself daily, well-executed, and planned smaller tasks in order to get there. Remember that the key to practice sessions is to do them regularly — one long day of rehearsals the day before the gig can't compare to daily 30-minute sessions, which will improve your playing a lot faster and, most importantly, reduce the possibility of injuries. Make regular practice a habit, and if you have a heavy promo schedule and can't take an instrument with you for a couple of weeks, or find a spare and private moment to sing, all is not lost — remember the benefits of mental rehearsal and try that instead.

Finally, amidst all of the techniques and practice strategies mentioned here, don't forget the intentions and bigger-picture goals you set in the previous chapter. These methods are tools that will enable you to improve your skill as a musician or vocalist, but, ultimately, your job is to communicate emotion to an audience or convey the broader intention of your music — both on an individual level for each song and for the performance as a whole. Remember to not get so caught up in the detail that you forget what you're trying to convey. Throughout your practice, maintain perspective by staying aligned with your original intention for each track, along with the reason you're playing music overall.

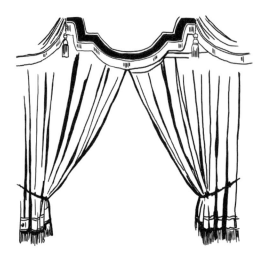

CHAPTER 16

PERFORMANCE ANXIETY

WHETHER YOU CALL IT performance anxiety, stage fright, or just plain old nerves, for some people, the feeling of fear and panic that surfaces in the minutes, hours, or days before they go onstage can be crippling, and can make or break an important gig.

Music performance anxiety (MPA) in its various forms is a massive issue within the music world and can affect musicians whether they've just started playing or have been performing for years.[1] Adele, Cat Power, Zayn Malik, Harry Styles, and Lorde are all high-profile performers who struggle with it, with some reporting pretty extreme experiences. "One show in Amsterdam, I was so nervous, I escaped out the fire exit," said Adele in 2011.[2] "I've thrown up a couple of times. Once in Brussels, I projectile-vomited on someone." Even veteran frontman Ozzy Osbourne has a story to share: "To say that I suffer from pre-show nerves is like saying that when you get hit by an atom bomb, it hurts a bit."[3]

Aaron Williamon, Professor of Performance Science at the Royal College of Music, says this reaction to appearing onstage is understandable. "**It's not a natural thing to do, going out and dealing with such high levels of stress in public.**"[4] Musicians can find this area particularly awkward if they've found themselves relying on substances to cope with the stress of performing. "It's after they get sober — that's when the stage fright kicks in," says Harold Owens, Senior Director of Grammy-supported music and health charity MusiCares in the US. "I've heard people say repeatedly, 'I've never played sober.' It's a huge issue. We have support groups to address what it's like to [perform] your first [sober] gig."[5]

Thanks to Williamon and other researchers in this field, we now have lots of tools and techniques to try and reduce or manage any MPA musicians may face. Whatever the cause of your anxieties, and however you might have found yourself dealing with them, in this chapter we'll introduce you to research-informed strategies that can help as well as direct you to appropriate therapeutic support if you need it. For those who need more information about drug and alcohol misuse and addiction, head over to the Substance Use and Addiction chapter, if you haven't already, and check out the resources section. For some, MPA can be a reason to stop performing, but that doesn't have to be the case for everyone and you may be surprised by how effective some coping techniques can be.

IDENTIFYING MPA

How would you describe MPA? Chances are, for every reader of this book, the answer to that question might be slightly different. There's no one size fits all approach to dealing with it, either, which can make it hard to find simple solutions. Copying what's worked for a friend, for instance, might not work for you. But there are some questions you can ask yourself that will help you bring this complex area into some focus.

- **What are the signs of anxiety you experience?**
- **How do they affect you mentally and physically?**
- **When specifically do these signs of anxiety appear?**
- **Does anxiety affect your performance in any way? If so, how?**
- **Are there any environments or situations that makes it better or worse?**
- **Is there anything you do that successfully manages the anxiety?**

There's a certain amount of trial and error that will go on here — not just in finding out how to manage MPA, but, just as importantly, in first learning to identify how it makes itself known to you. Recognising that it exists (and how it exists) is a vital first step to sorting things out.

For some people, for instance, it could be that their thoughts start spinning out of control before performance, with negative self-talk affecting confidence levels — thoughts like 'you're going to sing out of tune' (more on how to manage this later). For others, issues might be felt mainly in the body, so they may have a racing heart, sweaty palms, or a dry mouth. Other symptoms musicians might experience are behavioural, so you'll see people pacing up and down, fidgeting, picking their fingers, or shutting down verbally. The challenge you face as a musician is first working out which of these things affect you, as this will help with management. Of course, these symptoms don't necessarily result in a negative outcome — there are many musicians who will learn to interpret them differently and use them as excitement to create a positive 'buzz' for performance (more on this shortly).

Ways that performance anxiety can affect you [6]

Somatic
'Butterflies'
Shaky limbs
Sweaty palms
Increased heart rate
Needing to go to the toilet
Yawning
Dry mouth

Cognitive
Negative thoughts
Worries
Negative images
Difficulty concentrating

For former One Direction star turned solo artist Harry Styles, his MPA affects him in a very physical way, similar to Adele — he is known to throw up before and sometimes even during shows.[7] Lorde, meanwhile, talks about a feeling of "the most crippling fear" before she goes onstage but she also notes that it then "gets replaced by something magic."[8] She's talking about how low levels of anxiety can actually boost performance, as we've mentioned. For another former One Directioner Zayn Malik, the anxiety sometimes gets too much — in 2016, he was scheduled to play at Capital FM's Summertime Ball but had to pull out of the gig, writing to his fans on Instagram at the time: "Unfortunately my anxiety that has haunted me throughout the last few months around live performances has gotten the better of me... with the magnitude of the event, I have suffered the worst anxiety of my career."[9]

Even the seemingly most confident performers can be affected. Shaun Ryder, the larger-than-life frontman of Madchester band Happy Mondays, says stage fright made him question whether he was fit for being a musician at all. "When you've heard all the musicians talk, they go, 'I really come alive when I go out in front of the crowd,'" he says.[10] "With me, it was exactly the opposite. I would just shrivel up. I'm thinking, 'Am I a real writer, musician, because I don't thrive on being in front of everybody onstage?'" Ryder says he found it particularly hard in smaller venues when the performers and audiences were up close and personal. "The bigger the venue is, the less personal and the more showbiz it is. So, I never had a problem playing in front of 10, 20, 30, 60, 80 thousand people, or whatever."[10]

Ryder's comments echo those of many an artist: it's easier not to feel intimidated by an audience when you can't see the whites of their eyes, or when you're in the middle of stage lighting so elaborate and dazzling that you can't even see the crowd. But Ryder and all those artists know that you don't find yourself on an arena stage until you've spent a decent amount of time playing in venues considerably smaller.

If you've been reading this so far and have found yourself thinking that MPA isn't an issue for you, that's great. But don't skip to the next chapter quite yet. Studies have shown that a bit of MPA (or 'arousal') may help to improve your performance.

The term arousal is used because fear and excitement can be easily confused. Ever had that experience where you're nervous and you tell yourself you're excited instead? That's why. A particular level of arousal, be that high or low, may have benefitted your performance in the past. The key, as always, is knowing which one it is for you.

- **Have a think back to a time when you were nervous.**
- **Now think about a time when you were excited.**
- **What do you notice?**
- **Is there a big difference in physiological symptoms?**

You will probably notice that the physiological symptoms are extremely similar, if not identical. But the way you interpreted your arousal in one situation was positive, which is why we tend to appraise it as excitement. As a result, there is nothing to stop you from reframing your fear as excitement in the future.

INDIVIDUAL APPROACHES TO MPA

Managing performance states can be tricky — as we've already mentioned, everyone is different, but one useful approach can be the Individual Zone of Optimal Functioning (IZOF).[11] Performance psychologist Dr Ellis Pecen explains:

> "The IZOF model allows you to find your own optimal emotion and intensity of arousal. This 'optimal zone' can be different for everyone and it depends on the task and context. It can also change over time. Performers are encouraged to discover their emotion type and intensity, and experiment with emotional regulation techniques to get themselves into the desired state for performance."

Pecen suggests an exercise that might help you work out what your IZOF is:

- Think about good and bad past performances, and **write a log of what you did leading up to the event and how you were feeling.**
- Also write down any important 'other' information, like inspirational events or unusual things that happened leading up to memorably good or bad performances, and note the intensity of all emotions.

She continues: "Once performers discover which emotions work best for them at a particular phase in their career, they can work on getting themselves in that emotion and intensity. For example, I have had many clients who actually did their best when they were very anxious, or angry, or sad, or 'inspired'."

Another approach is to use the graph on the next page[12] to understand the relationship between arousal and performance 'quality' (which is quite a subjective term). On the left-hand side going up the graph, we have the quality of performance, and across the bottom, is arousal (or anxiety). What you can see is that with no anxiety, you'll turn in a show that's missing something

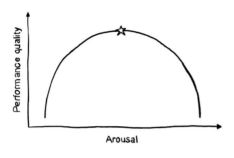

in terms of performance quality — but if there's too much anxiety, that's not great either. Where you want to be is somewhere in the middle, which is represented on the graph by a red star. The location of the red star is where a certain level of MPA can be a good thing — it's where you'll deliver a great performance. So if you're starting to experience anxiety before a show, it could be a sign that you're on your way to a brilliant performance, not a terrible one.

The ideal situation is to manage your levels of MPA so you'll hit that star. 'How on earth do I possibly achieve that?', you might ask. Well, that is one of the criticisms of this model. It doesn't take into account the individual differences in optimal states for performance, and some musicians have reported difficulties in hitting the red star consistently. The key takeaway from this model though is that **anxiety doesn't have to be bad for performance**. There has been a lot of discussion about the benefits of reframing anxiety as positive — sometimes the negative thought patterns that accompany unhelpful anxiety symptoms can cause more problems than the anxiety itself. So, if this is a problem for you, think about how you could reframe any anxiety as a positive 'boost' that is needed for performance. Another trick is telling yourself that you're excited (and not scared) when you start to feel those familiar feelings before going onstage.[13] Aaron Williamon puts it this way: "It's the way you interpret that different physical state which makes all the difference. Instead of seeing it as a signal that something's going to go wrong, treat the symptoms as a sign that your body is ready to perform."[14]

Finally, while we're on the subject of reframing, allow yourself to become curious about how you're viewing your experience. Are you telling yourself this is the most important gig you've ever done and that your life depends on it? Are you putting too much importance on something that isn't really such a big deal? And even if it *is* a huge deal, can you dial down the way you think about it? Overestimating the importance of an event can cause us all kinds of issues and make MPA worse. Sometimes, you can just take a step back and think: 'Yes this is important, but in the grand scheme of things, it's not *that* important.'

Williamon agrees that **MPA can helpfully be viewed as "as excitement, not as anxiety, and an opportunity to showcase what you can do."** He continues: "And, look, when you get out and do it, you do it. You deliver the things and your music in a way that you've prepared and rehearsed. Sometimes they go right. Sometimes they don't go right. But the audiences aren't as hypercritical as we often think they might be."[15]

That's a good point. You might have rehearsed a show to pinpoint precision, but it's only the people onstage who really know if a mistake has been made. Falling off stage might be difficult to conceal, but the more common concerns of performers (missing a big note, even remembering the exact words) are often missed by audiences, particularly if they're two pints in and enjoying themselves.

Where re-interpreting symptoms is not enough, some of the following may help: [16]

- **Thought-blocking**: stopping negative thoughts (such as 'I always get the phrasing wrong') as soon as they make an appearance, and replacing them with positive statements.
- **Positive self-talk:** using positive statements to boost confidence and feelings of control (e.g. 'It worked perfectly in rehearsal so there's no reason why it shouldn't do now', or just 'Go for it!'). Try creating statements to help focus on the artistic aspects of the work.
- **Mental rehearsal**: going over dance steps or instrument finger-work in your head can be a great help; it makes you feel like you've 'been there, done that' and more in control.

- **A good warm-up** can counteract muscle shakes or stiffness, help to use up some adrenalin, and steady the heart rate.
- **Relaxation exercises** can be effective, such as deep breathing. There are many different approaches to relaxation so find one that works for you.
- **Create a pre-performance routine** to help you feel more in control. Try to perform all your preparations in the same order for every performance, making them last up until you go onstage. Then you aren't leaving any spare time in which too much anxiety could build up.

SOURCES OF STRESS

Another approach to managing MPA is in identifying the sources of stress in performance and preparing accordingly. These sources of stress are as follows:

- **Task mastery**: in simple terms, this is all about how good we are at what we're performing. Have you ever gone onstage under-rehearsed, knowing you're winging it and that things could go wrong at any minute? Chances are, you were pretty nervous beforehand and taking more time to rehearse or learn the words could have made a real difference. We appreciate this is veering slightly into the territory of stating the obvious, but it's a common trigger for MPA and it's one of the easiest problems to fix. No matter what it is you're doing, make sure you're well-rehearsed (but remember, this is just one approach, and more practice won't always mean less MPA overall).

- **Situational stress**: imagine if you had to stand up right now and sing "Happy Birthday". If you're at home on your own, that suggestion probably won't even create a response. But if we asked you to head over to The O2 Arena in Greenwich tonight and sing it to 20,000 people, even though your task mastery for the event would be really high, you may not be used to performing in such an enormous venue, and you may find that you get incredibly nervous. A sudden change in venue size, a different audience, or an unfamiliar location can each create anxiety responses. On a practical level, things that can help alleviate some situational stress include getting to the venue in good time, having a walk around and, if possible, doing a rehearsal. If it's somewhere new, make friends with whoever's working the sound desk and be clear about what it is that you need, as sound issues can play into situational stress levels. If you can't get to the venue, have a look online and see if there are any pictures of the space or YouTube videos of previous performers at the same venue. Some venues even offer virtual tours, too. Then, start mentally rehearsing (see the Talent and Practice chapter for more on this), and try to get comfortable with the thought of performing there.

- **Trait anxiety**: do you get anxious on a regular basis? Do you ever find yourself getting nervous in social situations? If you do, then you may find that that you are more susceptible to MPA. As you might expect, there have been links shown between social anxiety and MPA, so if this is a problem for you, seeking professional help may be the best way forward. Studies have suggested that cognitive behavioural therapy (CBT) can be helpful here, or, if you have it, you may find that your existing therapy works. It's also worth assessing what's going on in your life generally when trying to predict your MPA levels. Relationship issues, financial difficulties, or even a stressful day can all play into your overall trait anxiety levels for the performance and are worth taking into account (but it can also be the case that some perform better during times of stress, as Ellis Pecen described with the IZOF approach).

REDUCING MPA OVERALL

We've established in the model above that there are three main sources of stress contributing to overall MPA levels. So how do you use that knowledge to your advantage? Let's think of these three concepts like sliders on a mixing desk — when the sliders are high, you're going to be experiencing more severe MPA. With this example, imagine that you're playing a song you've played many times before and you're incredibly well-rehearsed with it (slider one is therefore low). Now, imagine you're playing the song at your favourite local venue (again, slider two is low). Let's say that you don't tend to get anxious in social situations, and this isn't a general issue for you (slider three is low). When all the sliders are low, you can see that the likelihood of experiencing problematic MPA is quite unlikely (but remember it won't necessarily mean you'll give an optimal performance).

Now let's take another example — you have to play a song you don't know very well (slider one high), at Wembley Arena, having never played a gig that size in your life (slider two high), and you tend to get socially anxious (slider three high). This is an extreme example but you get the point. If you want to reduce your overall anxiety level, you need to try and get those sliders where they are optimal for you as a person and performer.

The good thing about the slider model is that it's easy to feel like you've made progress, even if you've only managed to address one of the issues. You don't always need to lower each of the faders — if you've just addressed, say, situational stress, or you've managed to get two of the sliders halfway down, you'll know you've made a big difference.

The other benefit of the slider model is that you may be able to anticipate how nervous you'll be in advance of the gig. If you have to perform at levels you're uncomfortable with, and there's nothing you can do to reduce the sliders any more, that's when it helps to know how MPA affects you. You can then put in place strategies that prevent your performance from breaking down. For example, if you know your memory goes blank and you can't remember the first chord to the song, why not put a piece of paper on the floor with basic chord structures? No one will know and it's there as a backup in case things go wrong.

Or, if you're a singer and you know remembering the first line of your words is going to be a real issue, why not place some of the lyrics on an amp towards the back of the stage? If you walked up to a corner of the stage and took a drink between songs, you could quite easily glance at a lyric sheet and remind yourself of the opening lines. Or, if you know you start shaking uncontrollably and don't want the audience to see, try leaving the microphone in the stand for the first song. It's good to start getting curious about how MPA affects you at its worst, so you can do your best to manage it and make sure it doesn't negatively impact your performance.

SELF-TALK

Negative self-talk or our 'monkey mind', as it has been called, can take us off to all kinds of self-sabotaging places we don't want to go, and often we're not even aware it is happening. If this is a problem for you, get curious about what's going on in your head before a performance and write down your thoughts, if it helps. **What are you telling yourself? How is it affecting you?** Aaron Williamon explains:

> "The issue I find is that breaking habits of negative thinking can be incredibly difficult to do. We, as musicians, perform a lot. We perform so regularly that we can develop habits quite quickly. And, unless we're consciously aware of wanting to do something about a negative habit, then we may not realise that we're dropping into that pattern of thinking."[17]

You can learn to calm your mind before performance and use intentional or instructional self-talk as a positive thing — it's a technique Taylor Swift employs to manage her anxiety before performing at festivals, where she knows that, unlike at a standard show, the audience may not have bought tickets to see her. She explains: "I get pretty nervous. You know when you talk to yourself in the mirror? I'm like, 'They're not going to throw things at you, it's going to be okay, it's going to be okay.'"[18] We'll delve deeper into positive self-talk in the Stage Strategies chapter.

INTENTION SETTING

Another way of managing MPA is to **be really clear about your intention when performing**. It's all too easy to go onstage and be consumed by self-focused thoughts; if you're coming across well, if your voice sounds good, or how you look. This can be quite a reactive state, and as MPA narrows our focus (so that we can become really obsessed by irrelevant things), it's totally natural. A way of overcoming this is to be crystal clear about your aim for the gig and to stay focused on that throughout the performance. If your music is pretty upbeat, the intention could be very simple — for everyone to enjoy themselves and have a great time, for example. Or, if your music is slow and sombre, it could be for the audience to have an emotional experience and feel something profound from your performance. Either way, making the intention something larger than yourself, and **focusing on the idea of 'giving' to your audience, can help to expand your sense of awareness to something greater than yourself**.

This approach can also help when motivation might be waning or when you're going through a tough time. Being very clear about why you're making the music you are, and what you're trying to achieve overall, can help to keep you on track during tough gigs and challenging periods. Thinking about the big picture — rather than allowing yourself to believe that this particular moment is the beginning, middle, and end of everything — can provide some welcome context and much-needed perspective.

OTHER WAYS OF MANAGING MPA: DRUGS AND ALCOHOL

Alcohol and drugs are some of the most common ways of coping with MPA for popular musicians. Having a drink before a show is often described as a way of taking the edge off MPA, and some musicians find it really helps, which is perfectly fine if you're gigging once every couple of weeks or so. However, if you start playing music professionally, and the number of gigs you need to do creeps up, suddenly you're drinking every night. Not only that, but over time your body gets used to the alcohol so you need more and more to get the same effect. Before you know it, you're going onstage drunk, which is really not ideal, and despite what you might think at the time, you're definitely not going to be playing to your full potential. And that's before you consider the negative implications for your health that long-term alcohol use brings.

You might be thinking now about great rock gigs you've seen where the singer's been totally out of it, but ask yourself: were they as out of it as they made it seem? Or could it have been the case that their show was a performance in more ways than one? There can sometimes be pressure in the music industry to display this kind of behaviour as part of the overall performance image of the band,[19] but this doesn't mean you have to live up to it, and many bands are proud of their sober or healthy and balanced approach to alcohol and music.

Legal drugs, such as beta-blockers, can help manage MPA in really extreme situations.[20] If you're finding there is nothing you can do to reduce MPA in any shape or form, consider having a chat with your GP about using them as a short-term remedy while you work with a therapist to find out why it is proving so problematic for you. But be warned – beta-blockers are not a cure and research has shown that in studies where musicians were taking them, audiences reported that the performances were 'flat' and often devoid of emotion. No-one wants to give a performance like this, so proceed with caution, but know that they are there as an option if you really need it.

SUPPORTIVE LIFESTYLE

It may seem obvious that lifestyle factors we've covered elsewhere all play into the amount and intensity of MPA you'll experience. It's therefore crucial to **get enough good quality sleep** and make sure that **you're taking time out to relax** between shows. In an industry where touring is often the most profitable aspect of a musician's career, it's crucial to balance out the significant levels of anxiety that may be experienced every performance. In a BBC Radio 4 documentary, researchers suggested that **performing live can be compared biologically to sky-diving in terms of the level of stress it creates in the body**. Professor of Psychobiology of Northumbria University, Mark Wetherell, explained:

> "If you're anticipating any kind of challenging or stressful event, your body mounts a response to help you deal with it. You release adrenaline, and people associate that with fight or flight response. Slightly longer-term, you also release a stress hormone called cortisol. That makes it sound very negative but these responses help us prepare for the demand that we think is going to happen."[21]

This is a great response when the body needs to prepare for an important one-off performance, but when it happens night after night, without a break, cortisol levels can stay heightened in the body. It's worth looking at your schedule and trying **to factor in some nights off so that you're not always putting your body in that high-alert state**. Long-term, these high cortisol levels can result in an increased risk of health issues, including anxiety and depression. So balance high-stress activities, such as performance with relaxation techniques, to provide quality recovery time. Some people find that mindfulness exercises and meditation or breathwork can help. Katy Perry once used beta-blockers to manage MPA but has now turned to transcendental meditation instead,[22] as well as a simple exercise: breathing through her nose and out through her mouth. There's a relaxation exercise you can use in the Stage Strategies chapter.

Bodywork such as Alexander Technique, Yoga, Pilates, and Feldenkreis may also help to reduce anxiety levels overall and are definitely worth checking out if they appeal to you. Running has been shown to reduce MPA, but as mentioned in the Vocal Health chapter, make sure you start training well in advance of a gig, otherwise there's a risk that you'll end up onstage exhausted.

Equally, be aware of how food and drink affect your anxiety levels. For some, necking a can of caffeine-packed Monster and having a bag of Haribo for lunch is likely to make things a whole lot worse. Once again, though, it all depends on what works for you. Ellis Pecen explains:

"Some performers may find that carbohydrates can blunt the stress response and give them energy without having the more excitatory effects of, for instance, caffeine. As performers are likely to be burning off a higher percentage of sugars through a prolonged elevated heart rate in performance, a planned and measured amount of simple carbohydrates consumed prior to performance may be beneficial for some. Again, the key is to find out what works for you and to make sure that you do not have underlying medical conditions that warrant a specific dietary approach. Always check with your medical professional, and make sure you test any dietary changes well before a performance to avoid unhelpful fluctuations in blood sugar under pressure."

PERFECTIONISM

A final word to mention on this topic is *perfectionism*, and how that can play into levels of MPA. Musicians often set really high standards and they want their gigs to go well. Obviously, this is an integral part of being a successful musician, but it's important to be aware of when those high standards start to sabotage your performance levels and work output. There are two types of perfectionism. The first (adaptive) gives you attention to detail and conscientiousness in your work, and helps you strive to be the best you can be. While research is still ongoing on the exact differences in behaviours, some useful characteristics have been explored. For instance, it has been suggested that adaptive perfectionists tend to:

- **Focus on their 'ideal self'** rather than on what is not good about themselves or avoiding their 'feared self'

- Focus on the **bigger picture**
- **Appraise positives** in their performance
- Have a **broad definition of success**
- Take part in behaviour experiments **and try things out** (rather than not doing something because it isn't perfect)
- **Frame positively**
- **Set achievable goals** they are satisfied with when these have been achieved

The second type of perfectionism (maladaptive) can seriously and negatively affect your ability to produce. It can prevent you from getting started on a project due to fear of failure, stop you from releasing perfectly good material, and contribute to high MPA levels. Overall, maladaptive perfectionism can suck the enjoyment out of performing and releasing music and is something you want to avoid as much as possible. If any of those feelings are familiar to you, try working through the exercise below, and if you feel you're setting impossible standards for yourself, seek professional help from a therapist.

ELLIS PECEN'S 'IDEAL SELF' EXERCISE TO MANAGE MALADAPTIVE PERFECTIONISM

- **What are the characteristics of my ideal self?** Rather than your feared self; try and use positive empowering words instead of stating what you do not want. What kind of words would describe the positive performer you aspire to become?

- **What do I care about meaning to others?** In a broad sense, what are the things you care about being and meaning? There are no wrongs here. This is about what you care about making other people feel, as a direct or indirect result of your aspirations and you as a person.

- **What is my broad definition of success,** as opposed to a narrow goal of winning a deal or competition, for example? What does success mean to you? Who do you think is successful and why? Can you 'broaden' the definition of success? For instance, from 'best performer' to 'most inspiring role model' to 'a person of integrity and inspiration'.

- **How can I think of ways to experiment,** rather than wait until I think it is perfect before I take any action. Can I click 'send' before I feel ready? Can I say 'yes' even though I don't feel like it? Ready never comes for a perfectionist so think of ways to practise saying 'yes' and putting things out there.

- **How can I frame this situation positively or differently?** Everything in life can be thought of as positive or negative, depending on how it's framed. What would an optimist say about this? What would a pessimist say about this?

If perfectionism creeps up in live performances, it's important to understand that, ultimately, the audience wants you to succeed, and if you do make a mistake, they'll understand that you're human. Williamon explains: "What we do find, because musicians are highly perfectionistic and they can be quite critical of things when they go wrong, they come off stage and they immediately start thinking, 'Well, where were the errors? Where were the mistakes? What happened? What could I do better?' And I think that's the wrong frame of mind to be in."[23]

This is exactly the frame of mind that writer, producer, and musician Catherine Anne Davies found herself in while experiencing a particularly bad bout of performance anxiety that made her want to call off a show. But she kept going, the performance went well, and she then had to reevaluate how realistic her anxiety had been. She explains:

> "I had to have a look at the perfectionism that I was placing on myself. I kept fixating on: 'What if I fuck up on the piano and everyone laughs at me?' I found it quite helpful to have friends who just said to me, 'Well, what if you did fuck up? What if you did play a wrong note? Let's think about gigs and shows you've been to where you know an artist that you love has done that.' And I remember seeing Rufus Wainwright doing that in the Royal Albert Hall — he fluffed a song and everyone loved it. It was the one moment of the show I remember because it was so sweet and endearing. So it was about reminding myself that **people will like the humanity of musicians and that I needed to stop thinking I had to be perfect**. I just told myself that, next time, I need to not put so much pressure on myself and almost allow myself the permission to mess up."

When it comes to evaluating how well a gig has gone, Williamon recommends avoiding doing so straight after the performance. He says to review performances "when we're in a situation where we can do so objectively." Instead of focusing on the negative, why not force yourself to ask a different question, like: 'What went well?' In that heightened state, focus on the positives and enjoy the post-performance buzz. There's plenty of time for detailed analysis later on. (For more about post-performance review, see the Stage Strategies chapter.)

CONCLUSION

Contrary to what might be immediately obvious, MPA is not something you want to get rid of completely. **Performers need to learn how to manage it, through a combination of environmental, lifestyle, and psychological factors**, including understanding their own zone of optimal functioning. There are musical factors, too, such as making sure you're well practised at what you're performing, along with understanding that certain environments or audiences may trigger different anxiety responses in you.

MPA is a complex subject and we've only scratched the surface here. The reasons why people are affected are diverse and not always obvious. For some, performing onstage and being 'seen' can trigger anxieties and fear stemming from negative childhood experiences, which can only really be worked through in therapy. For others, simple approaches, like those we've outlined, can make a big difference. There is also a new body of evidence suggesting that Acceptance and Commitment Therapy can be useful for managing MPA, so it may be worth exploring if you would like to find out more.[24]

A final takeaway on this topic is to make sure you **perform in front of an audience as much as possible**, as the dynamic live experience with an audience is totally different to the dry rehearsal room. Joanna MacGregor, Head of Piano at the Royal Academy of Music, explains: "Even if you're nervous, to make it as a performer, you still need to welcome the opportunity to sit in front of an audience and play to them."[25] Try incorporating some of the strategies we've described in low pressure gigs, so that when you're playing to a bigger audience, or at a gig where the stakes are higher, you'll be able to manage those rising anxiety levels. Ellis Pecen reiterates why this is important:

> "As anxiety increases, we typically experience changes in, for instance, brain activity, focus, and physiological responses. As a result, it can feel like a different person performing, because if you look at it from a neuroscience and physiology perspective, it really does put the individual in 'another state'. This means that performers need to practise their physical and psychological skills under a heightened level of arousal, before their skills can be transferred successfully to a high stakes performance context."

Finally, once you've managed your levels of MPA to optimise your performance, it's time to get out there, enjoy the performance, and show the audience what you're capable of. MacGregor concludes: "There's lots of training needed to be physically and mentally prepared, and emotionally flexible enough to be comfortable and creative on stage, but, ultimately, there has to be the desire to go out there and fly."[26]

Here are the key takeaways from this chapter:

- Music performance anxiety can be a big issue for musicians, but there are lots of proven ways of managing it successfully. The first step to doing that is **working out how it affects you.**

- You can then **start to manage it** by discovering your 'optimal zone' of emotion and intensity of MPA, reframing anxiety as positive (remembering that you need a certain level to deliver a great performance), and taking the pressure out of the situation by noticing how you view the importance of the performance.

- Other strategies include **thought-blocking, positive self-talk, mental rehearsal, warming-up, intention setting**, doing a **relaxation** exercise, and creating a **pre-performance routine.**

- You can also **identify sources of stress in performance** (task mastery, situational stress, and trait anxiety) and prepare accordingly while creating a **supportive lifestyle** (getting enough sleep, doing breathwork, keeping an eye on your diet, and practising relaxation techniques).

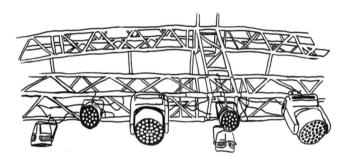

CHAPTER 17

STAGE STRATEGIES

OVER THE LAST FEW CHAPTERS, we've looked at getting clear about what you want to create in your career. Hopefully, you've set some goals, and if those include improving your ability as a musician, you'll now know the fastest and most effective ways to do that. We've covered performance anxiety, so you'll be armed with some strategies to manage that if it's a problem. The final piece in the performance jigsaw is the gig itself. We're now going to look at how to bring everything you've worked on together, and how to deliver an optimal performance night after night.

There are three fairly straightforward elements to this:

- Strategies to **prepare yourself just before the show.**
- Ways of **boosting your performance onstage**.
- **A process of review** afterwards, where you'll look at what went well and what can be improved next time.

When you consider these three aspects, you're able to get a handle on the external circumstances that are within your control, and focus on the job you have to do to the best of your ability.

BEFORE THE SHOW

As we said in the Touring chapter, performing live is the part of the job that many musicians love most, and it's where peak experiences happen that make all the travel, admin, and stress, worth it. However, along with the internal stressors mentioned in the Performance Anxiety chapter, there are also external stressors that can affect your mindset as you go onstage. If the venue's not what you expected, if you've missed your soundcheck because you were stuck in traffic, if you've just had a bust-up with a bandmate, or if you're simply not feeling your best, there could be a knock-on impact on your focus, concentration, and ability to perform. If you gig regularly, one of the greatest tools you can have is a process that helps you get into the right frame of mind for performing. It will also mean you can achieve consistency between shows, so if you suddenly scale up to a stadium when you're used to a room above a pub, you're able to get into a mindset that will help you take control of any situation, and even use any anxiety you feel to fuel your performance.

Mindset preparation is something we see a lot in athletes — legendary US swimmer Michael Phelps swings his arms three times and listens to Michael Jackson before a race. Tennis player Rafa Nadal has a cold shower before a match, and while doing it imagines feeling his power and resilience growing, allowing him to emerge from the shower focused and ready to play.[1] The New Zealand All Blacks rugby team have 'the Haka', which is a ceremonial Maori dance that involves stamping feet and shouting. It's performed before each match and designed to improve the players' state of mind and prepare them for action. There are examples of this in the music world, too — Marcus Mumford burns Palo Santo (a form of incense) before going on stage, Lorde takes a nap, and Led Zeppelin's Robert Plant does the ironing.[2]

Alongside the more informal approaches to performance prep above, we know that specially crafted pre-performance routines can be incredibly beneficial to musicians, thanks to a surge in music-related performance science research in the last 15 years. In *Musical Excellence*, authors Christopher Connolly and Aaron Williamon suggest developing pre-performance routines that warm up the body and voice (check back to Music and the Body and the Vocal Health chapters for more details on this) and, just as importantly, prepare the brain for the task ahead, creating consistency in performance. By consistency, we don't mean playing in exactly the same way night after night — you'll want to vary your performances and respond to the energy in the room each time. Instead, we mean consistency of quality — getting into the mindset that's right for you and being able to communicate effectively with each audience.

Pre-performance routines can be done just before you go onstage, or you might find there are things you do at other times on show day (for example, a vocal warm-up exercise first thing in the morning to check in with your voice, or going for a run during the afternoon). The important thing is finding a process that works for you and testing it in advance of a big show. If you're in a band, you may want to have your own individual pre-performance routine as well as something you do as part of a group. Coldplay like to have a band hug before going onstage, for example, while Rihanna leads everyone in group prayer.[3] Tour manager Suzi Green provides another example from one of the acts she has worked with, which started half an hour before showtime, when the band would play games in order to foster a connection that's then taken onstage. She explains:

"They would stand in a circle and throw balls to each other, playing word games. It was absolutely sacred, nothing ever ate into the half an hour. They always did something to connect, which meant that by the time they were walking up the steps to get them to the stage, they had already bonded and then they played better for it. I think that if you have that time to connect before you step out, you're in a better mental state for whatever you step out to; bad sound or rain coming onto the stage at your festival, or whatever. You are presented as a group, rather than lots of individuals not talking to each other."

Let's look in more detail at the key elements of a pre-performance routine so that you'll be able to craft one for yourself. We'll also introduce you to mental skills training tools that have been shown to prepare musicians' mindsets for performance.

WHAT WORKS FOR YOU?

There's general guidance and tools available that you can use to get into an optimal state for performance. We'll look at that shortly, but everyone is different and you may already know what works for you. Let's take a moment to reflect on what those things are, so that you can incorporate them into your routine.

You may have found that for your best gig ever, you had a light meal an hour before the show, and followed it with some deep breathing exercises that helped you get focused and in the zone (as we discussed in the Performance Anxiety chapter). Or, it could be that you listened to music on your headphones, dancing around the room, raising your overall level of energy and excitement ready for the set. Did you talk to fans by the stage door or did you keep to yourself? If you can't think of anything at the moment, it may help to pay attention to how you prepare at future gigs and whether you feel it has an impact — positive or otherwise — on your performance.

Successful gigs are the key — think about anything you did differently beforehand, or non-musical activities during the day, and incorporate them before your future shows (make sure you test them out in advance, though). A word of warning: you don't want to become so reliant on particular activities that they develop into unhelpful superstitions or beliefs, and you can't perform without having done a certain string of complicated procedures beforehand. Depending on where your optimal performance zone is, anything like this that increases anxiety around performance may not be helpful, so instead think about what you need, and try to include it if you can.

Here are some questions you can ask yourself to optimise performance preparation: [4]

- Think back to your **last really successful gig**.
- **How did you prepare physically?** (This could be related to various things, including food, exercise, hydration, and rest.)
- **How did you prepare emotionally?** (Perhaps you listened to some upbeat songs or had some alone time.)
- **How did you prepare mentally?** (Examples of this include positive self-talk, breathing exercises, and reframing anxiety.)
- **What worked well?**
- **What, if anything, do you want to change?**
- **What else could you have done?**

Hopefully, you now have some ideas that you can use as a starting point. Jot down factors that lift your mood, put you in a positive frame of mind, or that you might want to avoid. As we mentioned in the Performance Anxiety chapter, diet, in particular, can play a role in contributing to the anxiety you feel on the day of a show, so you might decide to cut out caffeine and sugar, for example, on show days. To reiterate, try out anything you're going to change or do differently in advance of the gig.

MENTAL PREPARATION

Now you have an idea of specific elements that work for you, let's look at general ways to prepare your mindset for optimal performance. Firstly, think back to some of the goals that you wrote down in the Setting Goals chapter. With any luck, live performance will in some way fit in with one of your overall goals. If so, have a think about how you can set an intention, or come up with ways of aligning with your original objective of why you are performing music. For some musicians, a major goal is to connect with people around the world through their songs, while others may want to lift the spirits of audiences to have an incredible experience through music. **Whatever your objective is, write it down, and make sure you connect to it before you go onstage.**

When you're mid-way through a long tour, motivation can tank pretty quickly, especially when you've been stuck in traffic, arrive stressed and late, and find that the venue is at half capacity. In that space, remembering why you do what you do can help you get back out there and provide the experience you want to give for the audience members who *have* come. In her book, *More Myself,* Alicia Keys describes how she aligned with her intention for performance before a landmark gig in New York's Times Square in 2016, performing to 15,000 people: "Just before I went out to meet the crowd I asked myself the question I ask before every performance – do you want to be good or do you want to be great? I answered by bringing my full self to that experience over the next hour and a half."[5]

A second approach is to **use a relaxation exercise** that can help increase alpha waves in the brain. These help you feel calmer and more focused, and some studies even indicate they boost creativity levels (particularly for introverts[6]), which can be a great state for performance, depending on the type of music you perform. The relaxation state will also shift your processing from the brain's left hemisphere (responsible for words, fears, criticism, and commentary) over to the right hemisphere (which will result in a quieter, more focused state). Dr Don Greene, author of *Performance Success,* explains:

> "Optimal performance and peak performance states are literally beyond words. They come from the quiet, Alpha mind-state in which clear images, beautiful sounds and wonderful feelings are allowed to flow."[7]

Using a relaxation exercise, like the one on the next page, is how you access these states. You may already have a relaxation exercise that works for you, or you might meditate before a performance (apps like Headspace and Calm have pre-recorded relaxation and meditation exercises). If you already have an exercise you use, go ahead and incorporate it into your pre-performance routine. If not, try recording the one we detail further on, and see if it works for you. Be aware that, for some, relaxation exercises may not be enough to manage anxiety levels effectively. If that is the case for you, check back to the Performance Anxiety chapter for more structured management approaches.

We discussed the benefit of mental rehearsal in the Talent and Practice chapter, but it can also be useful in this context if done in a slightly different way. Rather than imagining practising a certain section, after getting into a relaxed state, imagine yourself walking onstage in a confident manner and seeing the audience cheering as you effortlessly perform a brilliant set with ease. **Vividly imagining the gig going well can help prepare the brain to expect success** and will override negative chatter or beliefs that you're not good enough.

That negative chatter can be really distracting, so if you know it's a problem for you, take some time to write down what you say to yourself when you're under pressure. The results can be surprising. The key is to be aware that what you're experiencing are negative, irrational thoughts, and as they relate to events in the future, there's no way they can represent the truth. If you're able to catch yourself and notice it happening, step back, observe

INTRODUCTION TO RELAXATION [8]

The following steps can be used as a way to relax. You may want to ask someone to read them out loud to you, or record the instructions yourself, so that you can experience the effects without having to remember each step. With time and practice, the steps will come naturally.

- Sit down. Put your feet flat on the floor with your hands placed comfortably on your lap.
- Close your eyes.
- First, pay attention to the sounds outside of the room; then, within the room; then notice your own thoughts.
- Pay attention to the contact you make with the chair and floor, and notice your breathing.
- Take a deep breath in for four counts; hold it for four, and let it out slowly to the count of either four or eight.
- As you continue to breathe, pay attention to the muscles around your face: your forehead, the muscles around your eyes, cheeks, mouth, jaw, and neck. As you exhale, imagine all tension draining away through your shoulders and on through your arms, wrists, hands, and fingers. Notice how your chest relaxes, as well as your back, your stomach, waist, and pelvis.
- Pay attention to your thighs and notice any tension you may find in them. On your next out-breath, imagine all of the tension draining away through your knees, calves, ankles, feet, and into the floor, leaving you calm, relaxed, and alert.
- Remain in this state for a few minutes before taking three deep breaths, stretching, and opening your eyes.

the thoughts from a place of detachment and label what it is you're feeling. As musicians' psychotherapist Helen Brice said in the Criticism and Opinions chapter, The Awareness Continuum mindfulness exercise can be helpful if negative self-talk becomes a problem. To reiterate: if you're experiencing these thoughts, she suggests saying to yourself: "I'm aware of the thought, I'm aware of the feeling of discomfort. I'm aware of the emotion of anxiety." Coaching with a psychotherapist can be useful if you need more help with this, or refer back to the ACT strategies in the Performance Anxiety chapter.

Alternatively, to redirect negative self-talk, you can **come up with an empowering statement that can be incorporated into a pre-performance routine to help you stay aligned with your vision**. Essentially, this is a positive statement that reinforces how you want to feel. If you get nervous and find it hard to speak to audiences between songs, positive self-talk could be: "I am a confident singer and connect with the audience with ease." Equally, you may find it useful to have instructional self-talk, which is essentially telling yourself what you need to do from a practical point of view. Whichever way you choose to use it, managing self-talk can be a useful tool to counter any negativity that comes in.

Another tool available to prepare yourself for performance is the use of avatars, or 'alter-egos', as we mentioned in the Fame chapter. Beyoncé has Sasha Fierce, while Reginald Dwight becomes Elton John, and Adele uses one after a backstage conversation with Beyoncé led her to create her own version of Sasha Fierce mixed with singer June Carter, whom she calls Sasha Carter.[9] Standing onstage in front of thousands of people and being a larger than life character when, in reality, you just took the bins out that morning, can be a pretty weird experience. Some musicians, understandably, want to find ways to separate their everyday lives from their onstage personas, and this process can help with that. If you want to try it, have a think about the musicians who have inspired you. Think about how they walk on stage, how they use their body, and how they look. What aspects would you like to take for your own character? You can even use the benefits of the exercise without having to create a totally different persona

— just think of the best elements of performances you admire and incorporate those into your stage behaviour. If you want to try it, follow the exercise below.

ACTING 'AS IF' [10]

Acting 'as if' is like acting a part, performing as if you were someone or something else that represents a quality you want to emphasise in your performance. The someone or something will be very specific to you.

- Before starting, **think of someone who expresses a performance quality that you would like to recreate.**
- Use a **relaxation exercise** that works best for you.
- **Observe this person in a specific situation** where he or she expresses the quality you identified.
- Step into the situation yourself and **imagine being this person in this situation.** Notice physical sensations and what it feels like to be the person.
- Keep this image in your mind and **imagine playing or singing a piece of music you want to perform.** Notice what you see, hear, and feel, when you play like this person with the qualities they possess.
- As you finish the piece, let the scene fade. When you are ready, bring your attention back to your present environment and **jot down anything that you noticed about what you want to bring into your own performances.**

A word of warning on alter-egos — some artists have found that being a different person onstage to who they are in daily life can start to knock on to their promo sessions and interactions with fans, and before long, they're inhabiting the life of someone they no longer feel they are. That disconnect between who you think you need to be, and who you are on a daily basis, can take its toll over time, particularly if people on your team collude with this and stop treating you as 'you'. Some artists even feel unable to live up to the character everyone wants them to be — in an in-depth interview study on this topic, one participant described the pressure he felt over time to stay in the role: "You're trying to stay positive, trying to be that character that everyone wants you to be, and sometimes you can't do that, you can't be that character."[11]

In this study, three out of the five participants all used an artist character as a protective mechanism to distance themselves in their work, but struggled with the lack of authenticity and integrity they felt over time when engaging with it. More research is needed into this, but basically, when it comes to creating a totally separate alter-ego, proceed with caution, and if in doubt, or if you're already experiencing some kind of disconnect from the true, authentic version of yourself you want to be, have a chat with a therapist who will be able to guide you to doing this in a healthy way.

Depending on what kind of music you perform, creating an alter-ego and having a larger than life stage presence may be the last thing you want to do. If this is the case, instead, it could be that you want to connect to the audience with sincerity, honesty, and vulnerability. This requires bravery and can be tough to do, as researcher Brené Brown describes: "We're all taught to be brave and we're all warned growing up not to be vulnerable. When you have bravery with no vulnerability, you have all bluster, all posturing, no real courage."[12] For anyone who writes their own music, getting up on a stage, being truly seen, and presenting your inner world to the audience is an act of real courage. All staged art requires a level of persona-based performance, though, so expecting yourself to be the same, no matter the circumstances, is difficult. The solution perhaps lies in finding the balance that feels right to you — with enough persona-based 'activation' to give a good show, but whilst maintaining a level of integrity that feels comfortable. In the meantime, the previous exercise will help to boost the elements of your own performance you want to improve, so is a good and safe place to start.

The final ingredient in this mixture comes from American social psychologist and researcher Amy Cuddy. In her book *Presence*, Cuddy describes how our body language and posture can affect how we feel, and how holding confident stances (or 'power poses') before an important event can help to improve testosterone levels (responsible for confidence) and lower cortisol (the stress hormone). There have been some claims that her research wasn't quite the cure-all it was originally presented as; however, there is no doubt that posture affects how you feel so it's still worth mentioning, and a lot of people worldwide swear by her technique before performances to boost feelings of confidence before going onstage. To do it in the style Cuddy talks about, stand holding a 'Wonder Woman' or 'Superman' pose with your legs wide, hands on hips, chest out, and chin up for approximately two minutes, and see if you feel differently afterwards. Whether or not you choose to incorporate it into your pre-show routine, being aware that your posture affects your mental state before a performance might help if you struggle with confidence, and regularly spend the hour before a gig hunched over a phone, PlayStation controller, or laptop (not ideal).

PUTTING IT ALL TOGETHER

You've hopefully identified some activities that put you in a great headspace, you've aligned with an intention, and you have a relaxation method of choice. What do you do now? Well, you just need to put it all together to create your own individualised routine.

If you find a routine that works, write it down, or put it in your phone, so that you have a record of every step, then refer back to it before each performance to put you in the best state possible. **Review it on a regular basis, and if something doesn't work, change or adapt it.**

PERFORMANCE MAGIC – FLOW

So you've now stepped onstage, having prepared as best as you can. This is where the performance magic comes in. Have you ever had that feeling where you start playing and the world begins to disappear, leaving you fully immersed in the music with no thoughts distracting you, and time either speeding up or slowing down? Some put it down to mystical experiences onstage or describe how they're 'in the zone', and peak performance experts have described this using the concept of flow.[13] **In the state of flow, individuals perform at their very best and creative problem-solving abilities are heightened**, which is a perfect state for any musician wishing to perform live or improvise.

In his book about ultimate human performance, *The Rise of Superman*, researcher and flow expert Steven Kotler explains how these experiences are linked to neurochemistry — when you enter flow states, your brain releases five chemicals that improve performance, making you feel good in the process. These chemicals are:

- Dopamine (sharpens focus, engagement, and excitement)
- Norepinephrine (maintains focus, boosts skills)
- Anandamide (increases creativity, reduces fear)
- Endorphins (reduce pain)
- Serotonin (makes us feel good and come back for more)

In addition to receiving these performance-boosting chemicals, while performing in this state, your brain goes through a process call transient hypofrontality, which is where parts of the brain shut down. These are the parts responsible for introspection and self-awareness, so your brain essentially shuts off negative self-talk and improves confidence. This also allows you to rely on your intuition and find creative solutions to musical problems.

So how do you recreate flow in your next performance? Firstly, Kotler advises that you **enjoy the experience**. Without enjoying the task, accessing flow is much harder. You'll also need to be **focused and concentrated**, without your mind wandering all over the place. This can be cultivated with the relaxation exercises we mentioned earlier, or through mental skills training exercises such as

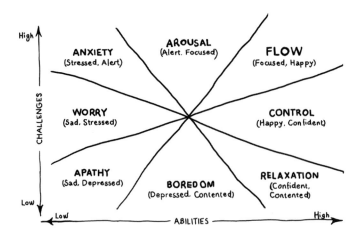

visualisation and mental rehearsal. Finally, you need to challenge yourself, but not too much. As Kotler explains: "Flow appears near the emotional midpoint between boredom and anxiety, in what scientists call the flow channel — the spot where the task is hard enough to make us stretch but not hard enough to make us snap."[14] The emotions and flow states graph[15] above outlines what Kotler is talking about. Think back to the last time you felt flow while performing and how you could recreate the skill level, enjoyment, and focus that you previously felt, and bring more of it into future performances.

A word of caution: flow may not be the panacea that Silicon Valley gurus proclaim — it can sometimes be difficult to access consistently, and some musicians find that they access flow in unlikely circumstances, or not at all. It's great to be aware of, and to strive towards, but if it doesn't feel like a manageable state for you, and the advice above doesn't resonate, don't get disheartened. It may be that other options such as the Individual Zone of Optimal Functioning (discussed in Performance Anxiety) are more helpful.

POST-PERFORMANCE REVIEW

After a successful performance, you'll definitely want to celebrate. However, if you want to continue improving as a stage performer and musician, **it's worth taking some time afterwards to review how the gig went**. This involves looking at what worked well, and why, and also at what didn't work and why. An effective post-performance review is not coming offstage and heading straight on to social media, judging success by the comments and videos posted. It's also not best done straight after the gig, as your emotions are likely to be all over the place. The ideal time is 24 to 48 hours after the gig, when your emotions have settled. However, a review of some kind is better than none at all, and if you'd rather do it straight away, go ahead. Try and avoid what Suzi Green describes as common practice with those she works with: "Most bands will quite often do debriefs by disappearing into the dressing room [straight after the gig] and analysing everything that they've messed up." The aim of having a post-performance review is to boost strengths and minimise weaknesses, and this is done by having an accurate assessment of your performance and a bit of emotional distance.

You might want to review short clips people recorded of the gig, but be aware that the sound quality will be appalling and you probably won't have sounded like the tinny speakers are suggesting. By all means, look at your posture, presence, use of the stage, and interaction with the band, but don't judge your vocal or musical ability on these videos. Leave that to your sessions with a coach.

Alongside the technical evaluation, you may also want to check in with any wider objectives or intentions set before the show. Sure, you messed up that solo, but how did the audience feel about the gig? If you wanted them to have a great time, and that was evident from where you were standing, in the wider context, those dropped notes probably weren't such a big deal. Keep aligned with the meaning and purpose of why you're performing and check in to see if you achieved that. It's also worth keeping a journal to track all of the things we've been talking about in this section — that way, you'll have your notes in one place to remind you of your wins and what to do (or not) next time.

There are lots of options available to you as a musician if you want to perform at your best and keep improving while playing live. Taking time to be mindful of what you do that makes you better (or worse) can help you avoid preventable mistakes in the future, improving your ability to perform at your best whenever you need to. **Find out what works for you, test it in advance, and refine along the way.**

Finally, remember these things:

- Having a process that helps you get into the best frame of mind for performing can help **alleviate the impact of stress and ensure you achieve consistency** between shows, regardless of the scale of the gig.

- The first step to curating your own process is to **work out what has an impact on your performance** and if there's anything you already do, or have done in the past, that helps you perform at your best.

- **Mental preparation** can involve connecting with your overall career objective before you go onstage, using a relaxation exercise that helps increase alpha waves in the brain (which make you feel calmer and more focused), and mentally imagining a confident and successful performance.

- You can try and **combat any negative thoughts** you might be experiencing by observing them, instead of being taken in by them, and countering them with an empowering positive statement.

- If it works for you, you can also **employ the use of an 'alter ego'** to help you step into the confident and competent performer that you want to be, and/or practise **holding confident 'power poses'**.

- **Accessing the state of flow** is another way of improving performance and confidence levels, which requires enjoyment, focus, and concentration.

- Finding a process that helps you perform at your best may change and evolve over time, so **keep an eye on what works and doesn't**, using a considered post-performance review process after the emotions of the gig have settled.

CHAPTER 18

CREATIVITY

HAVING AN OUTLET to express yourself creatively, is, without a doubt, one of the most rewarding parts of life as a musician. However, the ability to be creative isn't constant, easy or a given, and may be mired by factors like stress, pressure, time constraints, and too many voices in the room (which might even be yours). Inspiration can be elusive for short or long periods of time and it can arrive at unexpected moments. A spell in which you endure a painful period of writer's block might precede an exciting splurge of creativity, when an endless number of ideas seem to be exploding out of your brain morning, noon, and night. As Alicia Keys describes: "Creativity is inherently messy. It's chaotic and non-linear. It comes to life in fits and starts, disjointed and seemingly random."[1]

Whether you're a Grammy-winning singer like Keys or an independent emerging artist, the challenge lies in attempting to embrace and harness that chaos, whilst making sure the full force of your creativity isn't *too* controlled.

As well as enabling you to put your own stamp on the world we live in, research suggests that **practising creativity can pay dividends in terms of health**. It's said to contribute to both physical and psychological health, and to optimal human functioning.[2] Alongside keeping you healthy in mind, body, and spirit, and driving innovation and evolution, creativity can help deal with the challenges of life. Many a musician uses writing and making music to process all sorts of pain, sometimes even transforming that pain during the creative process. Jazz saxophonist Charlie Parker once said: "Music is your own experience, your thoughts, your wisdom. If you don't live it, it won't come out of your horn."[3]

Ed Sheeran echoes this sentiment, saying that writing, for him, is a therapeutic process. He explains: "I've never had a therapist and I think the reason is because I talk about all the shit that's in my head in a song. I'll have something happen to me, which will make me really sad, I'll write a song about it, I'll finish the song, and then I'll be really happy because I'm like, 'Oh, that song came out of that really shit situation' and then you look at that situation and go, 'I'm glad that happened' because you've got a song out of it. Creativity is very good for making people happy because at the end of it, you've got something that didn't exist 10 minutes ago."[4]

Writing music professionally, however, is not always a positive experience, and being under pressure to write a hit record within a fixed time period may create an immense amount of stress, particularly when the whole creative process is rarely understood. This is why we want to address the topic, so that you can better understand creativity and how to maximise your own. In this chapter, we're going to look at where to draw inspiration from, and the processes musicians use to harness their own creativity. We'll also discuss creative blocks, and ways of enhancing creativity, in the hope of providing you with some tools and ideas you can use to help curate an environment and state of mind that's conducive to the development of your own innate creativity.

THE ORIGINS OF CREATIVITY

First of all, where does creativity come from? Researcher and author Jenny Boyd, who conducted the largest interview study into creativity with 75 iconic rock and pop musicians, found that many participants spoke about the unconscious mind (as opposed to the rational mind) as the source of their creative spring. In Boyd's book *It's Not Only Rock 'n' Roll,* US singer and songwriter David Crosby (a founding member of The Byrds and Crosby, Stills & Nash) puts it like this:

> "Many of my best songs come out all in one blurt, and at those times I have the distinct feeling that this level of me is just a vehicle for some other level of me that has been sitting there, cooking this thing up. It often happens when I'm in between waking and sleeping. I'll be going to sleep, and I'll be sort of drowsy, and this motormouth mind will kind of shut down and then BAM! This stuff will start to come and I'll turn on the light quickly and write, write, write and play, play, write, and then 'Fantastic!' At about that time, my other mind is starting to kick back in and say, 'David, you're cool!'"[5]

The late Steve Jobs, former CEO of Apple, believed that you need to have rich life experiences as a cultural bank to draw upon in order to pursue creative endeavours. "**Creativity is just connecting things**," he said.[6] Jobs continued:

> "When you ask creative people how they did something, they feel a little guilty because they didn't really do it, they just saw something. It seemed obvious to them after a while. That's because they were able to connect experiences they've had and synthesise new things. The reason they were able to do that was that they've had more experiences,

or they have thought more about their experiences than other people."

Musician and writer Amanda Palmer agrees. She says: "We can only connect the dots that we collect, which makes everything you write about you. **Your connections are the thread that you weave into the cloth that becomes the story that only you can tell.**"[7] Keys, on the other hand, describes a more esoteric approach to making art. "During the creative process, I never know how a song is going to come to me, but every now and then, the universe sends me a gift. The lyrics and melodies just seemingly appear and I'm grateful whenever that happens."[8]

The ancient Greeks coined the concept of the muse and thought that creativity came to them through external 'daemons' that would visit. The Romans took the idea a bit further and believed there were spiritual entities that would assist creative people with their work, whenever they needed it. *Eat, Pray, Love* author Elizabeth Gilbert, who also wrote a book about how to unleash your creativity, titled *Big Magic,* explains why this was such a helpful approach for creators at the time:

> "The ancient artist was protected from certain things, like, for example, too much narcissism, right? If your work was brilliant, you couldn't take all the credit for it, everybody knew that you had this disembodied genius who had helped you. If you work bombed, not entirely your fault, you know? Everyone knew your genius was kind of lame."[9]

Gilbert describes how the Renaissance came and put the focus on the individual above the gods and universe, and how she believes that was a huge error. "Allowing somebody, one mere person to believe that he or she is the vessel, the source of all divine, creative, unknowable, eternal mystery, is just a smidge too much responsibility to put on one fragile, human psyche. It just completely warps and distorts egos, and it creates all these unmanageable expectations about performance."

David Byrne of Talking Heads fame, however, disagrees with the concept of the muse. He explains:

"I had an extremely slow-dawning insight about creation. That insight is that **context largely determines what is written, painted, sculpted, sung, or performed**. That doesn't sound like much of an insight but it's actually the opposite of conventional wisdom, which maintains that creation emerges out of some interior emotion, from an upwelling of passion or feeling, and that the creative urge will brook no accommodation, that it simply must find an outlet to be heard, read, or seen."[10]

The accepted narrative, according to Byrne, "suggests that a classical composer gets a strange look in his or her eye and begins furiously scribbling a fully realised composition that couldn't exist in any other form. Or, that the rock and roll singer is driven by desires and demons, and out bursts this amazing, perfectly shaped song that had to be three minutes and twelve-seconds — nothing more, nothing less." Instead, Byrne believes that we "unconsciously and instinctively make work to fit preexisting formats." He concludes: "**Opportunity and availability are often the mother of invention**." In her creativity bible, *The Creative Habit,* author Twyla Tharp (who has a background in choreography and dance) echoes Byrne's thoughts. She believes that **creativity is the result of preparation, routine, and constant effort, and that the cornerstones to achieving it are about honing your craft, cultivating genius, and overcoming fear.**[11]

As you can see, there isn't a concrete consensus on whether there is a mystical element involved in creativity, or if inspiration is simply the product of experience, rituals, organisation, and connection. The truth is, the source of creative zones could be multiple and various, even for one person, and what works for someone in a specific scenario might not lead to success in another. Similarly, trying to follow someone else's structured approach to being creative might lead to creative block through over-analysis of a process that often requires freedom of thought. This is worth bearing in mind as you read this chapter. **Your own personal approach to harnessing creativity may involve finding out what your optimal zone of functioning is for the task** (as we discussed in the Performance Anxiety chapter) and taking into account the nature of the music you have to produce. If you're a film composer, for example, you may have stricter parameters around the content you create, and performing elaborate rituals may not be appropriate when you're working in a room filled with producers. As ever, the key is to find out what works for you within whatever context you find yourself in.

FINDING INSPIRATION

Here are some examples of scenarios that have helped facilitate creativity for other musicians. Songwriter Wayne Hector, who has written a wildly impressive 30 number one hits for a long list of acts including One Direction, Westlife, and JLS, says he's inspired by working with others. He explains: "My inspiration generally comes from having a great artist in the room, somebody whose tone of voice really excites me, or somebody playing a set of chords." Alicia Keys says that her ideas can come from many different places: "A line I've read in a novel, a conversation I've overheard, or an abiding sense of calm I've felt during a Sunday stroll through Harlem's Mount Morris Park."[12]

For Keys, that initial inspiration is then furthered into a piece of creative work by **experimentation**. She continues:

> "In the case of the latter, I might return home, sit down at the piano, and play around with some chords that embody the feeling I've experienced. Or I might hear a beautiful chord in a song and think, 'What key is that?', and later try to pick it out on my keyboard. That chord might lead me to a different set of chords, which might later become the foundation for a melody. Other times, I may have some lyrics scribbled down on a random piece of paper, with no idea how they may fit together with notes."

To use Keys' approach, try experimenting or improvising with your instrument and see what emerges. It can be useful to record yourself while you're doing it, and then listen back and see what stands out.

Red Hot Chili Peppers' frontman Anthony Kiedis, on the other hand, has utilised **nature and solitude** as a way of accessing inspiration. As a participant in Jenny Boyd's study, he describes how, during a writing process in the south of Mexico, "I would go climb over these cliffs and sit on the rocks by the ocean. As I sat there, I had very little distraction from people or from cities, or anything like that, and I was able to just feel what it was that I feel about the world and write it down."[13]

The common thread in all these methods is **being present in the moment and remaining open to ideas**, whenever they might strike. As legendary American songwriter Jimmy Webb says:

> "I think that a writer has to constantly be aware of what is going on around them and ready to snatch an idea out of the air. Whether it's through a situation, an argument between two people in a restaurant, a phrase from your daughter, or something with rhythm that has a universal truth and is said in a slightly different way."[14]

As such, ideas can arrive when you're least expecting them — in bed, on a walk, during a conversation, or, as was the case with Ariana Grande's smash "thank u, next", in the shower.[15] That's why Webb advises songwriters to carry a notebook (or to anyone under the age of 40, a phone) everywhere. Hector uses an app called Recorder Plus to store his vocal ideas. Having a method of quickly capturing an idea is handy if you wake up in the middle of the night with what feels like a career-defining hit rattling around in your head. Most phones have an in-built voice recorder, and Apple's Music Memos will tell you what key you're singing in. Your rough recordings might even be useful as promo one day — some artists, like Taylor Swift, have included these early voice notes as bonus tracks on finished albums.

ORIGINALITY

When it comes to originality, it matters "not where you take things from — it's where you take them to", according to a quote widely attributed to film director, Jean Luc-Godard. And in the words of Picasso: "Good artists copy, great artists steal." Those aren't words we'd recommend trotting out if you're in court accused of plagiarism, and we're not saying outright stealing is a good idea in music making, but finding inspiration in what other people have already done can be a helpful part of any creative process. Michael Jackson and Bruno Mars were inspired by James Brown, while painter Frida Kahlo has been cited as an influence by Madonna and Florence Welch, and Prince paved the way for Frank Ocean, Alicia Keys, Janelle Monáe, D'Angelo, and many others besides. Additionally, there are persistent rumours that Oasis were quite keen on The Beatles. As Steve Jobs and Amanda Palmer said earlier, no one is an island — we're all creating new things that have been drawn from linking our personal connections, which results in something original.

However, as we've mentioned, there's a difference between 'being inspired by' and direct copying. It's best to avoid the latter, which can prove extremely costly, as Robin Thicke and Pharrell Williams will confirm. They were ordered to hand over a casual $5.3m in damages to the Marvin Gaye Estate, which said the duo's 2013 hit "Blurred Lines" emulated 'the vibe' of Gaye's '70s single "Got to Give it Up" (which Williams did admit was an inspiration during the recording process).[16] Some simple rules to avoid plagiarism include **clearing all direct samples with the owner of said song's sound recording** (no, simply manipulating the sample to try and disguise it is not sufficient), and not copying lyrics or melody.

Forensic musicologist Joe Bennett also suggests singing the melody of your work to someone who knows the prior work that you've drawn inspiration from, "and if they identify it as the prior work, then that probably is something that would be evidence in an accusation of plagiarism."[17] If similarities are found, the secret is to catch anything that might be considered inadvertent copying before it leaves the studio, says Bennett, "and then adapt, adapt and adapt until it's not recognisable." The tricky part, obviously, is that if your copying really is truly inadvertent, you won't even think about changing your work.

ACCESSING CREATIVITY AND NAVIGATING BLOCKS

You're not going to be brimming with brilliant ideas all the time, that's a fact (Lennon and McCartney managed to bang out some decent songs during their time in The Beatles, but think about how much time they spent *not* writing). Sometimes, you may even find it hard to believe that you ever thought of anything new at all, and feel that your creativity has dried up for good. If you're experiencing a creative block, first of all know that it's normal, especially under times of stress. During the coronavirus pandemic in 2020, some musicians found themselves with lots of time on their hands thanks to cancelled shows, and it might be easy to assume that sitting at home in lockdown was the perfect time to write new music. However, being able to use that time for creativity wasn't a given, due to high levels of anxiety brought about by the challenging circumstances. As journalist and music critic Richard Morrison said: "Note to artists: it's not a sign of weakness to be unable to work now. Recent research suggests that our brains work differently under extreme stress, shifting control from the cerebral cortex to the limbic system. We revert to instinctive survival thinking, suspending creative processes."[18]

It's difficult to be creative and productive during extreme and chronic states of stress, which can result in a person being neither relaxed nor deeply emotionally engaged enough to be in their optimal zone of creativity. However, there's a difference between extreme stress and intense negative emotions, and the latter can actually be helpful in fostering creativity. Performance psychologist Dr Ellis Pecen explains: "Limbic system activity can also be active during emotions like fear, sadness, grief, and so on, which can actually help some people produce and be highly creative. Creativity can come from both ends of the spectrum." This is why some artists found that they were incredibly productive in lockdown, and why some music creatives can produce something brilliant while being in a low mood and dealing with pain.

While negative experiences can inspire a creative process, it's important to note that low mood and emotional pain aren't a prerequisite for creativity and, as we discussed in the Mental Health chapter, living with generally good mental health is of utmost priority. Evanescence songwriter and frontwoman Amy Lee has found that, in the past, she was "in love" with her sorrow before the writing process for the band's 2006 album, *The Open Door*, challenged that mentality. She explains: "I get into these moods where I write music. It's not so much about being depressed, it's just the strange low that I ride. But at the same time, I want to be free and break through and be happy."[19] Lee managed to do that with a song on the album titled "Good Enough." She continues: "It was the bravest song to write and to bring to the table when we were recording the album. It's just really real, and it was saying what I felt, that for once I wasn't miserable, stuck, trapped, sad, or grieving. It was happy. I thought the guys (in the band) were probably going to hate it, and they loved it."

Another issue that stands in the way of creativity is being too busy. Dr Sandi Mann, who is a researcher at the University of Central Lancashire, says that **having the spare time to do nothing can be important when it comes to fostering creativity**. "Boredom is one of our most creative forces," she explains.[20] "If you ask people to do nothing to the point where they get really bored, they then become creative and start thinking in novel and productive ways." If you've got lots on your plate — is there any way you can carve out some time (however brief) where you can forget your to-do list? Perhaps go for a walk in nature or give yourself a chance to daydream, which can help to access the unconscious mind that David Crosby was talking about. It's surprising how rarely we give ourselves this sort of freedom. To put it another way, when was the last time you sat down without your phone, without the TV on, without a book, or music in the background and just stared into space? And what ideas might come into your mind if you did?

In her study, Jenny Boyd found there to be several factors involved in actualising creativeness, which can be embraced if you're going through a creative block. These include:

- **Recognising one's true gift**
- **Taking chances**
- **Developing the ability to concentrate**
- **Spending time alone to let the mind wander**
- **Learning to have faith in oneself and one's true expression, which encouragement from others can help nurture**

In order to start with this, Boyd recommends meditation. The late George Harrison, who was one of Boyd's interviewees, was a fan of the practice as a way to harness creative energy, and described meditation as "only a means to an end." He said: "In order to infuse energy and power and get it flowing through our bodies, we have to meditate. You infuse that energy into your being, and so when you are in activity, it rubs off onto that creatively. To really be in touch with creative energy, you will find that it lies within the stillness."

Lateral thinking is a process that is also said to spark creativity. Coined by physician and psychologist Edward de Bono, this style of thinking challenges the brain's automatic response to solving situations. It forces people to think in unconventional ways, moving from one known idea to creating new ideas, which can result in innovation. In music terms, the result might be finding a clever and new way of phrasing something in a lyric, or doing away with musical conventions to find a new style or combination of notes. You might even find a totally new way of approaching your career and making money. Like Steve Jobs said in the quote at the beginning of this chapter, having diverse exposure to different experiences fuels creativity. For musicians, exploring broad topics and diverse ways of thinking, outside of their extraordinarily absorbing jobs, could lead to something quite special. There are lots of lateral thinking exercises online and we've included a few below for you to try out.

- Choose a random topic or object and keep thinking of uses for it, no matter how absurd.
- Pick up a book, dictionary, or magazine, open it up to a random place and choose a word on the page that relates to whatever it is that you're working on. Use that to spark ideas.
- Think from the perspective of someone else — that could be a famous figure, friend, family member, or a fictional character you create.
- Source different perspectives by asking strangers for the solution to a problem — this doesn't have to be face-to-face, social media can help to ease any social awkwardness.

You can also use improvisation techniques to foster innovation, which could include:[21]

- **Try a call-and-response exercise** with a bandmate — compile a few melodies and play or sing them one at a time while your bandmate responds with something new. After a while, switch roles. You might come up with a new song as a result.
- For anyone who reads sheet music, mix it up by **learning a melody by ear instead**. This will probably take quite a bit of practice but helps you to become an effective improviser and diversify your style of playing.
- **Master a scale** so you can use that as a basis for improvisation, while not worrying too much about which note comes next.
- **Learn the part of another member in your band** — this can help you gain a different perspective and perhaps spark some creativity in the process.
- When you're doing a jam session, **rotate the lead role** so everyone gets a chance at controlling the music. This can

result in a more diverse and innovative piece of music and also improve the confidence of those who don't usually take the lead. This goes for songwriting too — if there's one person who usually leads a studio session, mix it up often to get the most interesting results.

Another tool to access your unconscious mind involves putting pen to paper and seeing what happens. This is a process that Nick Cave (of the Bad Seeds fame) endorses — he believes that "ideas are everywhere and forever available, provided you are prepared to accept them." Cave continues:

> "I have rarely sat down at my desk with something to say, other than I am ready. The sitting comes first, turning up with a certain alertness to possibility. Only then does the idea feel free to settle. It settles small and very tentatively, then, through your active attention, it can grow into something much bigger. Sitting in a readied state can sometimes last a long and anxious time. But you must not despair! I have never found a situation where the idea refuses to come to the prepared mind."[22]

Julia Cameron talks about this practice in her 12-week programme, *The Artist's Way*,[23] which incorporates 'morning pages'. She suggests the following:

- Write whatever comes to mind as soon as you wake up, trying to suppress the logical, critical side of your brain and letting your thoughts run free.
- Take yourself somewhere new on your own once a week for an 'artist's date'. The idea is to allow yourself to indulge your artistic side, encourage relaxation, new experiences and, again, let your mind wander.
- Find ways to explore the world around you. Seeking out new sights, smells, and experiences, is a way of expanding your creativity bank.

Still struggling to find that creative muse? Creative coach Clare Scivier recommends defining your motivations, and avoiding thinking too much and getting overwhelmed by the task at hand, whether that be writing a song, an album, or curating a performance. Twyla Tharp, on the other hand, recommends identifying what's not working and writing down your assumptions about it. Once you've done this, you can then challenge those assumptions by gathering new ideas.

Scivier also endorses the benefits of taking a break. Wayne Hector will attest to this: he wrote '90s smash "Flying Without Wings", which was first recorded by Westlife, within an hour after mindlessly singing the title line during a break for a breather while recording other music. It was a similar story for the song he co-wrote for The Pussycat Dolls, "I Hate This Part." He explains:

"We'd gotten to the end of the session, it was 1am, we'd written a song that was kind of all right but nobody was jumping up and down about it. Just before we left — and this happens a lot when you stop thinking about work — I was playing a melody very badly because I don't really play keys, and one of the guys said, 'What's that?' I dunno, I said, but let's put it down as a rough idea and we'll look at it tomorrow.

"[Co-writer] Lucas [Secon] said, 'Oh, you know what, I hate this part when we we're walking out the door and have a great idea.' I said: 'That's a great title, I hate this part, so what would it mean in terms of a relationship? Well, I hate this part when we're breaking up and having to say you don't want to be with somebody anymore.' That was the beginning of the story. So about half an hour in, we'd written the song, and in another half an hour we laid it down, and then spent about three hours head-banging in the studio because we were all so excited about the song."

A break doesn't just mean a breath of fresh air. For Hector — a prolific writer who churns out at least 400 songs a year (10% of which usually get picked up by artists) — lack of inspiration might be a sign he needs extended time away from work. He says:

> "I just stop for two, three, four weeks, whatever it takes until the ideas start coming on their own again. I always believe that your brain lets you know when it's ready. I'll call [my manager] Jackie and say, 'Cancel everything.' A few weeks later, I'll be listening to the radio, or there will be something going on, and I'll just start singing an idea and think: 'Okay, I'm in that place again.' Some people are good at fighting through it, but my belief is to stop, get away from music if necessary, do a bit of living, and eventually the ideas start coming in again."

Most of us don't have the luxury of being about to cancel all our commitments when overwhelm hits, but it might be worth looking ahead and booking some time off as soon as possible, however brief.

As well as the ideas recommended above, there are a few other tricks for getting over blocks. If you've got a big project to do, like an album, it's probably not helpful to start thinking about all the twelve-plus songs you've got to write. **Start with one small step at a time — one lyric, one melody, one song** — to avoid feeling overwhelmed and take the pressure out of the situation. This is a strategy musician Mike Rutherford of Genesis talks about in Boyd's study: "When I write, if I try too hard, it's completely hopeless; nothing happens. If I don't try to think about it, with the attitude of 'I'll give it 10 minutes', it all happens. It's frightening, because ideas come so fast. It's a wonderful feeling." Still feeling under-confident? Perhaps it's worth digging out some work you're really proud of to remind yourself that you're more than competent, and help to turn any paralysing negative thoughts into positive encouraging ones.

Along with taking a break and being in a relaxed state of mind, **get curious about what emotions help facilitate creativity**. Perhaps getting excited or feeling confident when you've been inspired helps aid further creativity, or being social and exchanging ideas (which is how this very book that you're reading came to be!). Does humour spark creative ideas? Think back to times when you've been productive and creative, recognise what emotions or states worked particularly well for you, and experiment with ways to recreate them.

PERFECTIONISM AND PRESSURE

It might also be a good idea to remove any ideas of writing something that's going to be the best thing ever, which is a sure-fire way of reaching brain block. Imogen Heap returns to explain:

> "We are being creative all of the time, but it's when we start to put it into a fine point of something that has to be magnificent and beautiful and the best poetry ever written and only then is it good… we put all that pressure on ourselves. I recently had the first weekend that I'd taken just for myself, and didn't know what to do, I was a bit confused, sat around, watched some Instagram movies, stuff on YouTube, then I was like, 'What am I doing? Why don't I just write a song?' I was a bit scared — what if I haven't got anything? But I was like, 'Fuck it, I'll just sit at the piano.' And I started playing it and of course out came a song, and then another one and another one, and suddenly I was the most confident person ever. [I was] allowing myself to not have all of that burden and baggage of being the best, and just exercise creativity in a safe space, in a relaxed state, like I did when I was 15 when there was no pressure or expectations."

Having high standards, attention to detail, and a conscientious approach to your work is known as *adaptive* perfectionism and we covered it in detail in the Performance Anxiety chapter. When this hits and it's hard to get going, experiment with Heap's and Rutherford's approach and just commit to 10 minutes of writing something. Once you get started, creative ideas may start to flow — the hardest part is often just getting started. Allow yourself to try, and fail, accepting that any bumps along the road are an important part of the process called life, and don't represent weakness or failure. Or, in the words of jazz legend Miles Davis: "Do not fear mistakes, there are none."[24] *Maladaptive* perfectionism is something different, and can be quite destructive. This is where those high standards tip over into unrealistic expectations and over time can have a negative impact on your health. As we said when discussing performance anxiety, if you're setting impossible standards for yourself and finding it hard to be freely creative as a result, it might be worth seeking some professional help to transform a destructive mindset into a positive one.

Pressure can come from external forces, too. That takes strength to drown out, but it's quite important to do so. Artists are frequently told by A&R people and managers that they need to write the big single, the radio or streaming hit, the album that's going to be as successful as the last (second album syndrome is real). But is that conducive to creating in a calm state of mind? (For any music executives reading this, is it helpful to tell an artist that they've got to write a hit song? Or that they are a major priority with a weight of expectation on their shoulders?) The truth is, no-one knows whether a song or artist is going to be a smash, commercially or critically, until it's put out into the world, and that's especially true in the age of streaming when the audience has more power than ever before. This isn't to say that all pressure is bad — we all need a deadline to motivate ourselves sometimes and helpful suggestions on a musical direction or lyric can complete a track. But when it comes to the initial creative process, **the only thing anyone can really do is make music they love and be curious about where it goes**.

ENVIRONMENTS AND STRUCTURE

As David Byrne suggested earlier in this chapter when discussing the importance of context, **curating your own environment can have a positive impact on creativity by providing a space where you feel comfortable and free**. This doesn't necessarily always have to be the same place — as musician Steve Jordan describes: "Sometimes you have to be somewhere other than your home to create; sometimes you can't create at all unless you're at home. Sometimes your place needs to look a mess; sometimes you can't do anything unless it's completely clean."[25]

Ellis Pecen says "the environment can have a huge non-conscious influence on productivity and creativity." She continues:

> "We can think that we have writer's block, when really we could have been perfectly fine writing in another environment that activated other non-conscious associations in us. For example, it's harder to procrastinate in a library when everyone else around is also reading or typing away. Or, I often hear artists say that once they go into a shared studio space with others, the ideas start to flow because everyone else is there doing the same."

If you struggle to get going, you may find that booking in a session with a co-writer helps to create the to-and-fro exchange of ideas that you need to inspire you. As Wayne Hector alluded to earlier, interactions with others can help to encourage new lines of thinking and broaden perspectives, which produces a larger bank of connections to draw upon creatively. Others don't necessarily have to be people who work with you — a conversation with a friend might be just as inspiring as a session in the studio.

On the other hand, songwriter and Eagles member Don Henley says that an important factor for his creative environment is solitude.[26] In *Letters to a Round Poet*, author Rainer Maria Rilke echoes this point: "What is necessary, after all, is only this: solitude, vast inner solitude. To walk inside yourself and meet no one for hours — that is what you must be able to attain."[27]

When it comes to time, psychologist Mihaly Csikszentmihalyi, who has done extensive research on how everyday happiness is achieved by looking into the lives of creative people who pursued their endeavours for purely intrinsic reasons, believes that "what matters is not whether one keeps to a strict or to a flexible schedule; what counts is to be a master of one's own time." Perhaps you're most creative in the morning and need peace and quiet to do your best work. Maybe, like Wayne Hector, you prefer to be in the studio working with others. You could concentrate best after everyone's gone to bed, and enjoy working in your bedroom, a home office, or outside on a walk. A thriving city could be conducive to your creative mind, or a peaceful spot in the countryside. Perhaps it's a combination of any of the above.

Whatever you discover works for you, musician Michael McDonald warns against too much of a structured process, which he believes calls upon the busy mind. "Creativity is not going to adhere to time restraints; it's not going to meet any specific standards you want to put on it," he says.[28] "It's like trying to put those stipulations on a three-year-old child, because in a way it's coming from that part of you." Legendary singer and songwriter Joni Mitchell agrees, but believes there does need to be some sort of structure:

> "If you're too reasonable, then creativity won't come around in you, because then you're not intuitive, and it requires a great deal of intuition. **You need a bit of all of it: you need to be emotional, otherwise your work will be chilly. If you're too emotional, your work will be all over place. You need to be rational for linear, architectural, orderly structural work, but if you stay there too long, the stuff will be chilly.** [Bob] Dylan will write a song and it will have abstract passages, and then it will have a direct phrase – like

bam – directly communicate, and then he'll go back into something more surrealistic."[29]

Like a lot of things we've discussed in this book, the key is to work out how and where you're most creative, and do what you can to make that creativity happen. As Boyd summarises at the end of *It's Not Only Rock 'n' Roll*: "**To be creative, we have to get out of our own way, to allow the unconscious to come through.**"

Here are some final points to conclude this chapter:

- Depending on where you stand, **creativity either comes** from the **unconscious mind, rich life experiences, the universe, external 'daemons'**, or **spiritual entities**. It can happen as a result of **opportunity, availability, preparation, routine**, or **constant effort**.

- **Finding inspiration is, therefore, a personal endeavour** that may involve working with others, finding ideas in the world around you, experimentation, improvisation, nature, and solitude.

- When creating new work, **make sure you're not directly copying what's gone before**, whether consciously or unconsciously. Clearing all direct samples, adaptation, and asking friends and family if a song sounds like anything they've heard before will help you here.

- **If you're struggling to be creative, unless you're experiencing extreme stress, there are some tactics that might help you to discover that spark of inspiration.** Try taking time out to access the unconscious mind and practise meditating, lateral thinking exercises, improvisation techniques, and just putting pen to paper, or hand to instrument, and seeing what happens.

- **Try removing any pressure** you're putting on yourself, or others are putting on you, by being willing to try and fail, and just committing to giving something a go for a short period of time.

- **Consider the environment you need to be most creative** (which might change often): do you need to be alone or with others? Is it important that your space is clean and organised? Do you need to go somewhere totally different for a change of scenery? Similarly, *when* do you do your best work?

- Remember that the suggestions above **aren't intended to offer you a foolproof guide to accessing creativity** that works every time (wouldn't that be nice?!), but should instead spark ideas that can be used to help you access creativity in lots of different ways, depending on the state of mind you're in.

END HERE

IF YOU'VE READ THROUGH this entire book to reach this point, hopefully you've found lots of useful information and feel better equipped to pursue a balanced approach to your career in music, whilst prioritising your health. We've covered a lot, so do keep hold of it to dip in and out of often. If you're a touring musician, it's also probably a good idea to take the book on tour — even if you don't pick it up, someone else in your touring party might find it handy.

When digesting all of this information, something to be wary of is what Yale happiness lecturer Laurie Santos calls the 'GI Joe fallacy'.[1] This is a nod to the American TV show and its strapline "knowing is half the battle". Or, more specifically, the idea that knowing something is *only* half the battle. Your mind might tell you that now you've read this book, you know enough to pursue happiness and health. But here's the problem — knowing this stuff is not enough. You have to practise it every day.

The chapter we're going to end on covers **perspective, failure** (which, as we'll explain, isn't necessarily a negative thing), **and life beyond music.** Because music is so present in most people's lives, and there are lots of high-profile examples of successful musicians, sometimes perspective in the popular music industry can get lost. It's easy to get carried away with chasing goals that aren't your own, or feel like a total failure because you haven't achieved some level of mainstream success. It's also easy to forget what truly makes you happy, or to pursue a path that's going to satisfy you, instead of your ego.

Unfortunately, **the large majority of musicians are not going to 'make it'** (according to the standards of 'making it' outlined by Imogen Heap's taxi driver referenced in the Setting Goals chapter). As we detailed in Money Management, the average salary for a working musician in the UK is £23k, which can be made up of income earned from playing and writing music, but also teaching, commercial deals, merchandise sales, and perhaps having a totally unrelated part time job, either through necessity or to achieve a change of scenery and a sense of perspective. Indeed, even acts who might look like they've hit the big time have been working a different job on the side.

Idles drummer Jon Beavis has been a restaurant manager and bar worker for the majority of the time he's been in the band, and couldn't afford to quit until the release of their second album in 2018. Bassist Dev (Adam) was a venue manager, guitarist Lee was a labourer and teacher, vocalist Joe was a social worker, and guitarist Mark was a (very tired) dentist. Beavis says: "On the 2017 tour, Mark would have to drive from his work in London up to shows and then, after the gig, would drive back down and work the next day, and drive up again because he couldn't take all the days off work. I don't know how he did that!" They all left their jobs in August 2018, around the time of a three-month tour.

Having a day job can be necessary in today's streaming age, when a lot of streams result in a relatively small amount of cash in your back pocket. According to *The Trichordist*, it would take over 3,000 streams per hour on Spotify to earn the equivalent of UK minimum wage, and over 1,600 on Apple Music.[2] The reality is, only a tiny fraction of acts are getting enough streams to make a living. Ever heard the stat that says half of the world's wealth is owned by the top 1% of people? That holds true in the music streaming world, too.[3] In 2017, 22,000 of Spotify's 'top-tier' aka. highest-earning acts made up just 0.7% of total artists on its platform (three million). So the remaining 99.3% were taking home either a medium or a low-level paycheque. Other sources of income, like touring and merchandise sales, take a while to build up, which is why most musicians are spinning multiple plates.

Case in point: Idles couldn't take a decent wage from music until nearly 10 years of hard work and frugality. "Album one was paid for by all of us in the band and for album two, we'd all saved up bits of money," Beavis explains. "Even when we first started way back in 2009, for every show that we did, we'd get paid about £50, and we'd always put it in a band pot and would never touch it. We'd use that pot for petrol or paying for t-shirts on the first merchandise run. There was always that business element, even though we were playing shows in pubs to about five people."

Because of the low chance of hitting the 'big time', **it's important to have realistic expectations from a career in music**. You may well be the next superstar, but do you have a backup plan just in case that doesn't work out? And at the end of the day, is that type of success, and all the nonsense that inevitably comes with it, even what you really want? Adam Ficek, who started his career as a member of Babyshambles and grew up with the ambition to 'make it' (whatever that meant), now balances life as a musician with his work as a trained psychotherapist.

He gets his music income from a combination of crowdfunding (thanks to a staunch fanbase who support his releases) and a small tour every few years. "It's working out quite nicely for me," he says. "There is no pressure, and I don't have to deal with some of the more commoditised aspects of the commercial music industry. I don't feel I have to strive to reach some kind of third party perspective, I can do it all how I want to do it, which is much more pleasurable, and I can be more creative with what I want to do."

If you do manage to achieve some big wins, Ella Eyre, who had a number one single and BRIT Award right at the beginning of her career, encourages artists to enjoy it but to also focus on the bigger picture. She says:

> "I've been in the industry from the age of 16 and my first experience was very shiny, glitzy, glam, and exciting. But it's really important to maintain perspective and goals and to take your craft seriously. When I was younger, I wish I had someone telling me to really **work on yourself and the music that you want to make, and make sure that as a brand and as a product, it's 100% something that you love** and would listen to and idolise. I think that it's really important, particularly when you're younger, to have your eye on the bigger picture and to have people around you who are aware of that bigger picture and aren't necessarily looking for quick numbers. Longevity takes a long time to make and to develop, and winning a BRIT and going to number one first time is not the reality of how the music industry works."

FAILURE

We hope that the overall tone of this book is supportive and encouraging (while being realistic), but the fact of the matter is, you're probably going to fail at some point. Some artists fail before they make it big — just ask Ed Sheeran, who failed his audition for cheesy ITV comedy-drama *Britannia High*, or Katy Perry, who was dropped before she eventually became a global pop superstar. Others (too many to mention) fail *after* they've hit the big time.

And in between there are setbacks big and small experienced by every artist you've ever heard of (and plenty you haven't). It's just the reality of a career which goes up and down in what can feel like minutes. You'll need a thick skin in this game and an ability to not take things too personally or too seriously. A sense of humour can really help. You're very likely to experience surreal 'Spinal Tap' moments — and if you haven't seen that satirical film about a fictional heavy metal band, we'd suggest it's essential viewing for any musician. In one pivotal scene, the band's manager bats away the suggestion that nosediving ticketing sales are evidence of the band's clearly waning popularity. "Oh no," he replies. "I just think their appeal is becoming more selective." It's a scene that'll ring true for any artist whose own manager has performed verbal acrobatics while attempting to deliver bad news.

In the grand scheme of things, it might be useful to know that the music industry, as a whole, is actually quite small. In the UK, the music business sustained 191k full-time jobs in 2018, with 73% of those belonging to music creators, according to a report from UK Music.[4] That means everyone *else* in the music industry would be about the size of the audience for a Wembley Stadium show by an act whose appeal was becoming 'more selective'. And to put *that* in context, people working full-time in the British music industry make up around 0.8% of the full-time UK workforce[5] (according to 2020 estimates), and the £5.2bn contribution music made to the British economy in 2018 represented just 4.7% of the £111.7bn made by creative industries as a whole[6] (which also includes film, TV, radio, photography, advertising, museums, galleries, and digital creative industries). We're not saying that music's numbers are insignificant in any way, but given the ubiquity of music in the world at large, it's perhaps surprising that they aren't higher.

That relatively small size means that the various facets of the music business are often based very much on networking, favours, and relationships. It can also be very competitive. These realities create a working environment that can feel like being part of a club where all the members are looking over their shoulders for a snake in the grass, while trying to protect their own standing. It's great if things are going well for you inside that ecosystem, but if they aren't, it's easy to feel like the loser in the school playground. And when few people are honest about what's gone right or wrong in their own careers, our own perceived failures can make us feel inadequate in an industry full of supposed 'hashtag-winners'. Thing is, just like all the fake faces and fake lives we see on Instagram, constant success is just not the reality for anyone.

Remember the story about The 1975 in the Criticism and Opinions chapter? They practised as a band for five years before finding their manager, and spent the next six years knocking on all those doors to get multiple "thanks but no thanks" responses, before finally hitting the top of the charts with their debut album. That's eleven years, from inception, via multiple refusals of support, to big notable success. It's a similar story for Idles, who ended up self-released their debut album with their manager after coming up against numerous closed doors. Jon Beavis explains: "I always joke with my friends that before we released [our debut album] *Brutalism*, I'd say every year that I was going to quit because it was too much. We were always away from our partners and friends, and we were just playing the same sort of pubs to the same sort of people. But there was always this part of me that said, 'Well, if this is what you want to do, this is what you want to do.' So I'd always come back and do the next show." The determination paid off — Idles found a label deal and reached number one with their third album, have since played Glastonbury, and are a multi-award-winning band that makes enough money through merchandise and touring to pay themselves a full-time wage.

At the beginning of her career, singer and songwriter Nina Nesbitt had to experience failure in a pretty devastating way. After releasing her first album, she spent the next two years in the studio writing music, most of which was deemed unacceptable by her label. Finally, a song got sent to radio and the video shoot was booked, only to be cancelled the night before for 'legal reasons'.

The next week she was dropped. "This [was] totally coming out of the blue," is her own recollection. "I thought we were working on a record together and then it turned out that someone in the finance department had decided they didn't want to spend the money [on me] again. I was like, 'Okay, that's fine, I just wish you had told me two years ago. The song's been announced now and it's publicly humiliating to be like, Oh, actually, it's not coming out anymore.' I guess a part of me was like, 'This song is going to come out and I hope it's going to do really well and they're going to change their mind.'"[7]

Nesbitt had to fund the song's release and video with the money she got from the label for being dropped to cover damages (rather grimly that sort of payout's called a parachute), and took her career into her own hands. That also wasn't easy at the beginning. She continues: "I noticed slowly but surely, some friends were dropping off, producers didn't really want to do a session, people were cancelling on me. Looking back now, I totally get it, because, as a writer, you want to write with artists who are signed to a major label. It's a business, it's your work. But at the time I was like, 'Oh my God, no one will work with me' and that was kind of upsetting. It made me feel like I mustn't be very good because I didn't understand the business side of it. And I slowly slipped into a depression. I just kind of sat in my room for about six months."

Psychotherapist Tamsin Embleton says this reaction to being dropped is quite commonplace. She explains:

> "The industry is all-encompassing, so your sense of who you are and your support network is often sourced within the industry. When that's wrenched away, it can be really devastating. You can be left with low self-regard, identity issues, issues around belonging, and relevance. There's a big loss of not just the role, your job, but maybe your identity or a sense of abandonment by the team, so you can be left feeling really hopeless and isolated, rejected and ashamed."[8]

Eventually, Nesbitt told her manager, mum, and boyfriend how low she was feeling, and picked herself back up again by getting back into the studio and writing for other artists, before embarking on the next stage of her artist career. She later signed to an independent label, and, at the time of writing, has 4.6m monthly Spotify listeners.

All of which is to say, **if you're going to be bold enough to put yourself and your creative vision out there, you've got to be ready for a few bumps along the way**. The key, according to science, is to keep trying and modifying. An extensive study by the Northwestern University, published in 2019, analysed 46 years of venture capital startup investments to try and determine what role failure plays in achieving success.[9] The takeaway, according to the professor who led the study, Dashun Wang, was that "every winner begins as a loser". The thing that eventually separates the winners from the losers? Trying again and learning from your mistakes. In music terms, modifying doesn't only mean changing (or honing) your creative output or approach — it could also mean shifting goals to be more manageable and working your way on from there.

It's also important to reiterate that **in a competitive industry, there can be a huge amount of luck involved in whether you are successful or not**. This sounds very unfair, but it's true. There are too many brilliant musicians out there for everyone to 'succeed' (in the commercial sense), and, as we said earlier, nepotism, connections, and privilege can still sometimes pave the way to a Top 10 charting record or high profile gig over pure skill and talent. So if you didn't achieve all of those lofty career goals, it might not be that you weren't good enough. Some of the best bands, DJs, and artists are never able to 'cut through' to the big time (and indeed, some don't want to), but many are still able to have long, sustainable careers, particularly when they are in control of their own copyrights and/or have a diverse portfolio career. It all comes back to that initial question of why you're doing what you're doing. If you can achieve success on your own terms, that's a pretty good way to live life — even if the taxi driver hasn't heard of you.

Sometimes, the hard work doesn't always pay off and you may end up in a place in your career that is wildly different from the glittering goals you set ten years ago. **Regardless of where you end up job-wise, it is still possible to access feelings of wellbeing, meaning, and happiness**. And if you do manage to get where you wanted to be, prioritising good mental health and wellbeing is paramount anyway, especially with all the ups and downs that are involved in a career in music. For this reason, we've included a summary of what some of the most recognised researchers and health providers believe to be the key factors to achieving wellbeing and happiness below, so that you can work out ways of incorporating them into your life, no matter where you end up.

- **Vitality**. Enough sleep,[10] regular exercise[11], and good nutrition — these are the first building blocks to take care of.
- **Social support**. Good relationships with the people around us play an important role in keeping us healthy[12] and happy.[13] Nurture those who are important to you and stay in touch when you're on the road.
- **Meditation**. Research suggests that mind-wandering is generally the cause, and not merely the consequence, of unhappiness.[14] Meditation helps to prevent this,[15] which can make us happier generally,[16] increase grey matter density in the brain, improve memory[17] and feelings of social connectedness.[18]
- **Regular engagement in a task**. Lots of research suggests that regular activity that engages your brain fully while you're doing it results in feelings of deep enjoyment.[19] People who achieve this often tend to report more positive states overall, and that their lives have more purpose and meaning.
- **Gratitude**. Writing a list of what you're grateful for in your life,[20] or reflecting on what went well in your day,[21] have both been shown to boost happiness levels.

- **Accomplishment**. Although fame and fortune won't make you happy, research suggests that some kind of accomplishment does.[22] The task doesn't need to be major — even a good day's work can help you feel positive. Learning new skills can also help boost wellbeing.[23]
- **Creating meaning in your life**. Understanding why you do what you do, and having a feeling of contributing to society in a broader sense, can help with happiness levels.[24]
- **Give**. Kindness[25] and giving make us feel good. This could involve volunteering,[26] donating to charity, practising random acts of kindness (where you do something nice for someone without anyone knowing), mentoring in the workplace, or helping others.
- **Prioritising time over money**. Research into how time and money shape happiness tells us that prioritising time over financial remuneration is related to greater subjective wellbeing.[27]
- **Mindfulness**. To fully appreciate the things you have in your life, it's worth practising the art of 'savouring'[28], which is a form of mindfulness.[29]
- **Positive emotions**. Whether it's dancing to your favourite song, stroking a dog, looking at a sunset, or reading a book you love, make sure you prioritise activities that bring you joy — and do it regularly.[30]

LIFE AFTER MUSIC

What if it all goes tits up and you can't, for whatever reason, continue working in music or as a musician? Fear not — there is a huge world out there. Your skills will reach far beyond the musical realm and can be adapted to many different roles. What else do you enjoy doing? What are the most satisfying elements of being a musician for you? What do your close ones say you are really good at? Is there something you'd enjoy doing that would help others? Perhaps the answers to these questions could direct you to a really fulfilling alternative career that doesn't necessarily have to spell the end of a musical one, like Adam Ficek, who splits his time between psychotherapy and music.

Alternatively, think about other music-related jobs that appeal — could you give instrument lessons or lecture about songwriting at a pop college? Perhaps you'd like to become a producer for other people or write library music for TV and film? There are so many jobs in music apart from being an artist, and, in many of them, a prior or concurrent performing career will help add credibility to what you do. If music-making doesn't appeal, how about transitioning to the business side of the industry? Many music professionals have had previous lives as artists and musicians, and having 'good ears' and an understanding of how to get the best out of artists can be a real asset in an industry that revolves around identifying and developing talent and hit songs.

If you do decide that it's time to put music behind you, or off to one side, be aware that there's likely to be some sort of adjustment period. Phil Jordan, who spent his twenties drumming for rock band The Music, found himself struggling with a lack of identity and an inability to deal with the more mundane elements of everyday life after the band fell apart. "It was a huge thing for me to readjust," he explains. "It's about ego — the way you are perceived by other people and how you perceive yourself. For all my life, I was 'the successful drummer' so everybody around me identified me with that and I identified *myself* with that. So to move away from that was a huge change in mindset."

Jordan retrained as a counsellor and, as a result, was able to do a lot of therapy himself. "Once the band started to fall apart, I could feel I needed to do that self-reflection to work out essentially who I am. I think the root of all of it is identity, and that's what I needed to do." He joined the band when he was 18, so for the next ten years was shielded from the realities of adult life by management and record label staff members. The point at which he really felt like 'an adult' for the first time was in his mid-thirties. "When I hit 35 or 36, I felt like I was actually independent and that I'd grown up," he recalls. "I felt like a man."

Psychotherapist Jodi Milstein confirms that transitioning out of life as a musician can be "quite a blow to the ego." The key is in reinvention. She explains:

> "It's okay to reinvent yourself, and sometimes when you do that, you find that you are this multi-faceted being instead of just this one person that you thought you were going to be. If you have a successful career as a musician and that's all you want to do and what you want to be, that's fine, but if you are finding that you need to earn money to support yourself and your family, well, then it's about not being afraid to reinvent yourself. If you love music, what can you do with music so you can still be involved? **We have to be flexible in life, life is long, and you have to be open to going on this ride.**"

Ultimately, it's up to everyone to continually evaluate whether what they are doing day to day is serving their overall health and happiness. There are going to be tough times and great times in any career, but if most days feel like a struggle, it might be time to think outside the box. As manager Jho Oakley says in the Music Manager Forum's Mental Health Guide, "There's no point having your dream job if you're going to let it kill you."[31] Equally, there's no point in achieving your dreams if you end up miserable because you were chasing the wrong things for the wrong reasons, or didn't stop to truly live life while you were getting there. **So get clear on what you want (and what you don't), both from career and health perspectives, and make sure that the route you're going to take on this journey will lead you to where you truly want to go.**

ACKNOWLEDGEMENTS

This book is the work of many hands, without whom, let's be honest, it probably would have been a total disaster.

Starting from the beginning, big thanks go to John Reid and Jo Dipple at Live Nation, and Selina Webb at Universal Music UK, for their blind belief when all we had to show for it was an idea and a Powerpoint presentation. Selina also swept in and saved the day with a last minute front cover, for which we are eternally grateful.

Similarly, Ferdy Unger-Hamilton and Daisy Greenhead, and Ben Cook were essential in getting Sony and Warner on board, respectively. John Blewett is legendary for championing us within the IFPI, as is Alison Bonny, who somehow managed to get some funding over the line at Spotify before swiftly exiting the building. Thank you also to kind souls Dot Levine at Vevo, Merck Mercuriadis at Hipgnosis Songs, and Stefi Pavlou at PRS for Music.

We owe immense gratitude to Lynne McDowell for selling the idea to PPL and Tom March and Ben Mortimer for Polydor's donation. There are lots of people beyond this within the business who encouraged us to pursue the idea by offering words of support and opening doors. Thank you to you all.

We are so grateful for our amazing editors. Here's to Gareth Dylan Smith for his sharp eye and invaluable experience as both an academic and musician, and Peter Robinson for providing some much-needed colour and nearly all the LOLs. Big thanks also go to marketing queen Sammy Andrews, Debra Geddes for press, our skilled and patient designer Steve Russell, and those responsible for the front cover at music agency.

Many proofreaders added vital contributions beyond this. Cherie Hu did a brilliant job on the final edit of our business and money chapters and Adam Webb and Simon Pursehouse also made excellent suggestions. Adam Ficek, Joanne Croxford, and Yasmine Ben-Afia pointed out vital omissions and edits for the substance use and addictions chapter, improving it immeasurably. We also really appreciate Adam's feedback and additions on mental health (a particularly tough chapter).

Thank you to Emmy Brunner for reading and approving our chapter on eating disorders and body image, and Rhian's sister Amy for her useful feedback (and for composing our melody for the creativity chapter). Big thanks go to Suzi Green for doing the same with touring. We're also hugely grateful for the time, contributions and feedback of Claire Cordeaux, Finola Ryan, Tori Burnay, Sam Parker, Ellis Pecen, Berenice Zammit, Sarah Upjohn, and Dane Chalfin.

Thank you to Rosie Perkins and Liliana Araujo, who are Lucy's co-authors of the original study that inspired this book, which is quoted throughout. In addition, Joe Hastings and Alex Mann at Help Musicians deserve a mention for providing expertise and suggestions whilst making the Elevate Music Podcast, which inspired topics within this book, as do the many contributors and artists who featured in the episodes, lots of which are mentioned in these pages.

Rhian's mum Lindsay deserves a special shoutout for her detailed and sweet edits, which went down a storm on social media. For anyone interested, her key advice for musicians is to set yourself up with a YouTube account to earn some extra cash and to practise resilience and faith. For the business, she'd like to see more human empathy, genuine love and concern for those that work within it. Lindsay for President?

Rhian would also like to extend a considerable amount of gratitude to the other captain at the helm of this ship, Lucy, for wholeheartedly starting this rollercoaster ride without hesitation and being a highly educated as well as supportive and encouraging voice throughout the process. In addition, Rhian's long-suffering partner, Gideon, is owed many drinks for celebrating the highs and always providing a listening ear throughout the lows.

Lucy is incredibly grateful to Rhian for her expert writing and editing skills, along with her tenacious driving of the project, and patience and understanding throughout the numerous (and unexpected) hospital visits and recovery periods during a tough 18 months. Let's just say the process hit home the value of good health even more than it did before. Thanks also go to Lucy's mum for proofreading, her Dad for providing a sounding board about the economics of publishing, and to Roddy for endless support, encouragement, and tea.

Finally, thank you to all those interviewed who gave us their time, honesty and advice, and to you, the reader, for picking up this book and supporting us for a project we feel so passionate about. Let us know what you think of it, and if you have any suggestions for future editions, via the Sound Advice social media pages @ soundadvicebook.

RESOURCES

GENERAL MUSICIANS' HEALTH AND WELLBEING

Help Musicians Health & Welfare team: 020 7239 9103 / help@
helpmusicians.org.uk
The Musicians' Union musiciansunion.org.uk
The British Association of Performing Arts Medicine bapam.org.uk
BAPAM Health Practice Resources bapam.org.uk/healthy-
practice-resources/
PRS Members Fund prsmembersfund.com
Music Support 0800 030 6789 / musicsupport.org
Royal Society of Musicians rsmgb.org
Incorporated Society of Musicians ism.org
Music Minds Matter 0808 802 8008 / musicmindsmatter.org.uk /
MMM@helpmusicians.org.uk

MIT Therapists & Coaches musicindustrytherapists.com
Samaritans Helpline 116 123 / samaritans.org
The Music Managers Forum Guide to Mental Health themmf.net/mental-health
The MU Guide to Mental Health musiciansunion.org.uk/Files/Guides/Equalities/Mental-Health_-A-Young-Freelancers-Guide-to-Mental.aspx
Mind's Wellness Action Plans offer guidance for employers and freelancers, including help for working at home mind.org.uk/workplace/mental-health-at-work/taking-care-of-your-staff/employer-resources/wellness-action-plan-download/
Mind 0300 123 3393 / mind.org.uk
Sane 0300 304 7000 / sane.org.uk
Calm 0800 585858/ thecalmzone.net
Shout giveusashout.org
NHS (England): 111
NHS Direct (Wales): 0845 46 47
NHS 24 (Scotland): 111

NAVIGATING THE INDUSTRY

Music industry terms by Kindness notion.so/MUSIC-INDUSTRY-TERMS-by-Kindness-8b7a605239b44067ba371531aeff34a8
MU guide to releasing your own product musiciansunion.org.uk/Home/Advice/Recording-Broadcasting/Releasing
The Creative Passport for music makers creativepassport.net
PRS for Music prsformusic.com
PPL ppluk.com
Music Week's top 5 tips for making the independent route work for you musicweek.com/labels/read/top-5-tips-for-making-the-independent-route-work-for-you/077515
The Featured Artist Coalition thefac.org
Music Managers Forum themmf.net
EmuBands emubands.com
AIM Start up Guide to the Music Business independentmusic.typeform.com/to/cZqz6j

Podcast on DIY artists audioboom.com/posts/7450810-diy-artist-imogen-heap-and-tim-ferrone

Sentric Music blog sentricmusic.com/blog

Music Business Worldwide musicbusinessworldwide.com

music:ally musically.com

How Did You Manage That? podcast podcasts.apple.com/gb/podcast/how-did-you-manage-that/id1459416501

On streaming, label deals, fan data and digital royalties MMF Dissecting the Digital Dollar: themmf.net/digitaldollar

Artist management platform Centralized centralized.me

Creative Differences (neurodiversity guide) umusic.co.uk/Creative-Differences-Handbook.pdf

Pride in Music prideinmusic.org

She Said So shesaid.so

She Is The Music sheisthemusic.org

Girls I Rate girlsirate.com

Women in Music facebook.com/groups/2295354417367787/about

Ladies Music Pub facebook.com/groups/462135697273378

Attitude is Everything attitudeiseverything.org.uk

Fresh on the Net freshonthenet.co.uk/tips

Next Stage Network attitudeiseverything.org.uk/artists/join-the-next-stage-network

Drake Music drakemusic.org

Heart n Soul heartnsoul.co.uk

Carousel carousel.org.uk

Shape Arts shapearts.org.uk

We Are Unlimited article about disability by Amble Skuse weareunlimited.org.uk/time-and-the-social-model

Access docs for artists accessdocsforartists.com

The OHMI Trust ohmi.org.uk

Constant Flux constantflux.co.uk/about

Parents in Performing Arts pipacampaign.com

Black Lives Matter blacklivesmatter.com

'The F-List' of female musicians available for festivals vbain.co.uk/the-f-list

Money Management, Social Media and Criticism and Opinions

The Musicians' Union tax advice musiciansunion.org.uk/home/advice/your-career/tax

Pensions info moneyadviceservice.org.uk/en/articles/pensions-for-the-self-employed

The Musicians' Union guide to live fees and payments musiciansunion.org.uk/Home/Advice/Playing-Live/Gigs-and-Live-Entertainments/Fees-and-Payment

The Musicians' Union Work Not Play campaign worknotplay.co.uk

PRS Foundation prsfoundation.com/funding-support/funding-music-creators

Musicians Union finance advice and rates musiciansunion.org.uk/Home/Advice/Your-Career/Finance

BPI Music Export Growth Scheme bpi.co.uk/news-analysis/music-export-growth-scheme

Arts Council England artscouncil.org.uk

Creative Scotland creativescotland.com

Creative Entrepreneurs Club creativeentrepreneursclub.co.uk

Step Change debt charity stepchange.org

Podcast on money for musicians audioboom.com/posts/7399110-money-hannah-peel-and-naomi-pohl

Podcast on social media and mental health in musicians audioboom.com/posts/7425428-mental-health-and-social-media-sk-shlomo-and-stephen-buckley

Amnesty International report on Violence Against Women on social media amnesty.org/en/latest/research/2018/03/online-violence-against-women-chapter-1

Jesy Nelson's *Odd One Out* bbc.co.uk/programmes/p07lsr4d

National Bullying Helpline 0845 2255787

Childline 0800 1111

Gurls Talk podcast on addiction to social media and FOMO gurlstalk.libsyn.com/ep-8-adwoa-talks-to-singer-mabel-comparison-coach-lucy-sheridan-about-our-addiction-to-social-media-and-living-a-life-without-fomo

Brené Brown Under The Skin with Russell Brand podcast on
vulnerability and power podcasts.apple.com/gb/podcast/85-
vulnerability-and-power-with-bren%C3%A9-brown/
id1212064750?i=1000442345382
Happy Place podcast with Alicia Keys podcasts.apple.com/gb/
podcast/alicia-keys/id1353058891?i=1000477115571
Ed Sheeran, Finding Peace at the Top of the Music Industry
youtube.com/watch?v=oxDLKVwFQ9Q

SUPPORTING HEALTH

Touring

MU touring abroad checklist musiciansunion.org.uk/Home/Advice/
Playing-Live/Touring
MU fair engagement guide for touring musiciansunion.org.uk/
Files/Guides/Playing-Live/MU-Fair-Engagement-Guide-for-
Performing-and-Tourin
BAPAM healthy touring checklist and rider bapam.org.uk/healthy-
touring-checklist-and-rider
Access rider for disabled artists weareunlimited.org.uk/creating-
your-own-access-rider
Viva La Visa vivalavisa.co.uk
Podcast on touring audioboom.com/posts/7320992-touring-
miles-kane-and-ben-perry
Tom Middleton's sleep hygiene tips djmag.com/longreads/power-
sleep
Attachment style quiz attachedthebook.com/wordpress/
compatibility-quiz/?step=1
Mental Health America tips on being a couple again mhanational.
org/being-couple-again

Vocal Health

British Voice Association (info on gastric reflux as well as Muscle
Tension Dysphonia and other issues) britishvoiceassociation.org.uk

Free voice care literature britishvoiceassociation.org.uk/free.htm
Info on voice clinics britishvoiceassociation.org.uk/voicecare_
voice-clinic-whos-who.htm
Vocal physiotherapy physioedmedical.co.uk
Podcast on vocal health audioboom.com/posts/7414238-vocal-
health-sophie-s-story-sophie-garner-and-tori-burnay
Voice warmup app from Vocal Process apps.apple.com/gb/app/
one-minute-voice-warmup/id1212802251 (a tailored warm up
from a vocal coach is advised)

Music and the Body

BAPAM performers advice on pain and posture bapam.org.uk/wp-
content/uploads/2020/03/FittoPlay_BAPAMfactsheet.pdf
BAPAM free health assessment clinics 020 7404 8444
Podcast on pain in musicians audioboom.com/posts/7461884-
pain-and-posture-chris-polglase-and-sarah-upjohn
Allegro Optical allegrooptical.co.uk

Hearing

British Tinnitus Association tinnitus.org.uk
British Tinnitus Association Plug'em campaign plugem.co.uk/how-
loud-is-loud
BBC Noise and Hearing Guide downloads.bbc.co.uk/safety/
documents/safety-guides/audio-and-music/Safety-Musician_
noise_guide_summary.pdf
BAPAM Hearing Conservation Guidelines bapam.org.uk/bapam-
hearing-conservation-guidelines-for-the-performing-arts
Action for Hearing Loss actiononhearingloss.org.uk
Musicians' Hearing Services musicianshearingservices.co.uk
Help Musicians Hearing Health Scheme hearformusicians.org.uk
ACS Custom acscustom.com/uk
Hearing advice soundadvice.info
Podcast on musicians' hearing audioboom.com/posts/7330869-
hearing-health-nigel-elliott-and-gladys-akinseye

Mental Health

See general health and wellbeing resources above for main organisations

Maytree suicide shelter 0207 2637070 / maytree.org.uk

Podcast on mental health in musicians audioboom.com/posts/7319415-mental-health-in-music-nina-s-story-nina-nesbitt-and-tamsin-embleton

Music and You mental health support musicandyou.co.uk

MITC Anxiety and Self-Isolation Guide musicindustrytherapists.com/resources

Substance Use and Addiction

NHS help for drug addiction nhs.uk/live-well/healthy-body/drug-addiction-getting-help

NHS help for alcohol misuse nhs.uk/live-well/alcohol-support

Narcotics Anonymous (NA) ukna.org

NA (links to virtual 24/7 NA meetings) virtual-na.org/meetings

NA UK helpline 0300 999 1212 (open 10am to midnight daily)

Alcoholics Anonymous alcoholics-anonymous.org.uk

SMART Recovery smartrecovery.org.uk

Frank talktofrank.com/contact-frank

MusiCares (for US-based musicians, artists, and crew) grammy.com/musicares

MusiCares 12 Step support group meetings (open to all music people internationally who are members of all 12 step fellowships) grammy.com/musicares/get-help/addiction-recovery

Turning Point – alcohol and drug support turning-point.co.uk

Amy Winehouse Foundation amywinehousefoundation.org

Steps 2 Recovery steps2recovery.org.uk

Podcast on addiction audioboom.com/posts/7411578-addiction-chula-goonewardene-and-adrianna-irvine

Mental Health America on co-dependency http://www.mentalhealthamerica.net/go/codependency

Co-dependents anonymous codauk.org

Eating Disorders and Body Image

NHS nhs.uk/conditions/eating-disorders
Beat beateatingdisorders.org.uk/support-services/helplines
Mind, eating disorders mind.org.uk/information-support/types-of-mental-health-problems/eating-problems/about-eating-problems
Mind, body dysmorphic disorder mind.org.uk/information-support/types-of-mental-health-problems/body-dysmorphic-disorder-bdd/about-bdd

IMPROVING SKILLS

Zig Ziglar's Seven Steps of Goal Setting worldofwork.io/2019/07/zig-ziglars-seven-steps-of-goal-setting
BAPAM's healthy practice diary (including a goal-setting framework) bapam.org.uk/healthy-practice-resources/
BAPAM performance anxiety factsheet bapam.org.uk/wp-content/uploads/2020/03/Icantgoon_PerformanceAnxiety_BAPAMFactsheet.pdf
Play: a psychological toolkit for optimal music performance ism.org/play
Podcast on performance anxiety audioboom.com/posts/7338162-stage-fright-shaun-ryder-and-aaron-williamon
The Bullet-Proof Musician (support for performance anxiety) bulletproofmusician.com
Warm-up from BAPAM bapam.org.uk/wp-content/uploads/2020/05/BAPAM-Factsheet-Warm-Ups-Dont-Cramp-Your-Style-2020.pdf
Optimising Performance through Pre-Performance Routines by Berenice Zammit and Aaron Williamon researchgate.net/publication/343214241_Optimizing_Performance_through_Pre-Performance_Routines_Preparing_to_Perform_in_Orchestras_and_Chamber_Ensembles
And The Writer Is... podcast andthewriteris.com
Song Exploder podcast songexploder.net

Creative Rebels podcast rebelscreate.com/podcast
Broken Record podcast brokenrecordpodcast.com
Sodajerker songwriting podcast sodajerker.com
The Happiness Lab podcast with Laurie Santos happinesslab.fm

PRACTITIONERS

Remi Harris remiharrisconsulting.com
Mike Burgess soundwithmike.com
Tim Ferrone wrappedupmusic.com
Darren Hemmings motiveunknown.com

Music Industry Therapists & Coaches musicindustrytherapists.com
Psychotherapist Helen Brice stimmungtherapy.com
Therapist Jodi Milstein jodimilstein.com
Comparison Coach Lucy Sheridan proofcoaching.com
Integrative Psychotherapeutic Counselor Liz Ritchie lizritchie.org
Clinical Psychologist Donna Rockwell donnarockwell.com
Psychotherapist Tamsin Embleton embletonpsychotherapy.com
Psychotherapist Adam Ficek musicandmind.co.uk
Mental Health and Wellbeing Consultant Sam Parker parker-consulting.co.uk
Psychotherapist Adrianna Irvine adriannatherapy.com
Psychotherapist and Spiritual Recovery Coach Emmy Brunner emmybrunner.com
Performance Consultant and Psychologist Ellis Pecen @ellisEP on Twitter
Coach Clare Scivier yourgreenroom.org

Vocal Coach Dane Chalfin vocalrehabilitation.com
Voice Specialist Speech and Language Therapist Tori Burnay finder.bupa.co.uk/Consultant/view/49719/mrs_victoria_burnay
Physiotherapist Sarah Upjohn spirehealthcare.com/consultant-profiles/ms-sarah-upjohn-n1906063
Clinical Audiologist Gladys Akinseye harleysthearing.co.uk
Naturopathic Nutritional Therapist Suzi Green greenvitality.co.uk

BOOKS

Music: The Business by Ann Harrison
All You Need to Know About the Music Business by Donald S. Passman
Slacker Guide to the Music Industry by Phil Taggart
How to Make It in the New Music Business by Ari Herstand
It's Not Okay to Feel Blue (and Other Lies) by Scarlett Curtis
Lost Connections by Johann Hari
Recovery by Russell Brand
Codependent No More by Melody Beattie
Eating by the Light of the Moon by Anita Johnston Ph.D.
8 Keys to Recovery from an Eating Disorder by Carolyn Costin and Gwen Schubert Grabb
Anti-Diet by Christy Harrison
Waiting for the Man by Harry Shapiro
Mental Health in the Music Industry by Rachel Jepson
Can Music Make You Sick? by Sally Anne Gross and George Musgrave
Isle of Noises by Daniel Rachel
Musical Excellence by Aaron Williamon
The Musicians' Way by Gerald Klickstein
The Singer's Guide to Complete Health by Anthony F. Jahn
Performance Success by Don Greene
The Science and Psychology of Music Performance by Gary McPherson and Richard Parncutt
Performance Anxiety by Eric Maisel
Musician's Yoga by Mia Olson
The Inner Game of Music by Barry Green and W. Timothy Gallwey
Creativity by Mihaly Csikszentmihalyi
Effortless Mastery by Kenny Werner
Peak by Anders Ericsson
It's Not Only Rock 'n' Roll by Jenny Boyd

REFERENCES

Start Here

[1]   Cooke, C. (2017). Help Musicians UK puts £100k into new mental health initiative. *CMU*. https://completemusicupdate.com/article/help-musicians-uk-puts-100k-into-new-mental-health-initiative/

[2]   Gross. S, Musgrave. G. (2016). Can music make you sick? Music and depression, a study into the incidence of musicians' mental health, part 1: pilot survey report. University of Westminster/Music Tank, p.13

Business Basics

[1]   Dobson, M. (2010). Insecurity, professional sociability, and alcohol: Young freelance musicians' perspectives on work and life in the music profession. *Psychology of Music, 38*(3), p.240-260.

[2]   Listen Entertainment & Help Musicians & Elevate. (2019, December 16). DIY Artist – Imogen Heap and Tim Ferrone. https://audioboom.com/posts/7450810-diy-artist-imogen-heap-and-tim-ferrone

[3]   @soundwithmike. (2020, August 14). A license deal CAN be better (...than an assignment deal), but a license deal that is forever-and-ever-amen, without any form ability to terminate is basically an assignment deal dressed up as a license. Any license deal you do needs a termination clause. That is non-negotiable. [Twitter post]. https://twitter.com/soundwithmike/status/1294276045709938689

4   Ezra, G. (2018). Episode 1 – Ed Sheeran. https://www.georgeezra.com/george-ezra-and-friends/george-ezra-friends-episode-1-ed-sheeran5

5   Gardner, E. (2019, March 4). Kanye West is contractually barred from retiring. *Hollywood Reporter*. https://www.hollywoodreporter.com/thr-esq/kanye-west-is-contractually-barred-retiring-1191995

6   Jones, R. (2015, July 3). Amy Winehouse: 'I felt so close to her. I thought I could get her through it.' *Music Business Worldwide*. https://www.musicbusinessworldwide.com/amy-winehouse-i-felt-so-close-to-her-i-thought-i-could-get-her-through-it/

7   UK Music. (2020). UK Music Diversity Report 2020. https://www.ukmusic.org/assets/general/UK_Music_Diversity_Report_2020.pdf

8   UK Music. (2018). Diversity Music Industry Workforce 2018. https://www.ukmusic.org/assets/general/UK_Music_Diversity_Report_2018.pdf, p.6

9   Stassen, M. (2019, April 4). Revealed: what major labels are paying women compared to men in the UK. *Music Business Worldwide*. https://www.musicbusinessworldwide.com/revealed-what-major-labels-are-paying-women-compared-to-men-in-the-uk/

10 Live Nation (Music) UK Limited. (2020). Gender Pay Gap Report. Gender pay gap service. https://gender-pay-gap.service.gov.uk/Employer/4OTzdjEg/2019

11 Universal Music UK. (January 2020). *Creative Differences*, p.22.

12 Youngs, I. (2019, February 19). Pop music's growing gender gap revealed in the collaboration age. *BBC News*. https://www.bbc.com/news/entertainment-arts-47232677

13 Coogan B, L. and Women in CTRL. (2020). Gender Disparity Data Report. https://www.canva.com/design/DAEE37rlDuc/-7R8D7IzU7EMdcnv9Snw3w/view

14 Bain, V. (October 2019). Counting the Music Industry: The Gender Gap. https://www.academia.edu/40898607/Counting_the_Music_Industry_The_Gender_Gap_A_study_of_gender_inequality_in_the_UK_Music_Industry

15 Blk, R. (2020, June 8). 'It's so sad that I've become a symbol of the black female struggle in the music industry'. *Music Week*, p.16.

16 The Musicians' Union. (2019, October 21). Preventing sexual harassment at work, protecting freelancers too. https://www.musiciansunion.org.uk/Home/News/2019/Oct/Preventing-Sexual-Harassment-at-Work-Protecting-Fr

17 (2019, January 23). Pride in music is working to make the music industry more LGBT-inclusive. *Attitude*. https://www.attitude.co.uk/article/pride-in-music-is-working-to-make-the-music-industry-more-lgbt-inclusive/20128/

18 Beaumont-Thomas, B. (2019, May 9). Survey into disabled musicians finds serious failings at UK venues. *The Guardian*. https://www.theguardian.com/music/2019/may/09/survey-into-disabled-musicians-finds-serious-failings-at-uk-venues

Money Management

1   Music By Numbers 2019. *UK Music*. https://www.ukmusic.org/assets/general/Music_By_Numbers_2019_Report.pdf

2   Pometsy, O. (2020, March 12). Average UK salary: ever wondered how you stack up? *British GQ*. https://www.gq-magazine.co.uk/article/average-uk-salary

³   Passman, D. (2011). *All You Need To Know About The Music Business,* p.85.

⁴   Ingham, T. (2020, March 5). The global recorded music business generated over $500m a day last year - and more than $2m of it went to DIY artists. *Music Business Worldwide.* https://www.musicbusinessworldwide.com/the-global-recorded-music-business-generated-over-50m-a-day-last-year-and-more-than-2m-of-it-went-to-diy-artists/

⁵   Teague, A., & Smith, G. D. (2015). Portfolio careers and work-life balance among musicians: An initial study into implications for higher music education. *Brit. J. Music. Ed., 32*(2), p.177–193. https://doi.org/10.1017/s0265051715000121

⁶   Shepard, S. (2019, June 7). Crowdfunding site PledgeMusic was an antidote to music biz middlemen—until it cheated artists out of millions. *Pitchfork.* https://pitchfork.com/thepitch/crowdfunding-site-pledgemusic-was-an-antidote-to-music-biz-middlemen-until-it-cheated-artists-out-of-millions/

⁷   Pursehouse, S. (2019, October 1). Ask The Music Industry 2019 Edition. *Sentric Music Publishing.* https://sentricmusic.com/blog/ 2019/october/17/ask-the-music-industry-2019-edition/

⁸   World Health Organization. (2019, May 28). Burn-out an "occupational phenomenon": International Classification of Diseases. https://www.who.int/mental_health/evidence/burn-out/en/

⁹   Heyman, L., Perkins, R. & Araújo, L.S. (2019). Examining the health and well-being experiences of singers in popular music. *Journal of Popular Music Education, 3*(2), p.173-201.

¹⁰   Puolakanaho, A., Tolvanen, A., Kinnunen, S.M. & Lappalainen, R. (2020). A psychological flexibility-based intervention for Burnout: A randomized controlled trial. *Journal of Contextual Behavioural Science, 15*, pp.52-67. https://contextualscience.org/article/a_psychological_flexibility_based_intervention_for_burnouta_randomized_cont

Criticism and Opinions

¹   Renshaw, D. (2014, February 26). NME Awards 2014 with Austin, Texas — full winners report. *NME.* https://www.nme.com/news/music/various-artists-1935-1231526

²   Jones, R. (2014, June 20). The underdog bites back. *Music Week,* pp.12, 13.

³   Stubbs, D. (2018, November 26). The 1975 – 'A Brief Inquiry Into Online Relationships' review. *NME.* https://www.nme.com/reviews/1975-brief-inquiry-online-relationships-review-2404007

⁴   Gunn, C. (2018, December 17). NME's albums of the year 2018. *NME.* https://www.nme.com/blogs/nme-blogs/best-greatest-albums-of-the-year-2018-2419656

⁵   Jones, R. (2019, March). What I wish I'd known. *Music Business UK,* pp. 44, 45.

⁶   Petridis, A. (2017, March 2). Ed Sheeran: 'I got hammered and cracked Justin Bieber in the face with a golf club'. *The Guardian.* https://www.theguardian.com/music/2017/mar/02/ed-sheeran-i-got-hammered-and-cracked-justin-bieber-in-the-face-with-a-golf-club

7 Blunt, J. (2009, May 4). At the Q Awards years ago, when @NoelGallagher was saying he was leaving Ibiza because I'd moved there, and @DamonAlbarn refused to be in the same picture as me, and @PaulWellerHQ was saying he'd rather eat his own shit than work with me, Keith Flint came over, gave me a hug, and [Twitter post]. https://twitter.com/JamesBlunt/status/1102642930207113216

8 Brown, M. (2019, February 1). 'Devoid of personality': BBC tells story of David Bowie's faltering early career. *The Guardian*. https://www.theguardian.com/music/2019/feb/01/devoid-of-personality-bbc-tells-story-of-david-bowies-faltering-early-career

9 Speed, D. (2020, January 16). The Art of Asking with Amanda Palmer. https://podcasts.apple.com/gb/podcast/the-art-of-asking-with-amanda-palmer/id1448695774?i=1000462870586

10 Allen, L. (2019). *My Thoughts Exactly*. London: Blink Publishing, p.98.

11 Allen, L. (2019). *My Thoughts Exactly*. London: Blink Publishing, p.109.

12 O'Connor, R. (2020, May 20). The 1975 review, Notes on a Conditional Form: new album is a parade of smug self-indulgence. *The Independent*. https://www.independent.co.uk/arts-entertainment/music/reviews/the-1975-notes-on-a-conditional-form-review-matt-healy-album-stream-a9523426.html

13 Allen, L. (2019). *My Thoughts Exactly*. London: Blink Publishing, p.100.

14 Temple-Morris, E., Halkes, N. (2018, April 25). S01E01 - Gary Numan. https://podcast2facbb.podigee.io/2-01-gary-numan

15 O'Connor, R. 2019. 'Bring Me The Horizon's Oli Sykes: 'Being cheated on makes you think the worst of people'. *The Independent*. https://www.independent.co.uk/arts-entertainment/music/features/bring-me-the-horizon-interview-oli-sykes-wife-amo-album-all-points-east-a8897876.html

Social Media

1 Lin, Y. L. et al. (2016, April). Association between social media use and depression among U.S. young adults. https://onlinelibrary.wiley.com/doi/abs/10.1002/da.22466

2 van den Eynde, J., Fisher, A. & Sonn, C. (2016, October). Passion & pitfalls and working in the Australian industry. *Victoria University*. https://www.headsup.org.au/docs/default-source/default-document-library/passion-pride-pitfalls_phase-1-reportba8c4adb5e846dcbbbd0ff0000c17e5d.pdf?sfvrsn=1408274d_0

3 Heyman, L. & Perkins, R. & Araújo, S. L. (2020). Examining the health and wellbeing experiences of singers in popular music. *Journal of Popular Music Education*, 3(2), pp.173-201.

4 Wise Buddah & Elevate Music (2019, November 27). Mental health and social media - SK Shlomo and Stephen Buckley. https://audioboom.com/posts/7425428-mental-health-and-social-media-sk-shlomo-and-stephen-buckley

5   Wise Buddah & Elevate Music. (2019, November 27). Mental health and social media - SK Shlomo and Stephen Buckley. https://audioboom.com/posts/7425428-mental-health-and-social-media-sk-shlomo-and-stephen-buckley

6   Brown, B. (2015, March 11). Brené Brown: the safe way to share your shame story. *Huffpost*. https://www.huffpost.com/entry/brene-brown-shame_n_4282679

7   Haig, M. (2018). *Notes on a Nervous Planet*. Edinburgh: Canongate, pp.101-103.

8   Day, E. (2020, January 15). How to Fail with Elizabeth Day. How to fail: Mabel, series 7 episode 3. https://howtofail.podbean.com/e/how-to-fail-mabel/

9   Wisebuddah & Elevate. (2019, July 29). Mental health in music: Nina's story - Nina Nesbitt and Tamsin Embleton. https://audioboom.com/posts/7319415-mental-health-in-music-nina-s-story-nina-nesbitt-and-tamsin-embleton

10   Adwoa, A. (2019, January). Adwoa talks to singer Mabel & comparison coach Lucy Sheridan about our addiction to social media and living a life without FOMO, episode 8. https://gurlstalk.libsyn.com/ep-8-adwoa-talks-to-singer-mabel-comparison-coach-lucy-sheridan-about-our-addiction-to-social-media-and-living-a-life-without-fomo

11   Day, E. (2020, January 15). How to Fail with Elizabeth Day. How to fail: Mabel, series 7 episode 3. https://howtofail.podbean.com/e/how-to-fail-mabel/

12   Mineo, L. (2017, April 11). Good genes are nice, but joy is better. *The Harvard Gazette*. https://news.harvard.edu/gazette/story/2017/04/over-nearly-80-years-harvard-study-has-been-showing-how-to-live-a-healthy-and-happy-life/

13   Haynes, T. (2018, May 1). Dopamine, Smartphones & You: A battle for your time. *Science in the News*. http://sitn.hms.harvard.edu/flash/2018/dopamine-smartphones-battle-time/

14   Kemp, S. (2020, January 30). Digital 2020: global internet use accelerates. *DataReportal*. https://datareportal.com/reports/digital-2020-global-digital-overview

15   Smith Galer, S. (2018, January 19). How much is 'too much time' on social media?. *BBC*. https://www.bbc.com/future/article/20180118-how-much-is-too-much-time-on-social-media

16   Bain, M. (2018, November 11). To feel less depressed and lonely, limit social media use to 30 minutes a day, researchers say. *Quartz*. https://qz.com/quartzy/1459609/limiting-social-media-use-reduces-depression-say-researchers/

17   Swift, T. (2019, March 6). 30 things I learned before turning 30. *Elle*. https://www.elle.com/culture/celebrities/a26628467/taylor-swift-30th-birthday-lessons/

18   Amnesty International. Toxic Twitter - a toxic place for women. Chapter 1. https://www.amnesty.org/en/latest/research/2018/03/online-violence-against-women-chapter-1/#topanchor

19   BBC. (2019, September 9). Jesy Nelson: 'I felt like the whole world hated me'. *BBC News*. https://www.bbc.co.uk/news/av/entertainment-arts-49626527/jesy-nelson-i-felt-like-the-whole-world-hated-me

Fans and Boundaries

1   Baym, N. (2018). *Playing to the Crowd: Musicians, Audiences, and the Intimate Work of Connection*. New York: New York University Press, p. 175.

2   Mailchimp. (2019). Average email campaign stats of Mailchimp customers by industry. *Mailchimp*. https://mailchimp.com/resources/email-marketing-benchmarks/

3   Godin, S. (2008). *Tribes: We Need You To Lead Us*. London: Piatkus Books, p.2.

4   Dacus, L. (2019, May 8). With love: please don't come to the stage door when we're loading in or out, don't try to enter the green room, don't wait by our van, and do not follow me places. Even if you're the absolute nicest person with the best and kindest intentions, it still feels like an invasion. [Twitter post]. https://twitter.com/lucydacus/status/1126170600899325958

5   Brand, R. (July 2019). Under The Skin with Russell Brand, vulnerability and power (with Brené Brown), #85. https://podcasts.apple.com/gb/podcast/85-vulnerability-and-power-with-bren%C3%A9-brown/id1212064750?i=1000442345382

6   Robinson, P. (2020, May 19). Lauv interview: "I'm trying to figure out a balance". *Popjustice*. https://www.popjustice.com/articles/lauv-interview-im-trying-to-figure-out-a-balance/

7   Violence Intervention and Prevention Center. (no date). Adapted from: how to create healthy boundaries: where you end and I begin. *University of Kentucky, Violence and Prevention Center*. https://www.uky.edu/hr/sites/www.uky.edu.hr/files/wellness/images/Conf14_Boundaries.pdf

8   Prism Health North Texas, as cited by Selva, J. (2019). Source reference: Selva, J. (2019). How to set healthy boundaries: examples + PDF worksheets. *Positive Psychology*. https://positivepsychology.com/great-self-care-setting-healthy-boundaries/

9   Prism Health North Texas, as cited by Selva, J. (2019). Source reference: Selva, J. (2019). How to set healthy boundaries: 10 examples + PDF worksheets. *Positive Psychology*. https://positivepsychology.com/great-self-care-setting-healthy-boundaries/

10 Prism Health North Texas, as cited by Selva, J. (2019). Source reference: Selva, J. (2019). How to set healthy boundaries: 10 examples + PDF worksheets. *Positive Psychology*. https://positivepsychology.com/great-self-care-setting-healthy-boundaries/

11 Bieber, J. (2016, March 23). Instagram. https://www.instagram.com/p/BDRkUVKAvIQ/?utm_source=ig_web_copy_link

12 Prism Health North Texas, as cited by Selva, J. (2019). Source reference: Selva, J. (2019). How to set healthy boundaries: 10 examples + PDF worksheets. *Positive Psychology*. https://positivepsychology.com/great-self-care-setting-healthy-boundaries/

13 Cotton, F. (2020). Alicia Keys. https://podcasts.apple.com/gb/podcast/alicia-keys/id1353058891?i=1000477115571

14 Baym, N. (2018). *Playing to the Crowd: Musicians, Audiences, and the Intimate Work of Connection*. New York: New York University Press, p. 201.

Fame

1   Evans, A. & Wilson, D. G. (1999). *Fame: The Psychology of Stardom*. London: Bath Press, p.1.

2   Kemp, S. (2020, January 30). Digital 2020: global internet use accelerates. *DataReportal*. https://datareportal.com/reports/digital-2020-global-digital-overview

3   3voor12 extra (2019). Billie Eilish answers her own questions on fame, dreams and her happy place. https://www.youtube.com/watch?v=CgwLSz1rQs4

4   Howard, T. (2015, November 13). Justin Bieber: the full NME cover story. *NME*. https://www.nme.com/features/the-justin-bieber-experience-nme-meets-a-pop-star-on-the-cusp-of-redemption-0-757005

5   Cowan, L. (2017, February 5). Lady Gaga on fame, family and football. *CBS News*. https://www.cbsnews.com/news/lady-gaga-on-fame-family-football-super-bowl-2017/

6   Gregoire, C. (2015, December 28). Why so many artists are highly sensitive people. *Huffpost*. https://www.huffpost.com/entry/artists-sensitive-creative_n_567f02dee4b0b958f6598764

7   Duckworth, L. (2002, June 17). Musicians found to have 'more sensitive brains'. *Independent*. https://www.independent.co.uk/news/science/musicians-found-to-have-more-sensitive-brains-5360670.html

8   Leopold, W. (2009, March 3). Musicians' brains 'fined-tuned' to identify emotion. *Northwestern*. https://www.northwestern.edu/newscenter/stories/2009/03/kraus.html

9   Evans, A. & Wilson, D. G. (1999). *Fame The Psychology of Stardom*. London: Bath Press, p.64.

10   Guardian music. (2016, January 11). Bowie in quotes: 'I wouldn't like to make singing a full-time occupation'. *The Guardian*. https://www.theguardian.com/music/musicblog/2016/jan/11/david-bowie-life-in-quotes

11   Rockwell, D. & Giles, D. C. (2009). Being a Celebrity: A Phenomenology of Fame. *Journal of Phenomenological Psychology*, 40, pp.178-210.

12   J. Maltby, J. Houran & L. McCutcheon. (2003). A Clinical interpretation of attitudes and behaviours associated with celebrity worship. *The Journal of Nervous and Mental Disease, 191*(1) https://www.researchgate.net/publication/10935546_A_Clinical_interpretation_of_attitudes_and_behaviors_associated_with_celebrity_worship

13   Pappas, S. (2012, February 24). Oscar psychology: why celebrities fascinate us. *Live Science*. https://www.livescience.com/18649-oscar-psychology-celebrity-worship.html

14   Tapper. J. (2006, February 6). Status-conscious monkeys shed light on celeb obsession. *ABC News*. https://abcnews.go.com/WNT/WaterCooler/story?id=623557

15   Drexler. P. (2014, August 12). Why we love to gossip. *Psychology Today*. https://www.psychologytoday.com/intl/blog/our-gender-ourselves/201408/why-we-love-gossip

16   Young, M. S. & Pinksy, D. (2006, October). Narcissism and celebrity. *Journal of Research in Personality*, 40(5), pp.463-471.

17   Fearne, C. (2020, May 11). George Ezra. *Happy Place*. https://podcasts.apple.com/gb/podcast/george-ezra/id1353058891?i=1000474187087

18   Wisebuddah & Elevate. (2019, July 28). Mental health in music: Nina's story - Nina Nesbitt and Tamsin Embleton. https://audioboom.com/posts/7319415-mental-health-in-music-nina-s-story-nina-nesbitt-and-tamsin-embleton

19   Alidina. S. (2010). *Mindfulness For Dummies*. Chichester: John Wiley & Sons, p.9.

Touring

1   Heyman, L., Perkins, R., & Araújo, L. S. (2019). Examining the health and well-being experiences of singers in popular music. *Journal of Popular Music Education*, 3(2), pp.173-201. https://doi.org/10.1386/jpme.3.2.173_1

2   Heyman, L., Perkins, R., & Araújo, L. S. (2019). Examining the health and well-being experiences of singers in popular music. *Journal of Popular Music Education*, 3(2), pp.173-201. https://doi.org/10.1386/jpme.3.2.173_1

3   Winkie, L. (2020, January 8). Touring is hard, and band therapists are here to help. *Vice*. https://www.vice.com/en_us/article/3a8n98/meet-band-therapists-the-pros-musicians-turn-to-when-their-mental-health-is-suffering

4   Embleton, T. (2018). What happens on tour stays on tour. An interpretative phenomenological analysis into the psychological impact of touring for contemporary British musicians. Unpublished masters dissertation, Regent's School of Psychotherapy, p.53

5   Light, A. (2017, January 23). How David Bowie brought Thin White Duke to life on 'Station to Station'. *Rolling Stone*. https://www.rollingstone.com/music/music-features/how-david-bowie-brought-thin-white-duke-to-life-on-station-to-station-125797/

6   Dolan, J., Grow, K., Doyle, P. & Hermes, W. (2019, December 18). Keith Richards' wildest escapades: 19 insane tales from a legendary life. *Rolling Stone*. https://www.rollingstone.com/music/music-lists/keith-richards-wildest-escapades-19-insane-tales-from-a-legendary-life-169242/oh-canada-1977-68956/

7   Yates, H. (2019, October). Eat to the beat. *The Musician*. https://www.musiciansunion.org.uk/Files/Publications/2019/The-Musician-Journal/The-Musician-(winter-2019)-No-AUF

8   Cizek, E., Kelly, P., Kress, K., & Mattfeldt-Beman, M. (2016). Factors affecting healthful eating among touring popular musicians and singers. *Medical Problems of Performing Artists*, 31(2), pp.63-68. https://doi.org/10.21091/mppa.2016.2013

9   Yates, H. (2019, October). Eat to the Beat. *The Musician*. https://www.musiciansunion.org.uk/Files/Publications/2019/The-Musician-Journal/The-Musician-(winter-2019)-No-AUF

10   BAPAM. Sensible Eating for Performers. https://www.bapam.org.uk/wp-content/uploads/2020/03/SensibleEatingforPerformers_BAPAMfactsheet.pdf

11   Yates, H. (2019, October). Eat to the Beat. *The Musician*. https://www.musiciansunion.org.uk/Files/Publications/2019/The-Musician-Journal/The-Musician-(winter-2019)-No-AUF

12 Listen Entertainment & Help Musicians & Elevate. (2019). Touring - Miles Kane and Ben Perry. https://podcasts.apple.com/gb/podcast/2-touring-miles-kane-and-ben-perry/id1469535660?i=1000444991741

13 *Miss Americana*. (2020). [Online]. Directed by Lana Wilson. United States: Tremolo Productions. Available from Netflix.

14 Yates, H. (2019, October). Eat to the Beat. *The Musician*. https://www.musiciansunion.org.uk/Files/Publications/2019/The-Musician-Journal/The-Musician-(winter-2019)-No-AUF

15 Carrington, D. (2019, June 13). Two-hour 'dose' of nature significantly boosts health - study. *The Guardian*. https://www.theguardian.com/environment/2019/jun/13/two-hour-dose-nature-weekly-boosts-health-study-finds

16 Walker. M. (2017). *Why We Sleep*. Penguin Books.

17 Walker. M. (2017). *Why We Sleep*. Penguin Books. pp.107-132.

18 Ezra, G. (2018). Episode 1 — Ed Sheeran. https://www.georgeezra.com/george-ezra-and friends/george-ezra-friends-episode-1-ed-sheeran

19 Listen Entertainment & Help Musicians & Elevate. (2019). Touring - Miles Kane and Ben Perry. https://podcasts.apple.com/gb/podcast/2-touring-miles-kane-and-ben-perry/id1469535660?i=1000444991741

20 Listen Entertainment & Help Musicians & Elevate. (2019). Touring - Miles Kane and Ben Perry. https://podcasts.apple.com/gb/podcast/2-touring-miles-kane-and-ben-perry/id1469535660?i=1000444991741

Vocal Health

1 Saner, E. (2019, November 11). Shakira: 'I needed surgery – or divine intervention.' *The Guardian*. https://www.google.co.uk/amp/s/amp.theguardian.com/music/2019/nov/11/shakira-interview-singing-el-dorado-tour-film-super-bowl

2 Warner, B. (2017, August 10). Why Do Stars Like Adele Keep Losing Their Voice? *The Guardian*. https://www.theguardian.com/news/2017/aug/10/adele-vocal-cord-surgery-why-stars-keep-losing-their-voices?

3 Cotton, F. (2018). Paloma Faith. https://podcasts.apple.com/ee/podcast/paloma-faith/id1353058891?i=1000405931362

4 Taylor, A. and Wasley, D. (2004). 'Physical fitness' in Williamon, A. (ed.) *Musical Excellence: Strategies and Techniques to Enhance Performance,* Oxford: Oxford University Press, pp.163-178.

5 Verdolini Abbott, K., Li, N. Y., Branski, R. C., Rosen, C. A., Grillo, E., Steinhauer, K., & Hebda, P. A. (2012). Vocal exercise may attenuate acute vocal fold inflammation. *Journal of Voice*, 26(6), 814.e1-814.e13. https://doi.org/10.1016/j.jvoice.2012.03.008

6 Glynne, J. (2019, June 27). https://twitter.com/JessGlynne/status/1144197318692016129?s=20

7 Chaffin R. & Lemieux A. F. (2004). General perspectives on achieving musical excellence, in A. Williamon (ed.). *Musical Excellence.* Oxford: Oxford University Press, pp.19-39.

8   Connolly, C. and Williamon, A. (2004). Mental skills training in A. Williamon (ed.), *Musical Excellence*. Oxford: Oxford University Press, pp.221–245.

9   Hughes, D. (2014). Contemporary vocal artistry in popular culture musics: perceptions, observations and lived experiences. New York: Springer, p.287–301.

10   Listen Entertainment & Help Musicians & Elevate. (2019). 9: vocal health: Sophie's story – Sophie Garner and Tori Burnay. https://audioboom.com/posts/7414238-vocal-health-sophie-s-story-sophie-garner-and-tori-burnay

11   Jahn, A. F. (2009). Medical management of the professional singer. *Medical Problems of Performing Artists*, 24(1), p.39.

12   Cohen, S. M., Jacobsen, B. H., Garrett, C. G., Noordzij, J. P., Stewart, M. G., Attia, A., Ossoff, R. H. and Cleveland, T. F. (2007). Creating and validation of the singing voice handicap index. *Annals of Otology, Rhinology & Laryngology*, 116(6), pp.402–06.

13   Smirke, R. (2014, May 19). La Roux returns with 'Trouble in Paradise' after 'burnout' and vocal problems: interview. *Billboard*. https://www.billboard.com/articles/columns/pop-shop/6092146/la-roux-interview-trouble-in-paradise-vocal-problems

14   Abitbol, J. (2019). *The Female Voice*. San Diego: Plural Publishing.

15   Abitbol, J. (2019). *The Female Voice*. San Diego: Plural Publishing.

16   Pestana, P., Vaz-Freitas, S. and Manso, M. (2017). Prevalence of voice disorders in singers: systemic review and meta-analysis. *Journal of Voice, 31*(6), pp.722–27.

17   Cotton, F. (2018). *Paloma Faith*. https://podcasts.apple.com/ee/podcast/paloma-faith/id1353058891?i=1000405931362

Music and the Body

1   Fishbein, M., Middlestadt, S. E., Ottati, V., Strauss, S., and Ellis, A. (1988). Medical problems among ICSOM musicians: overview of a national survey. *Medical Problems of Performing Artists*. 3 pp.1–8.

2   Raeburn, S. D., Hipple, J., Delaney, W., & Chesky, K. (2003). Surveying popular musicians' health status using convenience samples. *Medical Problems of Performing Artists, 18*(3), pp.113–119.

3   Ackermann, B., & Adams, R. (2003). Physical characteristics and pain patterns of skilled violinists. *Medical Problems of Performing Artists, 18*, pp.65–71.

4   Kenny, D., & Ackermann, B. (2014). Performance-related musculoskeletal pain, depression and music performance anxiety in professional orchestral musicians: a population study. *Psychology of Music, 43*(1), pp.43–60.

5   Clark T., Holmes P., Feeley G., & Redding E. (2013). Pointing to performance ability: examining hypermobility and proprioception in musicians, in A. Williamon & W. Goebl (eds.), *Proceedings of the International Symposium on Performance Science 2013,* pp. 605–610, Utrecht, The Netherlands: European Association of Conservatoires.

6   Jabusch, H., Zschucke, D., Schmidt, A., Schuele, S., & Altenmüller, E. (2005). Focal dystonia in musicians: Treatment strategies and long⊠term outcome in 144 patients. *Movement Disorders, 20*(12), pp.1623–1626.

[7] Mangar UK. 13 celebs you didn't know were living with arthritis. https://mangarhealth.com/uk/news/13-celebs-you-didnt-know-were-living-with-arthritis/

[8] Williamon, A., & Thompson, S. (2006). Awareness and incidence of health problems among conservatoire students. *Psychology of Music, 34*(4), pp.411-430.

[9] Rigg, J. L., Marrinan, R., & Thomas, M. A. (2003). Playing-related injury in guitarists playing popular music. *Medical Problems of Performing Artists, 18*(4), pp.150-152.

[10] Listen Entertainment & Help Musicians & Elevate. (2019). Pain and posture - Chris Polglase and Sarah Upjohn. https://podcasts.apple.com/gb/podcast/14-pain-and-posture-chris-polglase-and-sarah-upjohn/id1469535660?i=1000461071613

[11] Posturite. Ergonomic workstation set-up. https://www.posturite.co.uk/help-advice/useful-resources/learning-guides/ergonomic-workstation-setup

[12] Health, E. (2019, February 15). How to create the ideal ergonomic workstation setup in 2020. Ergonomics Health Association. https://ergonomicshealth.com/ergonomic-workstation-setup/

[13] VerticAlign. (2017, March 20). Texting neck pain: how to hold your phone. VerticAlign Posture Coaching. https://verticalign.com/2017/03/20/texting-neck-4-ways-hold-phone-avoid-painful-condition/

[14] Allegro Optical. Optometrist Amy's BAPAM registration is instrumental in helping musicians to see the music. Allegro Optical. https://www.allegrooptical.co.uk/optometrist-amys-bapam-registration-is-instrumental-in-helping-musicians-to-see-the-music/

[15] Dubois, B., & Esculier, J.-F. (2020). Soft-tissue injuries simply need PEACE and LOVE. *Br J Sports Med, 54*(2), pp.72-73.

[16] BAPAM. Fit To Play. https://www.bapam.org.uk/wp-content/uploads/2020/03/FittoPlay_BAPAMfactsheet.pdf

Hearing

[1] Kähäri, K., Zachau, G., Eklöf, M., Sandsjö, L., & Möller, C. (2003). Assessment of hearing and hearing disorders in rock/jazz musicians: Evaluación de la audición y de los problemas auditivos en músicos de rock y jazz. *International Journal of Audiology, 42*(5), pp.279-288. https://doi.org/10.3109/14992020309078347

[2] Yassi, A., Pollock, N., Tran, N., & Cheang, M. (1993, May). Risks to hearing from a rock concert. *Can Fam Physician*. 1993;39:1045-1050. https://pubmed.ncbi.nlm.nih.gov/8499785/

[3] Potier, M., Hoquet, C., Lloyd, R., Nicolas-Puel, C., Uziel, A., & Puel, J.-L. (2009). The Risks of Amplified Music for Disc-Jockeys Working in Nightclubs. *Ear and Hearing, 30*(2), pp.291-293. https://doi.org/10.1097/aud.0b013e31819769fc

[4] Listen Entertainment & Help Musicians & Elevate. (2019). Hearing health - Nigel Elliott and Gladys Akinseye. https://podcasts.apple.com/gb/podcast/hearing-health-nigel-elliott-and-gladys-akinseye/id1469535660?i=1000446131703

5   Turrill, K. (2019, February 10). Will.i.am health latest: The Voice judge's painful health condition revealed. *Express*. https://www.express.co.uk/life-style/health/1084177/will-i-am-health-latest-tinnitus-what-is-it-symptoms-the-voice-uk

6   Britt, R.J. (2006, January 4). Sound Science: Pete Townshend Blames Headphones For Hearing Loss. *Livescience*. https://www.livescience.com/522-sound-science-pete-townshend-blames-headphones-hearing-loss.html

7   Coleman, C. (2018. March 28). Musician Wins Ruling Over Hearing Damage. *BBC News*. https://www.bbc.co.uk/news/entertainment-arts-43571144

8   Press Association. (2017, May 5). Inspiral Carpets drummer killed himself after 20 years of 'unbearable' tinnitus. *The Guardian*. https://www.theguardian.com/society/2017/may/05/inspiral-carpets-drummer-craig-gill-inquest-tinnitus?CMP=share_btn_tw

9   BAPAM. (2020, April 1). BAPAM Hearing Conservation Guidelines For The Performing Arts. https://www.bapam.org.uk/bapam-hearing-conservation-guidelines-for-the-performing-arts/

10   Klickstein, G. (2009). *The Musician's Way: A Guide to Practice, Performance, and Wellness*. New York: Oxford University Press, p.283

11   Luke, L. (2018, March 16). About my hearing. https://www.youtube.com/watch?v=yfO2tnE1-CY.

12   Finlayson, A. (2017, June 22). A music-lover's guide to tinnitus. *Resident Advisor*. https://www.residentadvisor.net/features/2985

13   Klickstein, G. (2009). *The Musician's Way: A Guide to Practice, Performance, and Wellness*. New York: Oxford University Press, p.283

14   Finlayson, A. (2017, June 22). A music-lover's guide to tinnitus. *Resident Advisor*. https://www.residentadvisor.net/features/2985

15   Wartinger, F. (2017). Hearing wellness for musicians. *The Hearing Journal*, 70(4), p.42. https://doi.org/10.1097/01.hj.0000515659.73105.1d

Mental Health

1   Robson, D. (2019, February 21). How your belly could heal your brain. *BBC Future*. https://www.bbc.com/future/article/20190218-how-the-bacteria-inside-you-could-affect-your-mental-health

2   Iliades, C. (2018, October 16). How stress affects digestion. *Everyday Health*. https://www.everydayhealth.com/wellness/united-states-of-stress/how-stress-affects-digestion/

3   Lee, C.-H., & Guiliani, F. (2019). The role of inflammation in depression and fatigue. *Frontiers in Immunology, 10*. https://www.ncbi.nlm.nih.gov/pmc/articles/PMC6658985/

4   Jacka, N. F. & Berk, M. (2013, October 29). Depression, diet and exercise. *The Medical Journal of Australia*. https://www.mja.com.au/journal/2013/199/6/depression-diet-and-exercise

5   Keyes, C. (2010). Change in level of positive mental health as a predictor of future risk of mental illness. *American Journal of Public Health*, Vol 100, No. 12.

6   Bieber, J. (2019). Hope you find time to read this it's from my heart.[Instagram].

2 September. https://www.instagram.com/p/B17JfkkHEKt/?utm_source=ig_embed

[7] Malkin, M. (2018, November 9). Lady Gaga opens up about her 'mental health crisis'. *Variety*. https://variety.com/2018/scene/news/lady-gaga-mental-health-struggles-1203023093/

[8] MTV. (2015). Kendrick Lamar talks about 'u,' his depression & suicidal thoughts (Pt. 2). https://www.youtube.com/watch?v=Hu4Pz9Pjoll&feature=youtu.be

[9] Robinson, L. (2016, December). Cover story: Adele, Queen of Hearts. *Vanity Fair*. https://www.vanityfair.com/culture/2016/10/adele-cover-story

[10] Barr, S. (2019, August 31). Ariana Grande 'says her depression and anxiety have been at an all-time high'. *Independent*. https://www.independent.co.uk/life-style/health-and-families/ariana-grande-depression-anxiety-mental-health-panic-attacks-instagram-story-world-tour-a9086651.html

[11] Harman, J. (2015, May 27). Halsey opens up about being a reluctant role model. *Elle*. https://www.elle.com/culture/celebrities/q-and-a/a28577/halsey-music-bipolar/

[12] Dotiwala, J. (2017, March 1). Grime artist Stormzy on 'Gang Signs & Prayer'. *Channel 4*. https://www.channel4.com/news/stormzy-on-gang-signs-and-prayer

[13] Raeburn, S. D., Hipple, J., Delaney, W., & Chesky, K. (2003). Surveying popular musicians' health status using convenience samples. *Medical Problems of Performing Artists, 18*(3), pp.113-119.

Brodsky, M. (1995). Blues musicians' access to health care. *Med Probl Perform Art, 10*, pp.18-23.

Chesky, K., Kondraske, G., Henoch, M., et al. (2002). Musicians' health. In R. Colwell & C. Richardson (eds.), *The New Handbook of Research on Music Teaching and Learning*. New York: Oxford University Press.

Bellis M.A., Hennell, T., Lushey C, & Hughes, K.E. (2007). Elvis to Eminem: quantifying the price of fame through early mortality of European and North American rock and pop stars. *Journal of Epidemiolgy and Community Health, 61*(10), pp.896-901. https://doi.org/10.1136/jech.2007.059915

[14] Heyman, L., Perkins, R. & Araújo, L.S. (2019). Examining the health and well-being experiences of singers in popular music. *Journal of Popular Music Education, 3*(2), pp.173-201.

[15] World Health Organization. (2020). Mental health: strengthening our response. https://www.who.int/news-room/fact-sheets/detail/mental-health-strengthening-our-response

[16] Mind. (2017). Mental health problems – an introduction. https://www.mind.org.uk/information-support/types-of-mental-health-problems/mental-health-problems-introduction/about-mental-health-problems/

[17] McManus, S., Meltzer, H., Brugha, T. S., Bebbington, P. E., & Jenkins, R. (2009). Adult psychiatric morbidity in England, 2007: results of a household survey. The NHS Information Centre for health and social care.

[18] McManus S, Bebbington P, Jenkins R, Brugha T. (eds.) (2016). Mental health and wellbeing in England: Adult psychiatric morbidity survey 2014. Leeds: NHS digital.

[19] Chesky, K., Kondraske, G., Henoch, M., et al. (2002). Musicians' health. In R. Colwell & C. Richardson (eds.), *The New Handbook of Research on Music Teaching and Learning*. New York: Oxford University Press.

Gross. S, Musgrave. G. (2016). Can music make you sick? Music and depression, a study into the incidence of musicians' mental health, part 1: pilot survey report. University of Westminster/Music Tank, p.13

[20] Cooper, C. & Wills, G. (1987). Stress and Professional Popular Musicians. *Stress Medicine, 3*(4), pp.267-275.

Gross. S, Musgrave. G (2016). Can music make you sick? Music and depression, a study into the incidence of musicians' mental health, part 1: pilot survey report. University of Westminster/Music Tank, p.13

[21] Nusseck, M., Zander, M. & Spahn, C. (2015, March 30). Music performance anxiety in young musicians: comparison of playing classical or popular music. *Medical Problems of Performing Artists,* 30,(1), pp.30-37.

[22] Raeburn, S. D. (1999). Psychological issues and treatment strategies in popular musicians: a Review, part I. *Medical Problems of Performing Artists*, 14, pp.171-179.

Raeburn, S. D. (2007). The ring of fire: shame, fame, and rock'n'roll. *Medical Problems of Performing Artists, 22*(1), pp.3-9.

Wills, G. I. (2003). Forty lives in the bebop business: mental health in a group of eminent jazz musicians. *The British Journal of Psychiatry, 183*(3), pp.255-259.

[23] Cooper, C. & Wills, G. (1987). Stress and professional popular musicians. *Stress Medicine, 3*(4), pp.267-275.

[24] Cooper, C. Wills, G. (1989). Popular musicians under pressure. *Psychology of Music, 17*(1), pp.22-36. https://doi.org/10.1177/0305735689171003

[25] Dobson, M. (2010). Insecurity, professional sociability, and alcohol: young freelance musicians' perspectives on work and life in the music profession. *Psychology of Music, 39*(2), pp.240-260.

[26] *Everybody's Everything*. (2019). [Online]. Directed by Sebastian Jones and Ramez Silyan. United States: Gunpowder & Sky. Available from Netflix.

[27] *NME*. (2018, June 13). Avicii's death reported as suicide after family say: "He could not go on any longer". https://www.nme.com/news/music/how-did-avicii-die-2298210

[28] Hyman, D. (2018, November 15). Mac Miller's last days and life after death. *Rolling Stone*. https://www.rollingstone.com/music/music-features/mac-miller-legacy-loss-756802/

[29] BBC News. (2019, May 8). Keith Flint: Prodigy star took drugs before death. *BBC*. https://www.bbc.co.uk/news/uk-england-essex-48200575

SOUND ADVICE • REFERENCES

30 Grow, K. (2017, August 4). Chester Bennington's last days: Linkin Park singer's mix of hope, heaviness. *Rolling Stone*. https://www.rollingstone.com/music/music-news/chester-benningtons-last-days-linkin-park-singers-mix-of-hope-heaviness-124862/

31 Topping, A. (2013, January 8). Amy Winehouse died of alcohol poisoning, second inquest confirms. *The Guardian*. https://www.theguardian.com/music/2013/jan/08/amy-winehouse-alcohol-poisoning-inquest

32 Beaumont-Thomas, B. (2018, May 11). Police confirm death of Frightened Rabbit singer Scott Hutchison. *The Guardian*. https://www.theguardian.com/uk-news/2018/may/11/body-found-in-search-for-frightened-rabbit-singer-scott-hutchison

33 Kenny, D. T., & Asher, A. (2016). Life expectancy and cause of death in popular musicians: is the popular musician lifestyle the road to ruin. *Medical Problems of Performing Artists, 31*(1), pp.37–44.

34 Stack, S. & Lester, D. (2009). Suicide and the creative arts. New York: Nova Science Publishers. http://docshare02.docshare.tips/files/27602/276020147.pdf

35 Kyaga, S., Landén, M., Boman, M., Hultman, C.M., Långström, N. & Lichtenstein, P. (2013). Mental illness, suicide and creativity: 40-Year prospective total population study. *Journal of Psychiatric Research, 47*(1), pp.83–90.

36 Pavitra, K.S. Chandrashekar, C.R., Choudhury, P. (2007). Creativity and mental health: a profile of writers and musicians. *Indian J Psychiatry.* 49(1), pp.34–43.

37 Whitby-Grubb, S. (2015, June 26). The darkside of touring. *Drowned in Sound*. http://drownedinsound.com/in_depth/4149129-the-darkside-of-touring

38 Wisebuddah & Elevate. (2019, July 29). Mental health in music: Nina's story – Nina Nesbitt and Tamsin Embleton. https://audioboom.com/posts/7319415-mental-health-in-music-nina-s-story-nina-nesbitt-and-tamsin-embleton

39 Wisebuddah & Elevate Music. (2019, December 9). Wellbeing - Ayanna Witter-Johnson and Simone Willis. https://audioboom.com/posts/7441419-wellbeing-ayanna-witter-johnson-and-simone-willis

40 Hari, J. *Lost Connections*. London: Bloomsbury, p.313

41 Goulding, E. (2019). Sorry this is a little late, but I had to speak about about Mental Health Awareness, for what it's worth. [Instagram]. 14 October. https://www.instagram.com/p/B3mBD3UjTMM/?hl=en

42 Cotton, F. (2020, May 11). George Ezra. https://play.acast.com/s/happy-place/375bd29d-4115-44a0-b9fc-b013a530e05d

43 Wise Buddah & Elevate Music. Mental health and social media – SK Shlomo and Stephen Buckley. https://audioboom.com/posts/7425428-mental-health-and-social-media-sk-shlomo-and-stephen-buckley

44 BBCRadio 4. (2009, November 29). Play well: very loud science. https://www.bbc.co.uk/programmes/m000bfgq

45 Schumacher, H. (2019, March 18). Why more men than women die by suicide. *BBC*. https://www.bbc.com/future/article/20190313-why-more-men-kill-themselves-than-women

46 Ward, T. (2018, March 9). Loyle Carner: "People are caught up in certain ideas

of masculinity". *Vice*. https://www.vice.com/en_uk/article/9kz4g5/loyle-carner-calm-best-man-project-male-mental-health

47   Blake, J. (2019, October 9). 'How Can I Complain?'. *Penguin*. https://www.penguin.co.uk/articles/2019/oct/james-blake-on-mental-health.html

48   Heaf, J. (2019, September 19). Dave: 'Psychodrama was the album that I needed it to be, the album that was expected of me'. *GQ*. https://www.gq-magazine.co.uk/men-of-the-year/article/dave-music-interview-2019

49   Lewis, T. (2019, April 21). Loyle Carner: 'I was raised by women - they talked about feelings every day'. *The Guardian*. https://www.theguardian.com/music/2019/apr/21/loyle-carner-i-was-raised-by-women-talk-about-feelings-every-day-not-waving-but-drowning

Substance Use and Addiction

1   Shapiro, H. (2003). *Waiting for the Man.* London: Helter Skelter, pp. 13–18.

2   Bellis, M. A., Hughes, K., Sharples, O., Hennell, T., & Hardcastle, K. A. (2012). Dying to be famous: retrospective cohort study of rock and pop star mortality and its association with adverse childhood experiences. *British Medical Journal open*, 2(6), p.e002089.

Forsyth, A. J.M., Lennox, J., and Emslie, C. (2016). "That's cool, you're a musician and you drink": Exploring entertainers' accounts of their unique workplace relationship with alcohol. *International Journal of Drug Policy, 36,* pp.85–94.

Miller, K. E., & Quigley, B. M. (2012). Sensation-seeking, performance genres and substance use among musicians. *Psychology of Music, 40*(4), pp.389–410.

3   Bellis, M. A., Hughes, K., Sharples, O., Hennell, T., & Hardcastle, K. A. (2012). Dying to be famous: retrospective cohort study of rock and pop star mortality and its association with adverse childhood experiences. *British Medical Journal open*, 2(6), p.e002089

4   Forsyth, A. J.M., Lennox, J., and Emslie, C. (2016). "That's cool, you're a musician and you drink": Exploring entertainers' accounts of their unique workplace relationship with alcohol. *International Journal of Drug Policy*, 36, pp.85–94.

5   Butkovic, A. and Dopudj, D.R. (August 2016). Personality traits and alcohol consumption of classical and heavy metal musicians. *Psychology of Music, 45*(2), pp.246–256 DOI: 10.1177/0305735616659128

6   Wills, G.I. (2003). Forty lives in the bebop business: mental health in a group of eminent jazz musicians. *British Journal of Psychiatry*, 185,. pp.255–259.

7   Miller, K. E., & Quigley, B. M. (2012). Sensation-seeking, performance genres and substance use among musicians. *Psychology of Music, 40*(4), pp.389–410.

8   West, R. (2004). Drugs and musical performance. In A. Williamon (ed.), *Musical Excellence: Strategies and Techniques to Enhance Performance.* Oxford Oxford University Press, pp.271– 290

9   Cooper, C.L., & Wills, G.I. (1988). *Pressure sensitive: Popular musicians under stress.* London: Sage.

10   Miller, K. E., & Quigley, B. M. (2012). Sensation-seeking, performance genres and substance use among musicians. *Psychology of Music, 40*(4), pp.389–410.

11   Wesner, R. B., Noyes, R., & Davis, T. L. (1990). The occurrence of performance anxiety among musicians. *Journal of Affective Disorders, 18*, pp.177–185.

12   National Health Service. (2015, April 18). Addiction: what is it? https://www.nhs.uk/live-well/healthy-body/addiction-what-is-it/

13   Listen Entertainment & Help Musicians & Elevate. (2019, November 4). Addiction – Chula Goonewardene and Adrianna Irvine. https://audioboom.com/posts/7411578-addiction-chula-goonewardene-and-adrianna-irvine

14   National Health Service. (2015, April 18). Addiction: what is it? https://www.nhs.uk/live-well/healthy-body/addiction-what-is-it/

15   United Nations Office on Drugs and Crime. (June 2019). World Drug Report 2019. https://wdr.unodc.org/wdr2019/prelaunch/WDR19_Booklet_1_EXECUTIVE_SUMMARY.pdf

16   McManus, S., Bebbington, P., Jenkins, R., Brugha, T. (eds.) (2016) *Mental health and wellbeing in England: Adult Psychiatric Morbidity Survey 2014*. Leeds: NHS Digital. https://assets.publishing.service.gov.uk/government/uploads/system/uploads/attachment_data/file/556596/apms-2014-full-rpt.pdf

17   Brand, R. (2017). *Recovery: Freedom From Our Addictions*. New York: Henry Holt, p.32

18   Brand, R. (2017). *Recovery: Freedom From Our Addictions*. New York: Henry Holt, p.62.

19   Brand, R. (2017). *Recovery: Freedom From Our Addictions*. New York: Henry Holt, pp.201,202.

20   Lynskey, D. (2018, August 2). How the 1975's Matty Healy kicked heroin and took the band to new heights. *Billboard*. https://www.billboard.com/articles/news/magazine-feature/8468029/matty-healy-the-1975-billboard-cover-story

21   Press Association. (2018, October 10). Nearly 30% of young people in England do not drink, study finds. *The Guardian*. https://www.theguardian.com/society/2018/oct/10/young-people-drinking-alcohol-study-england

22   Brand, R. (2017). *Recovery: Freedom From Our Addictions*. New York: Henry Holt, p.66.

23   Mental Health America. Co-Dependency. https://www.mhanational.org/issues/co-dependency

Disordered Eating and Body Image

1   Richardson, W. M. (2019, February 1). How much energy does the brain use?. *Brain Facts*. https://www.brainfacts.org/brain-anatomy-and-function/anatomy/2019/how-much-energy-does-the-brain-use-020119

2   National Eating Disorders Association. Health consequences. https://www.nationaleatingdisorders.org/health-consequences

3   Karges, C. (2017, May 27). Can depression be caused by malnutrition from an eating disorder?. *Eating Disorder Hope*. https://www.eatingdisorderhope.com/blog/depression-caused-malnutrition

4   Harrison, C. (2019). *Anti-Diet: Reclaim your time, money, health, and happiness through intuitive eating*. New York: Little, Bown Spark, pp.23–49.

5   Snapes, L. (2020, March 10). Body of work: why Billie Eilish is right to stand her ground against shaming. *The Guardian*. https://www.theguardian.com/music/2020/mar/10/body-of-work-why-billie-eilish-is-right-to-stand-her-ground-against-shaming

6   Boyle, S. (2020, April 9). Liam Payne's furious mum 'hit him around the ear' over raunchy underwear shoot with model Stella Maxwell. *The Sun*. https://www.thesun.co.uk/tvandshowbiz/11366707/liam-payne-mum-underwear-stella-maxwell/

7   Sole-Smith, V. (2020, May 13). The pandemic is heightening diet culture for men. *Medium*. https://elemental.medium.com/the-pandemic-is-heightening-diet-culture-for-men-5af2c1ccfc8e

8   Arnold, C. (2020, June 25). Among people facing food insecurity, researchers find a hidden health issue: eating disorders. *Stat*. https://www.statnews.com/2020/06/25/eating-disorder-food-insecurity/

9   National Health Service. (2018, January 16). Eating disorders. https://www.nhs.uk/conditions/eating-disorders/

10   National Health Service. (2018, January 16). Eating disorders. Reviewed 16 January 2018. https://www.nhs.uk/conditions/eating-disorders/

National Eating Disorders Association. Information by eating disorder. https://www.nationaleatingdisorders.org/information-eating-disorder

11   Praderio, C. (2017, October 20). Demi Lovato shared powerful side-by-side photos to document her eating disorder recovery. *Insider*. https://www.insider.com/demi-lovatos-eating-disorder-recovery-photos-2017-10

12   Hiatt, B. (2017, October 4). The liberation of Kesha. *Rolling Stone*. https://www.rollingstone.com/music/music-features/the-liberation-of-kesha-123984/

13   Kesha. (2016, March 7). 'I've always tried to be a crusader for loving yourself'. *Elle*. https://www.elle.com/uk/life-and-culture/news/a29723/kesha-loving-yourself-elle/

14   Norman, P. (2019, October 6). Elton John's war with drugs, sex and bulimia – and his 20 cockle pot breakfast. *Mirror*. https://www.mirror.co.uk/3am/celebrity-news/elton-johns-war-drugs-sex-20526461

15   Munzenrieder, K. (2016, November 1). Zayn Malik struggled with an eating disorder during his time in One Direction. *W Magazine*. https://www.wmagazine.com/story/zayn-malik-struggled-with-an-eating-disorder-during-his-time-in-one-direction/

16   Willman, C. (2020, January 23). Taylor Swift opens up about overcoming struggle with eating disorder. *Variety*. https://variety.com/2020/music/news/taylor-swift-eating-disorder-netflix-documentary-miss-americana-1203478047/

17   Mind. (2018, November). Body dysmorphic disorder (BDD). https://www.mind.org.uk/information-support/types-of-mental-health-problems/body-dysmorphic-disorder-bdd/symptoms/

18   Veale. D. & Neziroglu, F. (2010). *Body Dysmorphic Disorder: A Treatment Manual*. New York: Wiley, p.38

19   Sturges, F. (2005, March 12). Shirley Manson: Shirley temper. *Independent*. https://www.independent.co.uk/arts-entertainment/music/features/shirley-manson-shirley-temper-5762.html

20 Kapsetaki, M. E., Easmon, C. (2017, July 14). Eating disorders in musicians: a survey investigating self-reported eating disorders of musicians. DOI: 10.1007/s40519-017-0414-9

21 Priory. Eating Disorder Statistics. https://www.priorygroup.com/eating-disorders/eating-disorder-statistics

22 Beat. (2017, September). Do I have an eating disorder? https://www.beateatingdisorders.org.uk/types/do-i-have-an-eating-disorder

23 National Health Service. (2018, January 16). Eating disorders. https://www.nhs.uk/conditions/eating-disorders/

24 Mind. (2018, November). Body dysmorphic disorder (BDD). https://www.mind.org.uk/information-support/types-of-mental-health-problems/body-dysmorphic-disorder-bdd/symptoms/

Setting Goals

1 Locke, E. A. (1996). Motivation through conscious goal setting. *Applied and preventive psychology, 5*(2), pp.11–124.

2 Lunenburg, F. C. (2011). Goal-setting theory of motivation. *International journal of management, 15*(1), pp.1–6.

3 Hay House. (2020, July 13). Ed Sheeran – finding peace at the top of the music industry. Chasing The Present. https://www.youtube.com/watch?v=oxDLKVwFQ9Q

4 Sheldon, K. M., & Kasser, T. (1995). Coherence and congruence: two aspects of personality integration. *Journal of Personality and Social Psychology, 68*(3), pp.531–543. DOI: 10.1037/0022-3514.68.3.531

5 Seligman, M.E.P. (2012). *Flourish: A Visionary New Understanding of Happiness and Well-being.* Random House Australia.

6 Clarke, J. (2020). Benefits of a Morning Routine. *verywellmind.* https://www.verywellmind.com/morning-routine-4174576

7 Speed, D. (2020, January 16). The Art of Asking with Amanda Palmer. https://podcasts.apple.com/gb/podcast/the-art-of-asking-with-amanda-palmer/id1448695774?i=1000462870586

8 Wikipedia. (2020, August 11). Paradise Syndrome. https://en.wikipedia.org/wiki/Paradise_Syndrome

9 Scott, P. (2013, August 5). How pop's most toxic love affair cast a shadow over SIX marriages: have Eurythmics' Annie Lennox and Dave Stewart finally got each other out of their systems? *Mail Online.* https://www.dailymail.co.uk/news/article-2384626/How-pops-toxic-love-affair-cast-shadow-SIX-marriages-Have-Eurythmics-Annie-Lennox-Dave-Stewart-finally-got-systems.html

10 BBC Newsround. (2019, November 29). How many records has Ed Sheeran broken?. https://www.bbc.co.uk/newsround/50219299

11 Hay House. (2020, July 13). Ed Sheeran – finding peace at the top of the music industry. Chasing The Present. https://www.youtube.com/watch?v=oxDLKVwFQ9Q

12 Hay House. (2020, July 13). Ed Sheeran – finding peace at the top of the music industry. Chasing The Present. https://www.youtube.com/watch?v=oxDLKVwFQ9Q

13   Kahneman, D., & Deaton, A. (2010, August 4). High income improves evaluation of life but not emotional well-being. PNAS. https://www.pnas.org/content/pnas/107/38/16489.full.pdf

14   Diener E., & Seligman M.E.P. (2002). Very happy people. *Psychological Science, 13*(1), pp.81-84. doi:10.1111/1467-9280.00415

15   Myers, D. G. (2000). The funds, friends, and faith of happy people. *American psychologist, 55*(1), pp.56-67.

16   Hay House. (2020, July 13). Ed Sheeran - finding peace at the top of the music industry. Chasing The Present. https://www.youtube.com/watch?v=oxDLKVwFQ9Q

Talent and Practice

1   Ericsson, A. & Pool, R. (2016). *Peak: Secrets from the New Science of Expertise.* New York: Random House.

2   Duckworth, A. L., Peterson, C., Matthews, M. D., & Kelly, D. R. (2007). Grit: Perseverance and passion for long-term goals. *Journal of Personality and Social Psychology, 92*(6), pp.1087-1101.

3   Ericsson, A. & Pool, R. (2016). *Peak: Secrets from the New Science of Expertise.* New York: Random House, p.113

4   Ericsson, A. & Pool, R. (2016). *Peak: Secrets from the New Science of Expertise.* New York: Random House, p.23

5   Chaffin, R., & Lemieux, A. F. (2004). General perspectives on achieving musical excellence. In A. Williamon, (ed.), *Musical excellence: Strategies and techniques to enhance performance.* Oxford: Oxford University Press, pp.19-39.

6   Freymouth, M. (1993). Mental practice for musicians: Theory and applications. *Medical Problems of Performing Artists,* 8, p.141-143.

7   Connolly, C. & Williamon, A. (2004). Mental skills training. In Williamon, A. (ed.). *Musical excellence: strategies and techniques to enhance performance.* New York: Oxford University Press, pp.221-245.

Performance Anxiety

1   Nusseck, M., Zander, M., & Spahn, C. (2015). Music performance anxiety in young musicians: comparison of playing classical or popular music. *Medical Problems of Performing Artists, 30*(1), pp.30-37. https://doi.org/10.21091/mppa.2015.1005

    Papageorgi, I., Creech, A., & Welch, G. (2012). Perceived performance anxiety in advanced musicians specializing in different musical genres. *Psychology of Music, 41*(1), pp.18-41.

2   Touré. (2011, April 28). Adele opens up about her inspirations, looks and stage fright. *Rolling Stone.* https://www.rollingstone.com/music/music-news/adele-opens-up-about-her-inspirations-looks-and-stage-fright-79626/

3   Osbourne, O. (2009). *I Am Ozzy.* London: Hachette UK.

4 Cox, D. (2015, September 8). It'll be alright on the night: how musicians cope with performance stress. *The Guardian*. https://www.theguardian.com/music/2015/sep/08/how-classical-musicians-cope-with-performance-stress

5 Britt, B. (2017, May 15). Musicians who grapple with stage fright. *Recording Academy*. https://www.grammy.com/grammys/news/adele-van-halen-among-musicians-who-battle-stage-fright

6 Walker, I., Nordin, S., & Clark, T. (2009). Losing yourself in the work, or lost to nerves?. *Trinity Laban*. https://www.trinitylaban.ac.uk/media/254741/anxiety%20information%20sheet.pdf

7 Palathingal, G. (2013). Lorde admits to crippling stage fright. *The Sydney Morning Herald*. https://www.smh.com.au/entertainment/music/lorde-admits-to-crippling-stage-fright-20131107-2x3ba.html

8 McAfee, T. (2013). Harry Styles throws up on stage at 1D Pittsburgh Concert. *Hollywood Life*. https://hollywoodlife.com/2013/07/10/harry-styles-throws-up-on-stage-video-one-direction-pittsburgh/

9 Sawa, J. (2017, October 1). Successful musicians who still suffer from stage fright. *Idolator*. https://www.idolator.com/7687627/successful-musicians-who-still-suffer-from-stage-fright/11?safari=1)

10 Listen Entertainment & Help Musicians & Elevate. (2019). Stage Fright - Shaun Ryder and Aaron Williamon. https://audioboom.com/posts/7338162-stage-fright-shaun-ryder-and-aaron-williamon

11 Hanin, Y. L. (2007). Emotions in sport: current issues and perspectives. Handbook of sport psychology, 3(3158), pp.22-41.

Hanin, Y. L. (1997). Emotion and athletic performance: Individual zones of optimal functioning model. *European Yearbook of Sport Psychology, 1*, pp.29-72.

12 Mindtools. *The inverted-u theory: balancing performance and pressure with the Yerkes-Dodson law*. https://www.mindtools.com/pages/article/inverted-u.htm

13 Brooks, A. W. (2018). Get excited: reappraising pre-performance anxiety as excitement. *AMPROC, 2013*(1), 10554. https://doi.org/10.5465/ambpp.2013.10554abstract

14 Listen Entertainment & Help Musicians & Elevate. (2019). Stage Fright - Shaun Ryder and Aaron Williamon. https://audioboom.com/posts/7338162-stage-fright-shaun-ryder-and-aaron-williamon

15 Listen Entertainment & Help Musicians & Elevate. (2019). Stage Fright - Shaun Ryder and Aaron Williamon. https://audioboom.com/posts/7338162-stage-fright-shaun-ryder-and-aaron-williamon

16 Walker, I., Nordin, S., & Clark, T. (2009). Losing yourself in the work, or lost to nerves? *Trinity Laban*. https://www.trinitylaban.ac.uk/media/254741/anxiety%20information%20sheet.pdf

17 Listen Entertainment & Help Musicians & Elevate. (2019). Stage Fright - Shaun Ryder and Aaron Williamon. https://audioboom.com/posts/7338162-stage-fright-shaun-ryder-and-aaron-williamon

18 CTV News. (2012, October 5). Taylor Swift Talks To Herself In Mirror

To Calm Nerves Before Shows. *CTV News*. https://www.ctvnews.ca/entertainment/taylor-swift-talks-to-herself-in-mirror-to-calm-nerves-before-shows-1.984420?cache=yes%2F5-things-to-know-for-wednesday-september-11-2019-1.4587785

[19] Novick, J., & Steen, R. (2014). Love is the drug: performance-enhancing in sport and music. *Sport in Society, 17*(3), pp.419-432.

[20] Brandfonbrener, A. G. (1995). Musicians with focal dystonia: a report of 58 cases seen during a ten-year period at a performing arts medicine clinic. *Medical Problems of Performing Artists, 10*, pp.121-127.

[21] Hawkins, C. (2019, November 4). Why playing live music is like jumping from a plane. *BBC*. https://www.bbc.co.uk/news/entertainment-arts-50238883

[22] Gander, K. (2018, April 28). Katy Perry says she treats her anxiety with meditation, not prescription drugs. *Newsweek*. https://www.newsweek.com/katy-perry-904893

[23] Listen Entertainment & Help Musicians & Elevate. (2019). Stage Fright - Shaun Ryder and Aaron Williamon. https://audioboom.com/posts/7338162-stage-fright-shaun-ryder-and-aaron-williamon

[24] Clarke, L. K., Osborne, M. S., & Baranoff, J. A. (2020). Examining a group acceptance and commitment therapy intervention for music performance anxiety in student vocalists. *Frontiers in Psychology, 11*. https://doi.org/10.3389/fpsyg.2020.01127.

[25] Cox, D. (2015, September 8). It'll be alright on the night: how musicians cope with performance stress. *The Guardian*. https://www.theguardian.com/music/2015/sep/08/how-classical-musicians-cope-with-performance-stress

[26] Cox, D. (2015, September 8). It'll be alright on the night: how musicians cope with performance stress. *The Guardian*. https://www.theguardian.com/music/2015/sep/08/how-classical-musicians-cope-with-performance-stress

Stage Strategies

[1] Hunter, A. (2016, August 8). Rituals and routines of Olympic athletes. *Get The Gloss*. https://www.getthegloss.com/article/rituals-and-routines-of-olympic-athletes

[2] BBC Music. (2017, April 27). 10 of music's oddest pre-gig rituals. *BBC*. https://www.bbc.co.uk/music/articles/a84df289-9e08-4a47-86e6-b91b7d94293f

[3] BBC Music. (2017, April 27). 10 of music's oddest pre-gig rituals. *BBC*. https://www.bbc.co.uk/music/articles/a84df289-9e08-4a47-86e6-b91b7d94293f

[4] Exercise adapted from Williamon, A. (ed.) (2004). *Musical excellence: Strategies and techniques to enhance performance.* New York: Oxford University Press.

[5] Keys, A. (2020). *More Myself: A Journey.* New York: Flatiron Books.

[6] O'Connor, P.J.,Gardiner, E., & Watson, C. (2016). Learning to relax versus learning to ideate: relaxation-focused creativity training benefits introverts more than extraverts. *Thinking Skills and Creativity, 21*, pp.97-108.

[7] Greene, D. (2012). *Performance Success: Performing your best under pressure.* New York: Routledge.

8   Adapted from Williamon, A. (ed.) (2004). *Musical excellence: Strategies and techniques to enhance performance*. New York: Oxford University Press.

9   Fullerton, J. (2011, April 22). Adele reveals Beyonce-inspired alter ego 'Sasha Carter'. *NME*. https://www.nme.com/news/music/adele-349-1296709

10 Adapted from Williamon, A. (ed.) (2004). *Musical excellence: Strategies and techniques to enhance performance*. New York: Oxford University Press.

11 Heyman, L., Perkins, R., & Araújo, L. S. (2019). Examining the health and well-being experiences of singers in popular music. *Journal of Popular Music Education*, 3(2), pp.173–201. https://doi.org/10.1386/jpme.3.2.173_1

12 (2018, February 8). Brené Brown — strong back, soft front, wild heart. *On Being*. https://onbeing.org/programs/brene-brown-strong-back-soft-front-wild-heart/#transcript

13 Csikszentmihalyi, M. (2020). *Finding Flow: The Psychology Of Engagement With Everyday Life*. London: Hachette UK.

14 Mindvalley. (2018, August 6). 13 strategies to get in flow based on the latest research by Steven Kotler. *mindvalley blog*. https://blog.mindvalley.com/how-to-get-in-flow/

15 Wikipedia. (2020, August 11). *Flow (psychology)*. https://en.wikipedia.org/wiki/Flow_(psychology)

Creativity

1   Keys, A. (2020). *More Myself: A Journey*. New York: Flatiron Books, p.61

2   Runco, M. (2004). Creativity. *Annual Review of Psychology*. http://people.wku.edu/richard.miller/creativity.pdf

3   goodreads.com. (2020). Charlie Parker Quotes. https://www.goodreads.com/author/quotes/265264.Charlie_Parker

4   Hay House. (2020, July 13). Ed Sheeran – finding peace at the top of the music industry. Chasing The Present. https://www.youtube.com/watch?v=oxDLKVwFQ9Q

5   Boyd, D. J. (2013). *It's Not Only Rock 'n' Roll - Iconic Musicians Reveal the Source of their Creativity*. London: John Blake Publishing.

6   Beahm, G. (2011). *I, Steve: Steve Jobs in his own words*. London: Hardie Grant Publishing.

7   "Connecting The Dots" - Amanda Palmer talks art & controversy @ Grub Muse conference. *GrubStreet*. https://vimeo.com/65681037

8   Keys, A. (2020). *More Myself: A Journey*. New York: Flatiron Books.

9   Pangambam, S. (2016, April 2). Elizabeth Gilbert on your elusive creative genius (full transcript). *The Singju Post*. https://singjupost.com/elizabeth-gilbert-on-your-elusive-creative-genius-full-transcript/2/

10 Byrne, D. (2012). *How Music Works*. New York: Three Rivers Press.

11 Tharp, T. (2009). *The Creative Habit: Learn it and use it for life*. New York: Simon and Schuster.

12 Keys, A. (2020). *More Myself: A Journey*. New York: Flatiron Books, p.61

13 Boyd, D. J. (2013). *It's Not Only Rock 'n' Roll - Iconic Musicians Reveal the Source of their Creativity*. London: John Blake Publishing.

14 Jones, R. (2016). Jimmy Webb interview. *The Works*.

15   (2019, February 9). Ariana Grande "thank u, next" interview. *Zach Sang Show*. https://www.youtube.com/watch?v=fpl8v3jiuNU

16   O'Connor, R. (2018, March 22). 'Blurred Lines' copyright ruling is a 'devastating blow' and sets dangerous precedent for musicians, judge warns. *Independent*. https://www.musicbusinessworldwide.com/robin-thicke-and-pharrell-williams-ordered-to-pay-5m-as-blurred-lines-copyright-case-comes-to-an-end/

17   Jones, R. (2015, September). Inspiration or infringement?. *M Magazine*. Issue 57. https://issuu.com/m_magazine/docs/m57

18   Morrison, R. (2020, April 2). Note to artists: it's not a sign of weakness to be unable to work now. *The Times*. http://www.thetimes.co.uk/article/ed2e951e-74ed-11ea-a7b2-0673a3ece2ba

19   Kawashima, D. (2006, November 15). Amy Lee talks about Evanescence's hit album, *The Open Door*, and her songwriting. *SongwriterUniverse*. https://www.songwriteruniverse.com/evanescence123.htm

20   Leake, J. (2020, April 5). Coronavirus lockdown: bored yet? Good — you're on the verge of a creative explosion. *The Times*. http://www.thetimes.co.uk/article/72ac7d9c-7641-11ea-a949-5bf33ccb8633

21   Cerullo, A. (2017, July 7). 5 effective improvisation exercises to practice with your band. *sonicbids*. https://blog.sonicbids.com/5-improvisation-exercises-to-practice-with-your-band

22   Cave, N. (November 2018). Are there times your creativity disappears and if so how do you coax it back / jump start it?. *The Red Hand Files*. https://www.theredhandfiles.com/creativity-disappears-coax-it-back/#:~:text=Creativity%20is%20not%20something%20that,are%20prepared%20to%20accept%20them.&text=You%20must%20prove%20yourself%20worthy%20of%20the%20idea.

23   Cameron, J. (2002). *The Artist's Way: A spiritual path to higher creativity*. London: Penguin.

24   Miles Davis Quotes. *goodreads*. https://www.goodreads.com/quotes/92796-do-not-fear-mistakes---there-are-none

25   Boyd, D. J. (2013). *It's Not Only Rock 'n' Roll - Iconic Musicians Reveal the Source of their Creativity*. London: John Blake Publishing.

26   Boyd, D. J. (2013). *It's Not Only Rock 'n' Roll - Iconic Musicians Reveal the Source of their Creativity*. London: John Blake Publishing.

27   A Quote From Letters To A Young Poet. *Good Reads*. https://www.goodreads.com/quotes/691965-but-perhaps-these-are-the-very-hours-during-which-solitude

28   Boyd, D. J. (2013). *It's Not Only Rock 'n' Roll - Iconic Musicians Reveal the Source of their Creativity*. London: John Blake Publishing.

29   Boyd, D. J. (2013). *It's Not Only Rock 'n' Roll - Iconic Musicians Reveal the Source of their Creativity*. London: John Blake Publishing.

End Here

1   Santos, R.L. & Gendler, T. (2014). What scientific idea is ready for retirement?. *Edge*. https://www.edge.org/response-detail/25436

2   Daly, R. (2020, April 19). New figures show how many streams artists need to earn minimum wage. *NME*. https://www.nme.com/news/music/new-figures-show-how-many-streams-artists-need-to-earn-minimum-wage-2649715

3   Ingham, T. (2018, March 25). The odds of an artist becoming a 'top tier' earner on Spotify today? Less than 1%. *Music Business Worldwide*. https://www.musicbusinessworldwide.com/the-odds-of-an-artist-becoming-a-top-tier-earner-on-spotify-today-less-than-1/

4   Music By Numbers 2019. *UK Music*. https://www.ukmusic.org/assets/general/Music_By_Numbers_2019_Report.pdf

5   Office of National Statistics. (2020). Employment in the UK: May 2020. https://www.ons.gov.uk/employmentandlabourmarket/peopleinwork/employmentandemployeetypes/bulletins/employmentintheuk/may2020#employment-in-the-uk-data

6   Department for Digital, Culture, Media & Sport. (2020, February 6). UK's Creative Industries contributes almost £13 million to the UK economy every hour. https://www.gov.uk/government/news/uks-creative-industries-contributes-almost-13-million-to-the-uk-economy-every-hour#:~:text=UK's%20Creative%20Industries%20contributes%20almost%20%C2%A313,the%20UK%20economy%20every%20hour&text=New%20government%20figures%20show%20the,%C2%A3306%20million%20every%20day.

7   Wisebuddah & Elevate. (2019, July 29). Mental health in music: Nina's Story – Nina Nesbitt and Tamsin Embleton. https://audioboom.com/posts/7319415-mental-health-in-music-nina-s-story-nina-nesbitt-and-tamsin-embleton

8   Wisebuddah & Elevate. (2019, July 29). Mental health in music: Nina's Story – Nina Nesbitt and Tamsin Embleton. https://audioboom.com/posts/7319415-mental-health-in-music-nina-s-story-nina-nesbitt-and-tamsin-embleton

9   Yin, Y., Wang, Y., Evans. A. J., Wang, W. (2019, October 30). Quantifying the dynamics of failure across science, startups and security. *Nature*. https://www.nature.com/articles/s41586-019-1725-y.epdf?

10 Dinges, D. F., Pack, F., Williams, K., Gillen, K. A., Powell, J. W., Ott, G. E., Aptowicz, C., & Pack, A. I. (1997). Cumulative sleepiness, mood disturbance, and psychomotor vigilance performance decrements during a week of sleep restricted to 4–5 hours per night. *Sleep, 20*(4), pp.267–277.

11 Blumenthal, J. A., Babyak, M., Moore, K., Craighead, E., Herman, S., Khatri, P., Napolitano, M., Doraiswamy, P. M., & Krishnan, K. R. (1999). Exercise Training and Major Depression. *Psychosomatic Medicine, 61*(1), pp.124–125. https://doi.org/10.1097/00006842-199901000-00218

12 Myers, D. G. (2000). The funds, friends, and faith of happy people. *American Psychologist, 55*(1), pp.56–67.

13 Diener E., & Seligman M.E.P. (2002). Very happy people. *Psychological Science, 13*(1), pp.81–84. doi:10.1111/1467-9280.00415

14 Killingsworth, M. A., & Gilbert, D. T. (2010). A wandering mind is an unhappy mind. *Science, 330*(6006), pp.932–932. https://doi.org/10.1126/science.1192439

15 Brewer, J.A., Worhunsky, P.D., Gray, JR, Tang, Y.Y., Weber. J., & Kober, H. (2011). Meditation experience is associated with differences in default mode

network activity and connectivity. *PNAS, 108*(50):20254-20259. doi:10.1073/pnas.1112029108

16 Fredrickson, B. L., Cohn, M. A., Coffey, K. A., Pek, J., & Finkel, S. M. (2008). Open hearts build lives: positive emotions, induced through loving-kindness meditation, build consequential personal resources. *Journal of Personality and Social Psychology, 95*(5), pp.1045-1062. https://doi.org/10.1037/a0013262

17 Mrazek, M.D., Franklin, M.S., Phillips, D.T., Baird, B., & Schooler, J.W. (2013). Mindfulness training improves working memory capacity and GRE performance while reducing mind wandering. *Psychological Science, 24*(5), pp.776-781. doi:10.1177/0956797612459659

18 Hutcherson, C. A., Seppala, E. M., & Gross, J. J. (2008). Loving-kindness meditation increases social connectedness. *Emotion, 8* (5), pp.720-724.

19 Csikszentmihalyi, M. (1999). If we are so rich, why aren't we happy. *American psychologist, 54*(10), pp.821–827.

20 Emmons, R. A., & McCullough, M. E. (2003). Counting blessings versus burdens: an experimental investigation of gratitude and subjective well-being in daily life. *Journal of Personality and Social Psychology, 84*(2), pp.377-389.

21 Seligman, M. E. P., Steen, T. A., Park, N., & Peterson, C. (2005). Positive psychology progress: empirical validation of interventions. *American Psychologist, 60*(5), pp.410-421. https://doi.org/10.1037/0003-066x.60.5.410

22 Seligman, M.E.P. (2011). *Flourish: A Visionary New Understanding of Happiness and Well-being.* London: Hachette UK.

23 National Health Service. (2019). 5 steps to mental wellbeing. https://www.nhs.uk/conditions/stress-anxiety-depression/improve-mental-wellbeing/

24 Seligman, M.E.P. (2011). *Flourish: A Visionary New Understanding of Happiness and Well-being.* London: Hachette UK.

25 Otake, K., Shimai, S., Tanaka-Matsumi, J., Otsui, K., & Fredrickson, B. L. (2006). Happy people become happier through kindness: A counting kindnesses intervention. *Journal of Happiness Studies, 7*(3), pp.361–375. https://doi.org/10.1007/s10902-005-3650-z

26 National Health Service. (2019). 5 steps to mental wellbeing. https://www.nhs.uk/conditions/stress-anxiety-depression/improve-mental-wellbeing/

27 Whillans, A. V., Weidman, A. C., & Dunn, E. W. (2016). Valuing time over money is associated with greater happiness. *Social Psychological and Personality Science, 7*(3), pp.213-222. https://doi.org/10.1177/1948550615623842

28 Paul E. Jose, Bee T. Lim & Fred B. Bryant (2012). Does savoring increase happiness? A daily diary study, *The Journal of Positive Psychology, 7*(3), pp.176-187, DOI: 10.1080/17439760.2012.671345

29 National Health Service. (2019). 5 steps to mental wellbeing. https://www.nhs.uk/conditions/stress-anxiety-depression/improve-mental-wellbeing/

30 Seligman, M.E.P. (2011). *Flourish: A Visionary New Understanding of Happiness and Well-being.* London: Hachette UK.

31 Music Managers Forum and Music Support. The Music Managers Guide to Mental Health. https://themmf.net/site/wp-content/uploads/2018/01/Mental-Health-Guide-Digital.pdf

ABOUT THE AUTHORS

RHIAN JONES is a respected journalist who specialises in writing about the music business. Titles she regularly contributes to include *The Guardian*, *Music Business Worldwide,* and *Hits Daily Double*. Born into a family of musicians, Rhian studied music at college before training as a journalist after realising performing was not her forte. She started her professional career at trade title *Music Week*, rising through the ranks to news editor, before embarking on a full-time freelance career in 2015. Other titles where you'll find her byline include *The Independent*, *Vice*, *The Sunday Telegraph,* and *Billboard*. This is her first book and proudest work to date.

LUCY HEYMAN is a vocal and performance coach and one of the UK's leading specialists in the health and wellbeing support of commercial recording artists. She studied music at Bristol University and holds an MSc in Performance Science from the Royal College of Music, where she now conducts research for a PhD. Lucy is the founder of industry health and wellbeing consultancy, Elevate, and host and creator of the health-focused *Elevate Music* Podcast, with guests including Imogen Heap, Miles Kane, Nina Nesbitt, and more. She is a member of the BRIT Award Voting Academy and a fellow of the Royal Society of Arts.